# Footnotes from the Page of Nature or First Forms of Vegetation

by Hugh Macmillan



Address:
HardPress
8345 NW 66TH ST #2561
MIAMI FL 33166-2626
USA
Email: info@hardpress.net

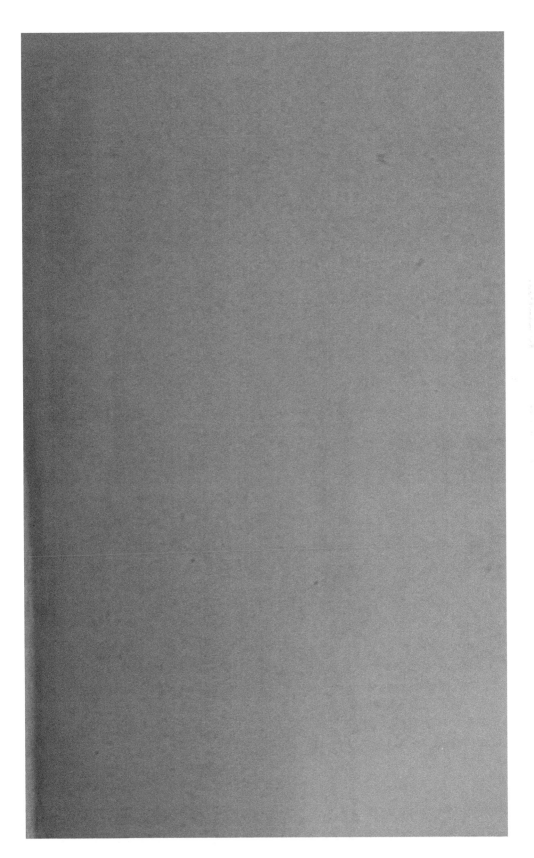

# FOOTNOTES

FROM

# THE PAGE OF NATURE.

PRINTED BY THOMAS CONSTABLE, EDINBURGH,

FOR

MACMILLAN AND CO., CAMBRIDGE.

DUBLIN: WILLIAM ROBERTSON.

EDINBURGH: EDMONSTON AND DOUGLAS.

GLASGOW: JAMES MACLEHOSE.

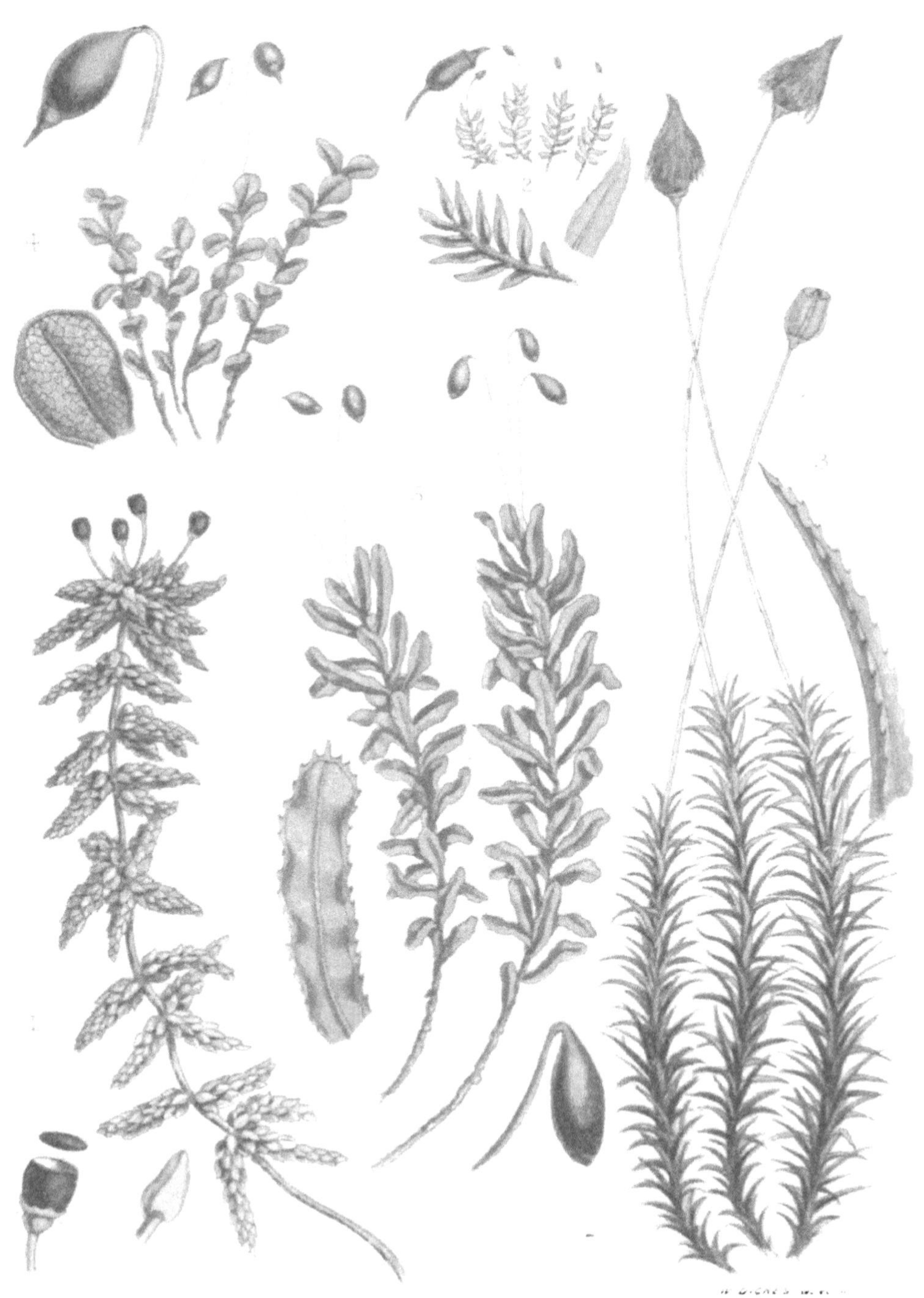

1. Sphagnum obtusifolium. 3. Polytrichum commune.
2. [illegible] 4. Bryum punctatum
5. Bryum ligulatum.

# FOOTNOTES

FROM

# THE PAGE OF NATURE

OR

## FIRST FORMS OF VEGETATION

BY

[illegible]

[illegible]

WITH ILLUSTRATIONS

Cambridge:
MACMILLAN AND CO.
HENRIETTA STREET, COVENT GARDEN,
London.
1861.

# FOOTNOTES

FROM

# THE PAGE OF NATURE

OR

## FIRST FORMS OF VEGETATION.

BY THE

REV. HUGH MACMILLAN,

FELLOW OF THE BOTANICAL SOCIETY OF EDINBURGH, ETC.

WITH ILLUSTRATIONS.

Cambridge:

MACMILLAN AND CO.

AND 23, HENRIETTA STREET, COVENT GARDEN,

London.

1861.

# PREFACE.

THE different chapters of this work were first composed and delivered in the form of a series of popular lectures. Re-written, and considerably extended, they are now published with the view of awakening the interest of the reader in a department of nature with which few, owing to the technical phraseology of botanical works, are familiar. Those who have derived pleasure and profit from the study of flowers and ferns—subjects, it is pleasing to find, now everywhere popular—by descending lower into the arcana of the vegetable kingdom, will find a still more interesting and delightful field of research in the objects brought under review in the following pages. This work is neither a text-book nor a guide to species, but simply a popular history of the uses, structural peculiarities, associations, and other interesting facts connected with the humblest forms of plant life; and, as such, it may be regarded as an introduction to more scientific treatises, which deal with particular orders and species.

H. M.

FREE MANSE OF KIRKMICHAEL.

# CONTENTS.

PAGE

INTRODUCTION, . . . . . . . . . 1

CHAPTER I.—MOSSES.

Beauty of Mosses—Classification—Appearance—Stems—Roots—Leaves—Harmonies of colours—Spiral arrangement of leaves—Organs of fructification—Antheridia, Pistilidia, and Phytozoa—Gemmæ—Proliferous mosses—Power of regeneration—General diffusion—Alpine mosses, and theory of their distribution—Particular limitations of mosses—Splachnum growing on animal substances—Social character of mosses—Bog-moss—Historical and personal associations—Illustrations of the beauty of mosses—Uses in the economy of man and of nature—Formation of peat—Liverworts—Structure and peculiarities—Lycopods—Hygrometric properties of Selaginella—Structure and fructification of Club-mosses—Uses—Analogical affinity—Geological facts connected with Lycopods, . . . . . . . 21

CHAPTER II.—LICHENS.

Viewed as æsthetic objects—Diversity of forms—Description and associations of Written Lichen—Huc and Gabet's Tree of Ten Thousand Images—Structure of lichens—Peculiar modes of Reproduction—Longevity—Geographical distribution—Lichens of Antarctic regions—Belts of vegetation on Chimborazo—Alpine lichens—Lichens as pioneers of all other plants—Adaptations of lichens to their circumstances—Uses on trees—Reindeer moss—Iceland moss—Tripe de Roche associated with Franklin—Manna of Israelites—Lecanora esculenta—Medicinal properties—Uses in arts and manufactures—Dye-lichens: Orchil, Cudbear, Perelle—Ruskin on lichens, . . . . . . . 61

CHAPTER III.—FRESH-WATER ALGÆ.

Importance of microscopic objects—Interest of Confervæ derived from the element in which they live—Forming the boundary line between plants and animals—Nature and structure of green

PAG

slime on ditches and streams—Curious mode of propagation—Uses in the economy of nature—River Lemania—Water-flannel—Moor-balls—Zygnema with spiral structure—Oscillatoriæ: their remarkable diversity; curious movements and resemblances to animals—Algæ in chemical infusions—Red snow—Green snow—Gory dew and associations—History of Blood-prodigies—Primitive algæ—Nostoc—Life within life—Algæ within animal bodies—Diatoms or Brittleworts; their universal diffusion in the atmosphere, waters, rocks, and soils; their geological history—Edible earths—Connexion with storms—Curious shapes—Anomalous position in nature—Extraordinary method of propagation, . . . . . . . . . 12

## CHAPTER IV.—FUNGI.

Autumn's peculiar plants—Origin—Chemical properties—Luminosity—Insensibility to the influence of light—Rapidity of growth and brevity of existence—Simplicity of organization—Capacity of regeneration—Enormous development—Variety of consistence—Qualities—Colours and forms—Illustrations of the curious shapes of Fungi—Description of structure and mode of propagation—Analysis of the classes and orders of British Fungi—Doctrine of spontaneous generation considered—Spores of Fungi in connexion with epidemic diseases—Geographical distribution—Ubiquitous habitats—Snow-moulds—Fungi on insects—Fly-disease—Silk-worm mould—Gold-fish disease—Mould protean in shape, and universal in distribution—Mycoderms of mucous and ulcerated surfaces—Fungi parasitic on man—Vinegar plant—Fungoid nature of Yeast—Uses of Fungi in nature and in human economy—Poisonous properties—Intoxicating Siberian Fungus—Edible Fungi—Morell—Truffle, etc.—Artificial propagation—Destructive effects—Cereal blights: smut, bunt, mildew, rust, and ergot—Potato-murrain—Grape disease—Black mildews—Dry rot—Means of obviating and removing Fungoid diseases—Fossil Fungi—Association of Fungi with Franklin's Expedition to the Polar Regions—Beauty and picturesqueness of Fungi, . . . . . . . 187

# BOTANICAL TERMS NOT EXPLAINED IN THE TEXT.

*Acrogens.*—Summit-growers, applied to mosses, etc., because they increase only by additions of matter to their top or their growing point.

*Archegonia.*—Spherical bodies originating in the small clusters or rosettes of leaves on the top of moss stems, containing internally a central nucleus from which arises the fructification of the moss.

*Cellular.*—The fleshy or succulent parts of plants are so called, because they are composed entirely of cells of irregular shape, forming a homogeneous mass, without a vestige of fibre.

*Cellulose.*—A substance closely allied to starch, forming an essential part of the structure of vegetable cells and vessels.

*Cilia.*—Minute hair-like filaments attached to cells, endowed with a vibratile motion.

*Coniferous.*—Cone-bearing; applied to structure consisting of punctuated, disc-bearing, woody tissue, like that of the pine tribe.

*Cryptogamic.*—Applied to all plants which are propagated by spores instead of seed, and which have no flowers.

*Cyphellæ.*—Collections of powdery reproductive matter, gathered into little cavities on the upper or under surface of lichens.

*Endochrome.*—Granular matter of a green colour occurring in the interior of the germinating shoots of mosses, and in the filaments of the fresh-water algæ.

*Filiform.*—Thread-like, slender.

*Flocculent.*—Woolly, presenting an appearance as if covered with down.

*Foliaceous.*—Applied to mosses, etc., because they exhibit leaf-like organs, like those of flowering plants.

*Frond.*—Cellular expansion of flowerless plants, resembling a leaf, but destitute of its fibrous structure.

*Fasciculate.*—Gathered into bundles.

*Homologous.*—Of similar structure, functions, and uses.

*Laticiferous.*—Vessels of plants, such as gutta percha, dandelion, lettuce, etc., are so called, because they contain a fluid like milk.

*Matrix.*—The substance upon which a plant grows.

*Membranous.*—Tissue which is composed uniformly of similarly-constructed cells is so called.

*Medullary rays.*—Lines which radiate from the pith to the bark all round the stem of common forest trees.

*Nidus.*—The nest or cavity in which a parasitic plant is developed.

*Phytozoa.*—Microscopic thread-like bodies, with movements resembling those of animals, occurring in the reproductive organs of the flowerless plants.

*Proliferous.*—Applied to plants which propagate themselves by forming new growths upon the old decaying bases.

*Phanerogamous.*—Applied to all the flowering plants, because they are propagated by conspicuous flowers and seeds.

*Scalariform.*—Tissue is thus called whose fibres are so broken up as to appear in the form of bars or lines, like the steps of a ladder, seen beautifully in tree-ferns.

*Sessile.*—Seated on the vegetative basis, without stem or pedicel.

*Sinuses.*—Deep grooves or hollows.

*Soredia.*—Collections of mealy powder scattered over the surface of lichens, and capable of propagating them.

*Spore.*—The ultimate germinating cell of flowerless plants, without lobes, resembling a particle of fine dust.

*Sporule.*—A minute round cell, capable of reproducing the parent plant, resembling buds in not being developed by a process of reproduction, but differing from them in being produced in special organs.

*Sporidia.*—The compound spores of lichens, containing minuter spores in their interior.

*Sporangia.*—The hollow cases or receptacles which contain the spores.

*Striæ.*—Delicate grooved lines or markings.

*Tartareous.*—Applied to the lime-like appearance and structure of some lichens.

*Thallogens.*—Applied to flowerless plants whose vegetative part consists of thin cellular expansions, increasing generally in a centrifugal manner.

*Vascular.*—Woody tissue, consisting of bundles of fine cylindrical fibres, often of great length, tapering at both ends.

" URNS of beauty, forms of glory,
Shapes with frosted silver hoary ;
Fair cups of light that pearls enfold,
Set in transparent gauzy gold ;
Lucid sprays of emerald dye,
Could e'en an empire's treasures vie,
With all these jewels that emboss
Each separate leaflet of the moss.
Voices from the silent sod,
Speaking of the perfect God.

" Fringeless or fringed, and fringed again,
No single leaflet formed in vain ;
What wealth of heavenly wisdom lies
Within one moss-cup's mysteries !
And few may know what silvery net
Down in its mimic depths is set,
To catch the rarest dews that fall,
Upon the dry and barren wall.
Voices from the silent sod,
Speaking of the perfect God."

# INTRODUCTION.

LIFE is everywhere. "Nature *lives*," says Lewes; "every pore is bursting with life; every death is only a new birth; every grave a cradle." "The earth-dust of the universe," says Jean Paul, "is inspired by the breath of the great God. The world is brimming with life; every leaf on every tree is a land of spirits." The tendency to vegetate is a ceaseless power. It has been in operation from the earliest ages of the earth, ever since living beings were capable of existing upon its surface; and so active in the past history of the globe has been this tendency, that most of the superficial rocks of the earth's crust are composed of the remains of plants. It operates with undiminished and tireless energy still. Vegetation takes place upon almost every substance; upon the bark of trees, upon naked rocks, upon the roofs of houses, upon dead and living animal substances, upon glass when not constantly kept clean, and even on iron which had been subjected to a red heat a short time before. Zoologists tell us, when speaking of animalcules, that not a drop of stagnant water, not a speck of vegetable or animal tissue, not a portion of organic matter but has its own appropriate inhabitants.

The same may be said of plants; for we can hardly point to a single portion of the earth's surface which is not tenanted by some vegetable form whose structure is wonderfully adapted to its situation and requirements. Even in the hottest thermal springs, and on the eternal snows of the arctic regions, peculiar forms of vegetation have been found. From the deepest recesses of the earth to which the air can penetrate, to the summits of the loftiest mountains; from the almost unfathomable depths of the ocean to the highest clouds; from pole to pole, the vast stratum of vegetable life extends; while it ranges from a temperature of 35° to 135° Fah., a range embracing almost every variety of conditions and circumstances.

The most cursory and superficial glance will recognise in every scene a class of plants whose singular appearances, habits, and modes of growth so prominently distinguish them from the trees and flowers around, that they might seem hardly entitled to a place in the vegetable kingdom at all. On walls by the wayside, on rocks on the hills, and on trees in the woods, we see tiny green tufts and grey stains, or parti-coloured rosettes spreading themselves, easily dried by the heat of the sun, and easily revived by the rain. In almost every stream, lake, ditch, or any collection of standing or moving water, we observe a green slimy matter forming a scum on the surface, or floating in long filaments in the depths. On almost every fallen leaf and decayed branch, fleshy gelatinous bodies of different forms and sizes meet our eye. Sometimes all these different objects appear growing on the same substance. If we examine a fallen, partially decayed twig, half-buried in the earth in a wood, we may find it completely covered with various representatives of these different vegetable growths; and nothing surely can give us a more striking or convincing proof of the universal diffusion of life. All these different plants belong to the second great division of the vegetable kingdom, to which the name of cryptogamia has been given, on account of the absence, in all the members, of those prominent organs which are essential to the production of perfect seed. They are propagated by little embryo plants called spores or sporules, generally invisible to the naked eye, and differing from true seeds in germinating from any part of their surface instead of from two invariable points. Besides this grand distinguishing mark, they possess several other peculiar qualities in common. They consist of cells only, and hence are often called cellular plants, in contradistinction to those plants which are possessed of fibres and woody tissue. Their development is also superficial, growth taking place from the various terminal points; and hence they are called acrogens and thallogens, to distinguish them from monocotyledonous and dicotyledonous plants. Popularly, they are known as mosses, lichens, algæ, and fungi. They open up a vast field of physiological research. They constitute a microcosm, an *imperium in imperio,* a strange minute world underlying this great world of sense and sight, which, though unseen and unheeded by man, is yet ever in full and active operation around us. It is pleasant to turn aside for a while from the busy human world, with its ceaseless anxieties, sorrows and labours, to avert our gaze from the splendours of forest and garden, from the visible display of green foliage and rainbow-coloured blossoms around us, and contemplate the silent and wonderful economy of that other world of minute or invisible vegetation with which we are so mysteriously related, though we know it not. There is something exceedingly interesting in tracing nature to her ultimate and simplest forms. The mind of man has a natural craving for the infinite. It delights to speculate either on the vast or the minute; and we are not surprised at the paradoxical remark of Linnæus, that nature appeared to him greatest in her least productions.

These plants once occupied the foremost position in the economy of nature. Like many decayed families whose founders were kings and mighty heroes, but whose descendants are beggars, they were once the aristocracy of the vegetable kingdom, though now reduced to the lowest ranks, and considered the *canaille* of vegetation. Geology reveals to us the extraordinary fact, that one whole volume of the earth's stony book is filled almost exclusively with their history. Life may have been ushered upon our globe through oceans of the lowest types of confervæ, long previous to the deposit of the oldest palæozoic rocks as known to us; and for myriads of ages these extremely simple and minute plants may have represented the only idea of life on earth. But passing from conjecture to the domain of established truth, we know of a certainty that at least throughout the vast periods of the carboniferous era, ferns, mosses, and still humbler plants, occupied the throne of the vegetable kingdom, and, by their countless numbers, their huge dimensions, and rank luxuriance, covered the whole earth with a closely-woven mantle of dark green verdure—from Melville Island in the extreme north to the islands of the Antarctic Ocean in the extreme south. The relics of these immense primeval forests, reduced to a carbonaceous or bituminous condition by the secret resources of nature's laboratory, amidst so many convulsions of the globe, are now buried deep in the bowels of the earth, packed into solid sandstone cases, and under huge shady covers, and stored up in the smallest compass by the mighty pressure of ponderous rock-presses, constituting the chief source of our domestic comfort, and of nearly all our commercial greatness. A coal-bed is, in fact, a *hortus siccus* of extinct cryptogamic vegetation, bringing before the imagination a vista of the ancient world, with which no arrangement of landscape or combination of scenery can now be compared; and gazing upon its dusky contents, our minds are baffled in aiming to comprehend the bulk of original material, the seasons of successive growth, and the immeasurable years or ages which passed while decay, and maceration, and chemical changes prepared the fallen vegetation for fuel. If the specimens of plants thus strangely preserved, teach us one truth more than another, it is this, that size and development are terms of no meaning when applied to a low or a high type of organization. The cryptogamia of the old world, the earliest planting in the new-formed soil, are in bulk, as well as in elegance and beauty of form, unrivalled by the finest specimens of the modern forest. The little and the great, the recent and the extinct, were equally the objects of nature's care, and were all modelled with a skill and finish that left nothing to be added.

And as in early geological epochs they occupied so conspicuous a position, so now in the annals of physical geography they are entitled to a prominent place. With the exception of the grasses—nature's special favourites—they are the most abundant of all plants, possessing inconceivable myriads of individual representatives in every part of the globe, from which unfavourable conditions exclude all other vegetation ; and thus they contribute, far more than we are apt from a superficial observation to imagine, to the picturesque and romantic appearances exhibited by scenery, and to the formation of that richly woven and beautifully decorated robe of vegetation which conceals the ghastly skeleton of the earth, and hides from our view the rugged outlines and primitive features of nature. They are the first objects that clothe the naked rocks which rise above the surface of the ocean ; and they are the last traces of vegetation which disappear under degrees of heat and cold fatal to all life. Their structure is so singularly varied and plastic, that they are adapted to every possible situation. In every country they form an important element in the number of plants, the proportion to flowering plants decreasing from, and increasing towards the poles. Taking them as a whole, and in regard to their size, they occupy a larger area of the earth's surface than any other kind of vegetation. There are immense forests of trees here and there in different countries, realizing Cowper's wish for "a boundless contiguity of shade ;" there are vast colonies of flowering plants ; but the range of the most ubiquitous tree or flower is vastly inferior to that of some of the humblest lichens and mosses. Although these plants occupy but a very subsidiary and unimportant position among the vegetation which surrounds us in our daily walks, and are concealed in isolated patches in the woods and fields by the luxuriance of higher and more conspicuous plants, yet they constitute the sole vegetation of very extensive regions of the earth's surface. Every part of the globe, within a thousand feet of the line of perpetual snow, is redeemed from utter desolation by these plants alone. Above the valleys and the lower slopes which form the step of transition from plain to mountain—inhabited by prosperous and civilized nations—is the domain of mist and mystery, the region of storm—a world which is not of this world, where God and nature is all in all, and man is nothing; and in this unknown region there are immense tracts familiar to the eye of wild bird, to the summer cloud, the stars and meteors of the night—strange to human faces and the sound of human voices, where the lichen and the moss alone luxuriate and carpet the sterile ground. The grandest and sublimest regions of the earth are adorned with garlands of the minutest and humblest plants; they are the tapestry, the highly-wrought carpeting laid down in the vestibules of nature's palaces. If we look at a map of the world, we see that Europe and Asia are held together as it were by a huge ridge or back-bone of mountain elevation, which, although suffering partial interruption, may be roughly described as continuous from one ocean to another. It begins with the mountains of Biscay in Spain, passes on through the Pyrenees with a slight interruption into the Alps, which throw off the important spur or rib of the Apennines; thence it divides into the Balkan and Carpathians. We trace the chain next in the Caucasus and the mountains of Armenia—with the interruption of the Caspian Sea—passing into the Hindoo Coosh and the Himalaya mountains, from whence the chain forks and takes a direction north and south, enclosing like walls the whole delta of China, and thence dips into the eastern ocean. In Africa also, at its widest part, there is a similar back-bone, beginning not far from Sierra Leone, and losing itself in the east in the mountains of Abyssinia; while in America the mountain-spine trends north and south from the Hudson's Bay territories, through the Rocky Mountains, uninterruptedly through the Isthmus of Panama, along the Andes to the Straits of Magellan. These vast mountain-systems, with their culminating regions in the Andes, Alps, and Himalayas, and their subsidiary branches or ribs in the Grampians, Doffrefels, Ural, and Atlantic ranges, are clothed on their sides, summits, and elevated plateaus, almost exclusively with cryptogamic vegetation, and enable us to form some conception of the immense altitudinal range of these plants. Then there are whole islands in the Arctic and Antarctic Oceans whose vegetation also is almost entirely cellular. The northern portion of Lapland, the continent of Greenland, the large islands of Spitzbergen, Nova Zembla, and Iceland, the extensive territories of the Hudson's Bay Company, the enormous tracts of level land which border the Polar Ocean from the North Cape to Behring's Straits, across the north of Europe and Asia, and from Behring's Straits to Greenland, across the north of America, a stretch of many thousands of miles; all these immense areas of the earth's surface—where not a tree, nor a shrub, nor a flower is seen, except the creeping arctic willow and birch, and the stunted moss-like saxifrage and scurvy grass—are covered with fields of lichens and mosses, far exceeding anything that can be compared in that respect amongst phanerogamous plants. Thus, to the rugged magnificence of Alpine scenery, and the dreary isolation and uniformity of the Arctic steppes, and the boundless wastes of brown desert and misty moorland, to these great outlets from civilisation and the tameness of ordinary life, which allow the soul to expand and go out in sublime imaginings towards the infinity of God, these humble plants form the sole embellishments.

So much for the distribution of these plants on the land; their range in the waters is still more extensive. Lichens and mosses cover the waste surfaces of the earth; diatoms and confervæ are everywhere miraculously abundant in the waters. In rivers and streams, in ditches and ponds, alike under the sunny skies of the south, and in the frozen regions of the north; on the surface of the sea in floating meadows, and in the dark and dismal recesses of the ocean only to be explored by the long line of the sounding-lead. The ocean swarms with innumerable varieties, without their presence being indicated by any discoloration of the fluid. The Arctic and Antarctic Oceans, covering areas larger than the continents of Europe and Asia, are peopled by myriads of diatoms; various inland seas and lakes are tinged of different hues by their predominance in the waters; while it has been ascertained, from the soundings obtained during the investigations connected with laying the electric telegraph cable between Ireland and Newfoundland, that the floor of the Atlantic is paved many feet deep with their silicious shields, preserving in all their integrity their wonderful shapes, notwithstanding their extreme delicacy and minuteness, and the enormous pressure of the vast body of water which rests above them. Such is the wide space which these organisms occupy in the fields of nature —a prominence which is surely sufficient to redeem them from the charge of insignificance. They are inferior in majesty of form to palms and oaks, but in their united influence it is not too extravagant to say that they are not less important than the great forests of the world.

This vast profusion of minute and humble vegetable life serves the obvious purpose of preparing the way for higher orders of vegetation. Nature is incessantly working out vast ends by humble and scarcely recognisable means. The features of the earth are being continually altered by the germination and dispersion of the algæ, mosses, and lichens. Bare and sterile mountains are clothed with verdure; rocks are mouldering into soil; seas are filling up; rivers and streams are continually shifting their outlines; and lakes are converted into fertile meadows and the sites of luxuriant forests, by means of the vast armies of nature's pioneers. Hard inorganic matters are reduced to impalpable atoms; waters and gases are decomposed and moulded into new forms and substances having new properties, by vegetable growth. Minute as these plants are, they are intimately related to the giant forms of the universe. It has been observed that as the great whole is indissolubly connected with its minutest parts, so the germination of the minutest lichen, and the growth of the simplest moss, is directly linked with the grandest astronomical phenomena; nor could the smallest fungus or conferva be annihilated without destroying the equilibrium of the universe. It is with organic nature as with the body politic or the microcosm of the human frame, if "one member suffer all the members suffer with it," and the loss of one class or order would involve that of another, till all would perish. Our comfort and health, nay our very existence more or less immediately depend on the useful functions which they perform. Before we can have the wheat which forms our daily bread, or the grass which yields us, through the instrumentality of our herds, our daily supply of animal food, or the cotton and lint which form our clothes, countless generations of lichens and mosses must have been at work preparing a soil for the growth of the plants which produce these useful materials. And as on the dry land, so in the great waters, this wonderful chain of connexion exists in all its complexity. Before the reader can peruse these pages by the light of the midnight lamp, or the gay party can indulge their revels under the brilliant glare of spermaceti tapers, myriads of minute diatoms and confervæ, floating in the waters of the sea, must have formed a basis of subsistence for the whales and seals whose oil is employed for these purposes. Man's own structure is nourished and built up by the particles which these active plants have rescued from the mineral kingdom, and which once circulated through their simple cells;

and thus the highest and most complex creature, by a vital sympathy and a close physical relation, is connected with the lowest and simplest organism, to teach him humility, and inspire him with a deep interest in all the works of his Maker!

> "Nothing in this world is single;
> All things, by a law divine,
> In one another's being mingle."

It may be asked by a class of individuals, unfortunately too numerous, What is the use of these minute plants? In the business language of the world things are called useful when they promote the profit, convenience, or comfort of everyday life; and useless when they do not promote, or when they hinder either of these desired ends. But this definition is extremely partial and one-sided. There are higher purposes to serve in this world than mere subservience to the physical wants of man. There is a much higher utility than the mere temporary and worldly one. The useful things of external life, indeed, should not be undervalued; they are the first things required, but they are not the sole or the highest things necessary. Man must have food and clothing in order to live; but it must also be remembered that man does not live by bread and the conveniences of external life alone. When any one does live by these alone, he has forfeited his claim to the higher form of life which is his glorious privilege, and by which he is distinguished from the lower animals. Nature throughout her whole wide domains gives no countenance to such a materialistic exclusiveness. She is at once utilitarian and transcendental. Uses and beauties intermingle. All that is useful is around us; but how much more is there beside? There is a strange superfluous glory in the summer air; there is marvellous beauty in the forms and hues of flowers; there is an enchanting sweetness in the song of birds and the murmur of waters; there is a divine grandeur and loveliness in the landscapes of earth and the scenery of the heavens, the changes of the seasons, the dissolving splendours of morning, noon, sunset and night, utterly incomprehensible upon the theory of nature's exclusive utilitarianism. "The tree which shades the wayfarer in the noontide heat adorns the landscape; and the flower which gives honey to the bee sheds its perfume on the air. A leaf no less than a flower fulfils the functions of life, ministers to the necessities of man, yet clothes itself, and adorns the earth in tapestries richer than the robes of kings." All things proclaim that the Divine Architect, while amply providing for the physical wants of his creatures, has not forgotten their spiritual necessities and enjoyments; and having implanted in the human soul a yearning for the beautiful, has surrounded us with a thousand objects by whose charms that yearning may be gratified. And one of the most striking examples of this Divine care is to be seen in the profusion of minute objects spread around us, which apparently have no direct influence at all upon man's physical nature, and have no connexion with his corporeal necessities. These objects, subserving no gross utilitarian purpose, are intended to educate man's spiritual faculties by the beauties of form, the wonders of structure, and the adaptations of economy which they display. Their beauty is sufficient reason for their existence were there no other. When their varied and exquisitely symmetrical forms are presented to the eye under the microscope, a thrill of pleasure is experienced, calm and pure, because free from all taint of passion, and felt all the more intensely because nameless and indefinite. We are brought face to face with perfection in its most wonderful aspect—the perfection of minuteness and detail; with objects which bear most deeply impressed upon them the signet-mark of their Maker; and we observe with speechless admiration that the Divine attention is acuminated and His skill concentrated on these vital atoms; the last visible organism vanishing from our view with the same Divine glory upon it, as the last star that glimmers out of sight on the remotest verge of space.

These organisms further justify their existence to the utilitarian, inasmuch as their study is well calculated to exercise an educational influence which should not be overlooked or despised. While they try the patience, they exercise the faculties by forcing attention upon details. Their minuteness, their general resemblance to each other, their want in many cases of very prominent or marked characteristics, render it a somewhat difficult task to identify them. Long hours may often be spent in ascertaining the name of a single species, and assigning it its proper place in the tribe to which it belongs. One species may often be confounded with another closely allied, and days and weeks may elapse before the eye and the mind, familiarized with their respective details, can observe the distinctions between them. This difficulty of identification greatly sharpens one's knowledge, induces a habit of paying attention to minutiæ, and creates a power of distinguishing between things that differ slightly, which is exceedingly valuable and important. For the eye and mind thus educated to detect resemblances and differences in objects, which to ordinary observation appear widely dissimilar or precisely the same, there will be abundant scope in the practical details of common everyday life, as well as in the higher walks of literature, science, and art.

The study of these plants has also a tendency to elevate and enlarge our conceptions of nature ; its vastness and complexity, its incommunicable grandeur, its all but infinity, opening before us newer and more striking vistas with every descending step we take. The farther we advance, and the wider our sphere of observation extends, wonder follows on wonder, till our faculties become bewildered, and our intellect falls back on itself in utter hopelessness of arriving at the end. Minute as the objects are in themselves, contact with them cannot fail to excite the mind, to call it forth into full and vigorous exercise, to enlist its sympathies, and to expand its faculties. Many eloquent pages have been written to show this elevating influence upon the mind, of contact with, and contemplation of the phenomena of nature ; but it is not the great and sublime objects of nature alone that produce this effect—the sublimity of mountains, the majesty of rivers, and the repose of forests,—the very humblest and simplest objects are calculated to awaken these emotions in a yet higher and purer form. "The microscope," as Mr. Lewes has well observed, "is not the mere extension of a faculty; it is a new sense."

There are also peculiar pleasures connected with the study of these objects. There is first the pleasure of novelty and discovery—of exploring a realm where everything is comparatively new, and every step is delightful; where the forms are unfamiliar, and the modes of life hitherto unimagined. There is next the more subtle and refined pleasure of observing the strange truths which they unfold, the beautiful laws which they reveal, and the resemblances and relations which they display. The false romanticism of vulgar fancy requires something pretentious and unnatural to gratify its taste; but to the true poetical mind, the humblest moss on the wall, or the green slime that creams on the wayside pool, will suggest trains of pleasing and profitable reflection. He who has an observing eye and an appreciating mind for these minute wonders of nature, need never be alone. Every nook and corner of the earth, however barren and dreary to superficial minds, has companions for him; and on every path he will find what the Indians call a rustawallah, a delightful road-fellow.

To the cryptogamic botanist nature reveals herself in her wildest, and also in her fairest aspects. He enters into her guarded retreats—retiring spots of luxuriant, refreshing, and enticing beauty, that are hidden from every other eye; where the great world of strife and toil speaks not, and its cares and sorrows are forgotten, and nature wakes up the dead divinity within, and rouses the soul to purer and nobler purposes. The peculiar haunts of the objects of his search are found on the sides and summits of lofty mountains, amid the dark lonely recesses of forests, in the bright bosom of rivers and lakes and waterfalls, on far-off unvisited moors, where heaven's serene and passionless blue is the only thing of beauty, and in the mossy retreats of dell and dingle, where Titania and her fays might sport away the dreamy noontide hours. There he finds the pictures which the soul treasures most lovingly; and in these by-ways does he gain the truest insight into the mysteries of life. In thus penetrating into the very heart of nature, with much toil and exertion it may be, he seems to win her confidence, and to earn the right to look into her arena. By minute contact and continued commune with her alone in the wilderness, he feels in all its fulness and depth the beautiful relationship that exists between the outer and the inner life of creation. To others the landscape may be the mere background of a picture, in the foreground of which human figures are acting; to him its charms are agencies and influences acting on his heart and mingling with his life. The sportsman in search of game frequently wanders into regions that seem primeval in their solitude, and where "human foot had ne'er or rarely been;" but so absorbing is the pursuit in which he is engaged, that he seldom pauses to watch the features of the surrounding scenery, or to notice combinations of objects and effects of light and shade which nature never displays except in such unfrequented spots. But to the cryptogamist, on the other hand, these very scenes of nature lend a nameless charm and interest to the lowly plants he gathers, and are ever after indelibly associated with them in his memory, and are renewed every time he witnesses their faded remains. Hardly a moment passes over the solitary collector amid such secluded scenes, without some grand effect being produced in the surrounding landscape, or in the appearance of the sky above him; some wonderful transformation of nature, as though the spot where he stands were her tiring-room, and she were trying on robe after robe to see which became her best; some striking incident, which might well inspire him with the wish to catch the happy moment, and give it a permanent existence. Such are the simple, refining, and enduring pleasures which the cryptogamic botanist enjoys in the pursuit of his favourite study amid the scenes of nature.

Add to all these recommendations this last important advantage, that these plants can be observed and collected without interruption throughout the whole year, and in situations where other vegetation is reduced to zero. They can be studied alike under the cloudy skies of December, as when illumined by the sunshine of June. When the flowers and ferns have vanished, when the lights are fled, and the garlands are dead, the deserted banquet-hall of Flora is still relieved by the presence of these humble retainers, whose fidelity is proof against every change of circumstance, and whose better qualities are displayed when the storm is wildest and the desolation most complete. They are no summer friends. As Ruskin has beautifully observed, "Unfading as motionless, the worm frets them not, and the autumn wastes not. Strong in lowliness, they neither blanch in heat, nor pine in frost. To them, slow-fingered, constant-hearted, is intrusted the weaving of the dark eternal tapestries of the hills ; to them, slow-pencilled, iris-dyed, the tender framing of their endless imagery. Sharing the stillness of the unimpassioned rock, they share also its endurance ; and while the winds of departing spring scatter the white hawthorn blossoms like drifted snow, and summer duns in the parched meadow the drooping of its cowslip-gold, far above among the mountains, the silver lichen-spots rest, starlike on the stone, and the gathering orange-stain upon the edge of yonder western peak reflects the sunsets of a thousand years."

# FOOTNOTES

FROM

# THE PAGE OF NATURE.

---

## CHAPTER I.—MOSSES.

"And upon the top of the pillars was *lily-work*."
1 KINGS VII. 22.

THERE is nothing more calculated to strike the thoughtful mind with astonishment than the boundless prodigality with which the riches of nature are thrown broadcast over the whole surface of the earth. The most lovely objects are, as it were, carelessly scattered here and there in waste spots and lonely unvisited haunts, where there is no hand to gather, and no eye to admire them. The great temple of Nature is like the magnificent and gorgeous old temple of Solomon,—upon the top of every pillar is lily-work. The massive and rugged foundation stones of the earth are almost completely concealed by a profusion of graceful and beautiful things,—the grass, the flowers, the forests ; while the craggy pillars have their capitals enwreathed with exquisite garlands of ferns and mosses. Not a rock peeps above the surface of the soil but has its steep sides clothed with rainbow-hued lichens, and its summit enveloped in verdure. In the smallest and most insignificant of these objects, there is as much of beauty and ingenuity of structure displayed as though it were the only object in the universe. Nay, God seems to bestow more abundant honour and glory upon those objects whose smallness and insignificance would otherwise cause them to be overlooked.

Of all the minute flowerless plants with which Nature, as it were, points her flowery sentences, fills up her vacant spaces, and balances and tones her landscapes, mosses are by far the loveliest and the most interesting. As regards form and structure they are the most beautiful of all plants; nature having bestowed upon them this compensation for want of the varied and gorgeous colouring imparted to the higher tribes of vegetation. In them the most exquisite symmetry and beauty are developed, a beauty not of a glaring or obvious character, but refined and spiritual, consisting in delicacy of tint, in the imperceptible gradation by which one hue is blended with another, in the filmy transparency of the structure, and in the endless diversity and perfection of the form; a beauty generally invisible to the careless or the casual observer, but brightening like a star upon the view when attentively and minutely examined, finding an unconscious interpreter in every heart, and affording, when fully perceived, to every thoughtful mind, a purer and more subtle joy than is communicated even by the rose or the lily. Regarded *en masse*, what can be lovelier than a closely-shaven mossy lawn, over which the golden sunbeams, and the light-footed shadows of the fleecy clouds overhead, chase each other throughout the whole summer day in little rippling waves, like smiles and thoughts over a human face! What can be pleasanter than the soft yielding carpets of greenest verdure and weirdest patterns, woven by these tiny plants on the floor of shadowy old forests, "stealing all noises from the foot," and imbuing the mind with reverence and awe in the pillared aisles of nature's cathedrals! What can be more picturesque than the varied hues which mosses impart to the ivied ruin, the grey old wall, or the decaying tree; or what object can be more romantic than a fantastic rock crowned with pines or birches, with mosses hanging down in waving clusters from its edge, and forming beautiful festoons like draperies of green and brown silk over the pillars of some oriental palace! Truly these little plants originated in a high ideal of creative wisdom and love.

Mosses belong to the foliaceous or highest division of flowerless plants. Although consisting entirely of cellular tissue, and increasing by simple additions of matter to the growing point or the apex of parts already formed, they point to far higher orders of vegetation; they are prefigurations of the flowering plants, epitomes of archetypes in trees and flowers. There is nothing in the appearance or structure of the lichens, fungi, or algæ, to remind us of higher plants; they form, as it were, a strange microcosm of their own—a perfectly distinct and peculiar order of vegetable existence; but when we ascend a step higher and come to the mosses, we find for the first time the rudimental characters and distinctions of root, stem, branches, and leaves—we recognise an ideal exemplar of the flowering plants, all whose parts and organs are, as it were, sketched out, in anticipation, in these simple and tiny organisms. Through the small densely-cushioned, moss-like alpine flowers, they approximate analogically to the phanerogamous plants in their leaves and habit of growth; and through the cone-like spikes of the club-mosses, they approximate to the pine tribe in their fructification. From both these classes of highly organized plants, however, they are separated by wide and numerous intervening links. But still it is curious and interesting to find in them an exemplification of the universal teleology of nature—the humblest typical forms pointing to the grand archetypes, the simplest structures anticipating and prefiguring the most highly organized and complicated!

In no tribe of plants is there so great a similarity between the different species as in the mosses. In them is strikingly displayed the grand characteristic feature of God's work in creation—unity of type with variety of development. A simplicity and uniformity of structure runs throughout the entire family. The whole appearance, the general air, the manner of growth, is the same in all the species; so much so, that it is perhaps easier to distinguish a species of moss than a species of any other plant. This remarkable similarity conjoined with remarkable diversity, has led to the popular belief that there is only one kind of moss;—all the species, of which no less than 500 exist in this country alone, being confounded in one general appearance. Minutely and attentively examined, however, by an educated eye, their exceeding variableness of form will at once appear, some being slender hair-like plants; some resembling miniature fir-trees, others cedars, and others crested feathers and ostrich plumes. In size they vary from a minute film of green scarcely visible to the naked eye, to several feet in length. Nor are their colours less variable, ranging from white, through every shade of yellow, red, green, and brown, to the deepest and most sombre black.

Though most of the peculiarities of mosses are visible to the naked eye, it is on the stage of the microscope that they appear to the greatest advantage. The modifications of structure to suit the requirements of their economy thus revealed, cannot fail to excite our admiration and astonishment. The stems of mosses, though serving the same purposes, are widely different from those of flowering plants. We are ignorant of the manner in which they are developed. Probably, like endogenous plants, which is the least complicated of the two natural processes of increase in the vegetable kingdom, they grow by successive additions to the summit, always proceeding from the interior, never increasing the diameter after their outer layer has been formed. They are solid, and composed entirely of cellular tissue, which gradually becomes softer and more porous near the centre, uniform in every part, having neither medullary rays, nor true outward bark, nor central pith, nor even the scalariform vessels observable in the stems of ferns. Of the course taken by the ascending and descending sap, we are equally ignorant, if indeed there really exist in them currents similar to those of flowering plants, which may be more than doubted. The roots are exceedingly delicate organs, and yet they take as firm a hold of the earth, in proportion to their size, as the roots of many trees. In some cases they consist of small thread-like fibres, or long creeping underground stems; while in others they are aërial, like those of orchids, being developed in the form of a thick silky down of a pale brown colour, imbedded among the leaves close to the stem. This last variety of root is to be seen chiefly in species that grow in moist or watery places, where they act as sponges to attract and preserve the humidity of the plants, when the moisture around them is dried up. In connexion with their roots we observe a striking provision of nature for the welfare of mosses in unfavourable circumstances. As the most delicate fibres hardly penetrate beyond the surface of the soil, which in dry, sultry weather speedily parts with its moisture, the mosses would perish were they entirely dependent for their nourishment upon their roots. But every part of them, and especially the leaves, is endowed, to a remarkable degree, with the power of imbibing the faintest moisture from the air, and reviving, even when apparently withered and dead, on the recurrence of a shower of rain. The roots therefore, in most instances, serve only to attach the plant to its growing-place, the functions of nutrition being performed indiscriminately by its whole surface.

The leaves of mosses are their most prominent parts. To the careless and superficial eye, accustomed to look at a tuft of moss as merely a patch of velvety greenness, creeping over an old tree or dyke, the leaves of all mosses may appear precisely similar; but the attentive observer who examines them under a microscope, will find that the leaves of different kinds of trees are not more distinct from each other than are those of the mosses. Indeed, so remarkable and so constant is this dissimilarity, that it has formed one of the principal bases of their arrangement and classification; and the botanist who has studied them thoroughly can identify under the microscope, in some cases, the smallest fragment of a leaf, although almost invisible to the naked eye. The leaves of some mosses are quite plain and pellucid, exhibiting no structural arrangement whatever; others are furnished with a nerve which runs through the centre and terminates above or below the apex; some are either ribbed and notched like a saw on the edge, or quite plain and even; and others present the most beautiful and varied net-work of cells. Some are linear like miniature pine-needles, others ovate and round like the leaves of our common deciduous trees. The harmonies of colours are beautifully exhibited in their appendicular parts. The stem, in almost all the species, is of a pale wine-red colour, while the leaves are generally of a delicate pea-green hue. In some species the leaves are of the deepest and most vivid green, while their margins and nerves are of a deep blood-red colour. The fruit-stalk and fruit-vessel are sometimes red or orange-coloured, while the leaves are brown; and sometimes dark brown, when the leaves are of a golden yellow. Unlike the leaves of ferns, which are mere foliaceous expansions of the stem, and developed in one plane, the leaves of mosses are quite distinct from the stem, and are arranged around it on all sides, most frequently in an alternate manner, so that a line joining their bases would form a spiral more or less elongated.

The organs of fructification, however, with which mosses are furnished, are perhaps the most wonderful parts of their economy. When the requisite conditions are present, these are generally developed during the winter and spring months, and may be easily recognised by their peculiar appearance. At first a forest of hair-like stalks, of a pale pink colour, rises above the general level of the tuft of moss, to the height of between one and three inches, giving to the moss the appearance of a pin-cushion well provided with pins. These stalks, through course of time, are crowned with little urn-like vessels called capsules, which are covered at an early stage with little caps, like those of the Normandy peasants, with high peaks and long lappets,—in one species bearing a remarkable resemblance to the extinguisher of a candle,—a curious provision for protecting them alike from the sunshine and the rain, until the delicate structures underneath are matured. When the fruit-stalk lengthens and the capsules swell, this hood or cap is torn from its support, and carried up on the top of the seed-vessel, much in the same way as the calyx of the common garden annual, the *Eschscholtzia Californica*, is borne up on the summit of the cone-like petals before they expand. When the seed-vessel is riper it falls off altogether, and discloses a little lid covering the mouth of the capsule, which is also removed at a more advanced stage of growth. The mouth of the seed-vessel is then seen to be fringed all round with a single or double row of teeth, which closely fit into each other, and completely close up the aperture. It is a circumstance worthy of being noticed, that the even numbers which prevail in the formation of microscopic cells, are also found in these organs, the teeth being arranged in each row in the geometrical progression of 4, 8, 16, 32, or 64, there never being by any chance an odd number; thus illustrating the general doctrine that a system of types runs throughout the whole works of nature, furnishing evidences of supreme intelligence, and wonderfully adapted not only to the objects to which it is applied, but also to the same or similar principles in the constitution of man's mind.

FIG. 1.—BRYUM SERPENS.

(*a*) Veil. (*b*) Fringe. (*c*) Leaf. (*d*) Capsule with lid. (*e*) Stem.

These teeth are highly sensitive to the changes of the weather, opening in sunshine, and closing during moist or rainy weather, for the obvious purpose of ripening the minute dust-like seeds with which the interior of the capsule is filled; and it is a remarkable circumstance that, in one or two genera of mosses which are *not* provided with hygrometric teeth, the lid that closes the capsule is permanent, being thrown off only when the seeds are ripe and ready to be dispersed. By placing a capsule, the teeth of which are closed, near the fire or in the warm sunshine, the teeth will be seen to open with a graceful and gradual motion; while the slightest moisture of one's breath invariably causes the little teeth instantly to close over the mouth. This beautiful and extremely simple mechanism, of which a somewhat similar example occurs in the Rose of Jericho, is one of the most wonderful contrivances of nature, one of the most extraordinary adaptations of means to an end, to be found in the whole economy of vegetation. Within the capsule the seeds surround a slender pillar or columella, and are enclosed in a membraneous bag. Elevated as the seed-vessels are by their stalks, they are freely exposed to the ripening effects of sun and wind; and it is a curious sight to see these straight footstalks gradually bending, reversing the seed-vessels, and emptying the seeds they contain as from a pitcher, to be carried by the wind to some congenial spot, where through course of time they may spring up and form a new colony of mosses, which in their turn will carry on the circle of life, from the seed to the full-grown moss, and from the full-grown moss to the seed, the beginning and the ending, the ending and the beginning!

Besides these curious capsules, there are other organs of fructification which clearly demonstrate the sexuality of mosses. Their real nature has only recently been accurately ascertained. They are called antheridia and pistilidia, from the strong resemblance which they bear to the stamens and pistils of the flowering plants, and from their being supposed to perform the same or analogous functions. They are small spherical bodies, fixed by short footstalks, concealed in cup-shaped receptacles among the perichætial or uppermost leaves, and often occur in abundance along with the capsules on the same plant. Examined under the microscope, they are found to consist of a bag, whose membrane is formed of somewhat oblique cells, containing granular matter arranged around a bright red nuclear body, which divides into a number of small vesicular bodies of precisely the same character. This granular matter, under a higher power of the microscope, is resolved into a mass of apparently living animalcules called phytozoa, somewhat similar to the spermatozoa which occur in the reproductive matter of animals. These tiny organisms have short slender bodies, with long spirally-twisted tails, and display the most active and lively movements, each whirling upon its own axis, and quickly running about the field as if from an intense feeling of sensuous enjoyment. These movements generally cease in the course of two hours after the discharge of the phytozoa from the antheridia; but sometimes they are observed to move actively even after the lapse of two days. It is impossible to determine whether these tiny bodies are animals, as they appear to be, or simply modifications of vegetable tissue. They are furnished with cilia like animalcules; and their motion is such as would undoubtedly be attributed to ciliary action if seen in an animal structure. But as Dr. Lindley says, "It is so improbable that animals should be generated in the cells of plants, unless accidentally, that we cannot but entertain grave doubts whether, notwithstanding their locomotive powers, these bodies are really anything more than a form of vegetable matter. As to the motion, how are we to tell that it is not a hygrometrical action, like that of the teeth which fringe the mouth of the capsule?" Be their nature, however, what it may, they are extremely curious objects, and well worthy of the most careful examination. In the same receptacle, among the upper leaves of the moss, may be seen antheridia in every stage of development, those in the centre appearing to ripen first, even while some of those at the outer edge are of small size and quite green. There is thus a constant succession of phytozoa produced; a provision which tends to insure their application to the pistilidia at the proper time. Several species of mosses are furnished with gemmæ or pseudopodia, which consist of powdery or granulated heads terminating an elongated and almost leafless portion of the stem. These organs are usually developed only in unfavourable circumstances, being formed at the expense of the fruit which is then abortive. They appear to be simply a mass of naked seed, without the ordinary protection and mechanism of an enveloping seed-vessel, and as such, afford a remarkable illustration of the simplicity of the means by which nature, when placed at a disadvantage, effects her vital purposes. It is worthy of remark, that there are several mosses which possess the power of maintaining and spreading themselves without the aid of any of these organs of fructification. There is one remarkable species, the male plant of which exists only in Europe, so far as can be ascertained, and the female only in America, and yet they propagate themselves with as much facility as though they grew side by side in the same crevice of rock.

Almost all the mosses, which cover extensive areas of mountain and lawn, and occupy large tracts of bogs and watery wastes, are barren; it being a rare thing to find on them capsules or any of the other compensating organs. They are exceedingly proliferous, throwing out young shoots from their sides or summits, and thus often increasing many feet in depth, forming layer above layer, the uppermost stratum alone being vital; the rest decomposed into peat, forming a rich organic soil for its nourishment.

Mosses possess in a high degree the power of reproducing such parts of their tissue as have been injured or removed. They may be trodden under foot; they may be torn up by the plough or the harrow; they may be cropt down to the earth, when mixed with grass, by graminivorous animals; they may be injured in a hundred other ways; but, in a marvellously short space of time, they spring up as verdant in their appearance and as perfect in their form as though they had never been disturbed. The necessity of such a power of regeneration as this is abundantly manifest, when we consider the numberless casualties to which they are exposed in the bare shelterless positions which they occupy.

Mosses also possess the power of resisting, perhaps to a greater extent than all other plants of similar structure, the injurious operation of physical agents; and this likewise is a wise provision to qualify them for the uses which they serve in the economy of nature. The influence of heat and cold upon them is extremely limited, for the same species flourish indiscriminately on the mountains of Greenland and the plains of Africa. They have been found growing near hot springs in Cochin-China, and fringing the sides of the geysers of Iceland, where they must have vegetated in a heat equal to 186 degrees; while, on the other hand, they have been gathered in Melville Island at 35 degrees, or only just above the freezing-point. Though frozen hard under the snow-wreaths of winter for several months, their vitality is unimpaired; and though subjected to the scorching rays of the summer's sun, they continue green and unblighted. Even when thoroughly desiccated into a brown unshapen mass that almost crumbles into dust when touched by the hand, they revive under the influence of the genial shower, become green as an emerald; every pellucid leaf serving as a tiny mirror on which to catch the stray sunbeams. Specimens dried and pressed in the herbarium for half a century, have been resuscitated on the application of moisture, and the seed procured from their capsules has readily germinated. They grow freely in the Arctic regions, where there is a long twilight of six months' duration; and they luxuriate in the dazzling uninterrupted light of the tropics. They are found thriving amid moist steam-like vapours, with orchids and tillandsias, in the deep American forests; and they may be seen in tufts here and there on the dry and arid sands of the Arabian deserts. It matters not to the healthy exercise of their functions whether the surrounding air be stagnant or in motion, for we find them on the mountain top amid howling winds and driving storms, and in the calm, silent, secluded wood, where hardly a breeze penetrates to ruffle their leaves. The range of flowering plants is circumscribed by conditions of light, temperature, elevation above the sea, geological character of the district, and various other physical causes; but the wonderful vital energy with which the mosses are endowed, enables them to resist the most unfavourable influences, to grow freely and luxuriantly even in the bleakest circumstances, and to acclimatize themselves, without changing their character, in any region of the earth, and every kind of situation upon its surface; while, owing to the extreme minuteness and profusion of their germs of reproduction, they are almost universally disseminated by the winds and waves. There is no spot so barren and desolate where some species or other may not be found. Although often growing in great abundance within the tropics, carpeting the ground, and covering the trunks of the trees, and sometimes attaining very luxuriant proportions, the temperate zones, however, are the proper regions of the mosses. Unlike the ferns, the size and number of which gradually diminish in passing from tropical to temperate countries, the maximum of mosses is found in cold climates, increasing in luxuriance, beauty, and abundance as we approach the North Pole. Like the ferns, moisture and shade are essential to their growth and wellbeing, hence, as a class, they are principally confined to islands and the vicinity of rivers and lakes; the interior of continents, unless when well wooded and watered, being in a great measure destitute of them. Their favourite habitats appear to be rocky dells or ravines at the foot of mountains, with streamlets murmuring through them, and dense trees interweaving their foliage over their sides, and creating a dim moist twilight in the recesses beneath. In such hermit seclusions the botanist may expect to reap the richest harvest of species. Mosses occasionally select very singular places of growth; and notwithstanding the minuteness and profusion of their seeds, the facility with which they can be disseminated, and their insensibility to ordinary physical conditions, are, specifically considered, sometimes very much restricted in their geographical range. Several kinds are found in this country only on the summits of the highest Highland mountains, covering the barren soil with a thin film of verdure, or creeping over the weather-beaten rocks in tenacious dark-coloured clusters or tufts. These species are identical with those found on the plains of the Arctic regions and the hills of Lapland and Greenland, where they occur not merely in isolated tufts, as we find them in this country, but carpeting the ground for many yards, and imparting a verdant hue to the mountains and valleys. This circumstance would indicate that their original centre of distribution exists in these dreary regions, and that from thence they have been disseminated over the British and European mountains. The Alpine species are exceedingly restricted, seldom being found lower than 3000 feet, and often ascending to a height of 4000 feet on the British hills, and 8000 feet on the Alps of Switzerland and the Pyrenees; the isothermal line of these altitudes corresponding with the plains of Lapland and the level of the sea-shore in the Arctic regions. Along with the small moss-like Alpine flowers with which they grow, they must have been wafted down to the Highland mountains, either as germs or as full-sized plants, growing undisturbed in their native soil, when these mountains existed as islands in the midst of an immense glacial sea which swept over what is now the continent of Europe. When this sea retired, owing to the elevation of the land, and its islands became mountain peaks and ranges, the tiny plants which imparted to them their first faint tinge of verdure still remained, finding the same conditions of temperature, shade, and moisture among the clouds as they formerly found on the shore of an icy sea. Thus all the Alpine plants found on the summits of our loftiest hills are Norwegian or Arctic species. They are besides the oldest living plants in the world, each of them, even the very humblest moss or saxifrage, having a pedigree which extends into the misty past, thousands of years before the creation of man. What an intense, almost human interest, gathers around these tiny mosses and fragile flowers, which bloom like lone stars in a midnight sky, in the very hoof-marks of the storm, when we reflect that they are the last of their race, the scanty remains of what was once for many ages the general Flora of the whole of Europe. True patriots, they have clung to their native homes, although they have changed their very nature; retiring before the inroads of the host of gaudy flowers which invaded our valleys and woods from the east, to the storm-scalped summits of the Highland mountains, and behind the icy battlements of the Arctic regions! Upwards of thirty-four species are confined to the lofty ranges in the centre of Scotland, especially the Braemar and Breadalbane mountains, which form the most important part of the great Grampian range, and contain the most extensively and uniformly elevated land in Great Britain. These species are pre-eminently Arctic and Norwegian, and present many striking peculiarities which distinguish them at a glance from the mosses of the woods and the valleys. Though confined to the shoulders and the summits of our loftiest mountains, they are common hyperborean mosses, growing most luxuriantly and spreading in wide patches on the rocky plains of Spitzbergen, and in the upland woods of northern Norway. A few of them are found on the highest mountains of Wales and the south of Ireland; while the remaining representatives of these Alpine and Arctic mosses cover the projecting rocks which tower up through the glaciers of the Alps and the avalanches of the Pyrenees. No less than nine are exclusively restricted to the very highest summits of the most elevated peaks in Britain, never, except when brought down by streamlets in isolated tufts along their course, descending to a lower altitude than 4000 feet; while upwards of twenty of the rarest species are found on Ben Lawers and the lofty hills in the neighbourhood, of which no less than thirteen are to be found nowhere else in this country.

Mosses, in many instances, are limited in their range to rocks and soils of the same specific character; their limits of distribution, and of the rocks and soils possessing such character, being identical. For instance, some are confined to limestone districts and chalk cliffs; a calcareous soil being indispensable to their existence. Others affect granite; numerous species luxuriate in soil formed by the disintegration of micaceous schist; while not a few are found growing chiefly on sandstone and clay. Some are found only on and near the sea-shore; others are confined to the beds of streams and cliffs moistened by the spray of cascades, where, however impetuous the torrent may be, they cling tenaciously to the rocks, and form carpets of greenest verdure for the white glistening feet of the descending waters. Some are restricted exclusively to trees, whose trunks and boughs they clasp like emerald bracelets; others lead a lonely, hermit-like existence, in the dim moist caves and crevices of rocks, where they are discovered only by the glistening of a stray adventurous sunbeam on the drops of dew trembling upon their shining golden-green leaves. One species has actually been found covering the half-decayed hat of a traveller who had perished in a storm on Mount St. Bernard. There is a very peculiar genus called *Splachnum*, whose members are only found on organic remains, on the blanched and polished skulls and bones of hares and sheep which had furnished a meal to the fox or the eagle, or on droppings of game and cattle which browse upon the higher hills. This is the only vegetable we find to be contemporary with or posterior to the creation of animals, with the exception of minute microscopic entophytes which grow within the bodies of men and the lower animals. It is worthy of remark—though it may seem a digression—that there was an obvious necessity for the universal precedence of plants in creation, for the hard inorganic elements of the rocks had first to be converted by the vital energies of plants into organic substances, before animals could be sustained. It is true that the first created plant and the first created animal derived their origin alike from the inorganic soil, and were endowed alike with the power of converting heterogeneous matter into their own proper substance. But here the resemblance between them began and ended. The plant still possesses its original power of deriving its nourishment from the soil, while the animal has no such power, and is dependent for its support upon matter previously organized to a certain degree by the plant. Thus it is the peculiar function of the plant to effect that important change by which inorganic matter is converted into living substance; it is in the organs of the plant that matter becomes vital. This is by far the most wonderful operation which is going on in the world; for in all that afterwards takes place there is no such radical change, there is simply development into more highly organized substance. Yet in what the operation consists, or by what process it is accomplished, is involved in the greatest mystery.

Mosses are sometimes found in an isolated state as single individuals, but they are far oftener found in a social condition. It is a peculiarity of the family to grow in tufts or clusters, the appearance of which is always distinct and well-marked in different species, and often affords a specific character. This disposition to grow together, which is exhibited in no other plants so strongly, redeems them from the insignificance of their individual state, and enables them to modify in many places the appearance of the general landscape. As social plants they often cover vast districts of land. Along with lichens they give a verdant appearance to the desert steppes of northern Europe, Asia, and America. Mixed with grass they luxuriate in parks, lawns, and meadows, particularly in moist, low-lying situations. They spread in large patches over the ground in woods and forests; and at a certain elevation on mountain ranges, they take exclusive possession of the soil, forming immense beds into which the foot sinks up to the ankle at every step, bleached on the surface by the sunshine and rain, blackened here and there by dissolving wreaths of snow which lie upon them through all the summer months, and gradually decomposing underneath into black vegetable mould. The shoulders, ridges, and elevated plateaus of all the Highland mountains are covered with huge luxuriant masses of the woolly-fringe moss (*Trichostomum lanuginosum*), growing continuously over whole acres of ground, and banishing every other plant from its domains. Mountain peat, which is of a dry, friable nature, is formed almost exclusively by the decay of this moss. It seems intended by nature to serve as a covering to the soil—in the absence of grass and heather—as it is found most luxuriantly and in the greatest profusion in spots considerably above the heather line, as well as the point where grass ceases to be a social plant, and occurs only in scattered tufts here and there. In these bleak and desolate spots, it sometimes furnishes materials for an extemporaneous couch to the belated traveller compelled to sleep in the shade of a rock on the hills; although care must be taken in arranging the couch to place the dry surface uniformly uppermost, otherwise the wet decomposed portions will here and there obtrude, and render the repose of the tenant exceedingly uncomfortable. The common hair moss[1] (*Poly-*

[1] See Frontispiece.

*trichum commune*), which is the strongest and wiriest of the British mosses, often covers large tracts of moorland, in moist places, and frequently attains a height of between two and three feet. In Lapland it forms almost the only verdure of the plains, and is occasionally used by the inhabitants when on long journeys for a bed, a large portion of the mossy turf, cut from a neighbouring spot, being employed as a covering. The fountain apple-moss (*Bartramia fontana*) also grows in great profusion wherever it occurs. It completely fills up the sources of springs, for many yards around, with a bright green deceptive verdure, through which the unwary foot sinks into the coldest water and the blackest mud. The course of Alpine streamlets, near their commencement, may be traced for a considerable distance by the beds of this moss, through which the waters languidly flow. But of all the members of this family the *Sphagna*[1] or bog mosses are the most social. They are everywhere most abundant on heaths and mossy soils, where they spread in such immense masses that they give a singularly light appearance to the whole moorland landscape; and by the accumulation of their remains fill up the beds of ancient lakes, bogs, and marshes, with dense, spongy, continuous cushions, of a pale green, dirty white, or dark red colour. This is the principal moss in the marshy plains of Lapland, and within the whole of the Arctic Circle; and nothing can be more dreary and desolate than the scenery where this moss exclusively prevails. Melville Island, the most western point ever navigated in the Polar Sea, though

[1] See Frontispiece.

nearly as large as Scotland, is principally covered with mosses, these plants forming more than a fourth part of its whole flora; while the black lifeless soil of New South Shetland, one of the most southern points in the Antarctic regions, is covered with faint specks of mosses struggling for existence. In the extreme north and the extreme south, they thus form the principal vegetation of large portions of the earth's surface.

Mosses are seldom associated with historical or personal incidents. There are two species, however, which derive an additional interest from this connexion. It has been ascertained that the hyssop, which formed the lowest limit in the descending scale of Solomon's botanical knowledge, and which was frequently employed in the temple service of the Jews for purposes of purification by water or blood, is identical with the little beardless moss (*Gymnostomum truncatulum*), which is abundant on banks, walls, and fallow fields in this country. It has been found in little scattered tufts on the walls of Jerusalem, the kind of situation indicated in Scripture as its natural growing place. It is little more than half-an-inch in height, but it is very much branched, and forms sometimes large continuous patches, which could easily be employed as sponges. The specimens found in the East are considerably larger than those which occur in this country; so that there is every probability that the reference of Hasselquist, who called it *Hyssopus Solomonis*, is correct. The moss which so deeply interested the feelings of Mungo Park in the African desert, as to revive his drooping spirits when overcome with fatigue, has been found, by means of original specimens, to be the little fern-like fork-moss (*Dicranum bryoides*),[1] a frequent denizen of moist banks in woods in this country, although, from its very minute size, often overlooked. There is one peculiar species, the cord moss (*Funaria hygrometrica*), called *la charbonnière* in France, from its growing in the woods where anything has been burned, and particularly abundant on old walls, whose stem possesses the curious hygrometric action observable in the teeth of other species. In dry weather it becomes corded, while it uncoils and straightens in moist weather, and thus forms an excellent natural hygrometer. As particular illustrations of the beauty of mosses, which can be perfectly seen and appreciated by the naked eye, may be instanced the *Splachnum rubrum* of the North American bogs, with its large, bright red, flagon-shaped fruit-vessel, and its broad, pellucid, soft green leaves; the common long-leaved thyme moss[2] of our own woods, with its exquisite, prominent undulated foliage, like a palm-tree in miniature; and the *Neckera crispa*, which is perhaps the loveliest of all the species, investing rocks and trunks of trees with its richly-coloured and glossy leaves. When spreading over trees, it is of a dark, dull green colour; but when occurring on dry lichen-clad rocks, over which its closely-adhering stems and leaves creep for many a yard, it assumes a bright yellowish-green, glossy hue, changing gradually and imperceptibly downwards, until the old leaves become of a singularly rich dark brown or red colour. When the sunbeams and shadows are flickering over its crisped and silken leaves, it forms

[1] See Frontispiece. [2] *Ibid.*

one of the most beautiful objects upon which the eye can rest.

Mosses directly serve very few purposes in the economy of man. They are often employed for packing articles, for which they are admirably adapted; and Linnæus informs us that the Swedish peasantry fill up the spaces between the chimney and the walls in their houses with a particular kind, which prevents the action of the fire by the exclusion of air. Another species is sometimes employed in the manufacture of mats and brooms. The bog-moss supplies materials for mattresses. The Laplanders use it instead of clothes for their new-born babes, packing their cradles firmly with it; and in seasons of scarcity it enters into the composition of their bread. The dense fork moss, when twisted, is used by the Esquimaux for lamp-wicks, a purpose which it very inadequately performs. But this is about all that can be said of their value to man. In the economy of nature, however, they are extremely useful. They contribute to the diffusion and preservation of vegetable life, both by the soil which their decay supplies, and by the shelter which they afford to the roots of trees and plants in very hot or very cold weather. Peat is almost entirely composed of mosses. This substance is usually found in great basin-shaped hollows, or valleys among the hills, formerly covered with indigenous forests of birch, alder, and hazel, or with the waters of a mountain lake. In the former case, the rotting of the fallen trees produced a rich black mould where mosses luxuriated; these mosses acted like sponges, and absorbed the moisture from the atmosphere, and retained the rains when they fell, forming shallow marshes around the fallen trees. More mosses were developed by this moisture, and more moisture was accumulated by these mosses; and thus the mutual process went on, one layer of moss decaying in its lower parts, and increasing by additions to its tops—the dead giving birth to the living—until at last the fallen trees were completely entombed, and a stratum of upwards of twenty feet of solid peat, in some instances, deposited above them. When, on the other hand, the basin-shaped hollows were originally occupied by lakes, the *Sphagnum* or bog-moss abounded in the waters, and spread so extensively, even from great depths, as through course of time to transform the lakes into quaking bogs, which, by the accumulation of drift, dust, and rubbish, and the decay of the original plants and the formation of new, became ultimately compressed into solid peat, covered upon the surface with heather, or a green vesture of grass or moss. The *Sphagnum* or bog-moss by which this great change was effected is of a singularly pale, almost snowy-white colour, a peculiarity exceedingly rare among plants, and sometimes attains a length of six or seven feet in deep water, its large air-cells imparting the necessary buoyancy to it. Its structure is in many respects different from that of all other mosses. Its branches are fasciculate and disposed around the stem in spirals; it has no roots whatever, but floats unattached in an upright position in the water; its cell-walls are perforated, and the leaf-cells contain a well-developed spiral; while the stem is composed of tissue, which, under the microscope, bears a close resemblance to the glandular structure of the stems of coniferous trees. The seed-vessel is sessile among the leaves, and bursts in the centre, the lid flying off when the seed is ripe with considerable force, so as to give a distinctly audible report on a still summer day. It is extensively distributed in temperate regions, being almost unknown in the tropics, where the peat is formed by the decomposition of shrubby plants like the common heather. The peat of Tierra del Fuego, the Falkland Islands, and the Galapagos Archipelago, is composed of this bog-moss. We may be able to form some idea of the vast importance of this moss, when we consider that peat-bogs occupy a tenth part of the whole of Ireland, and furnish in the Highlands of Scotland the largest proportion of the fuel consumed by the inhabitants. It is a singular fact that we owe our coals to the carbonized remains of ferns and their allies; and our peats to the decomposed tissues of mosses—two of the most useful and indispensable materials in our social economy to two of the humblest families in the vegetable kingdom. How true it is, that things which we are apt to despise or overlook on account of their minuteness and apparent insignificance, are not only full of lessons of beauty and wisdom, but are also made the means, in the hands of a kind Providence, of the greatest good to His creatures!

The plants whose peculiarities have been described in the preceding pages are called urn mosses, their fructification being urn-shaped, furnished with teeth, and closed with a lid. There is another large class, called scale mosses or liverworts (*Hepaticæ* or *Jungermanniæ*), so closely allied to the true mosses that they are frequently confounded even by an educated eye. Of these there are nearly a hundred species indigenous to Great Britain and Ireland, some of which are so small as to be scarcely visible, and others much larger than any of the true mosses. With the exception of a few prominent species, which are found in every moist wood and on every shady rock, they are very local and limited in their distribution, many of them being remarkably rare, and confined to remote and isolated localities. Perhaps the greatest number of species occurs in the tropics; and no-

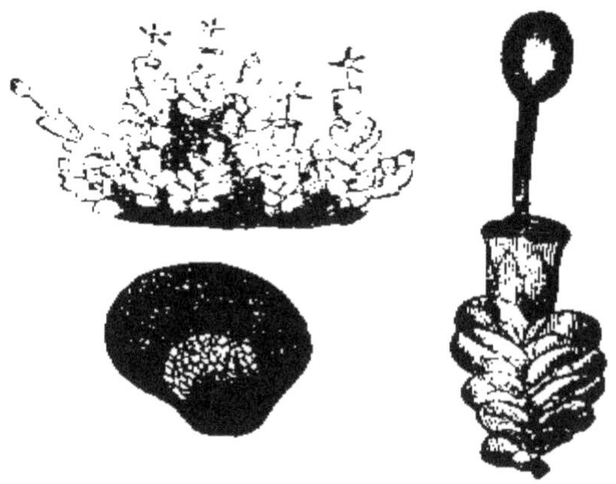

Fig. 2.—Jungermanniæ complanata.

where do they luxuriate so much as in the dark woods and mountain ravines of New Zealand. Some of them grow in the bleakest spots in the world, and are to be found even at a higher altitude than the urn mosses on the great mountain ranges of the globe. They form the faintest, dimmest tint of green on the edges of eternal glaciers, and on the bare storm-seamed ridges of the Alps and Andes, where not a tuft of moss or a trace of other vegetation can be seen; and this almost imperceptible film of verdure, when cleansed from the earth and moistened with water, presents under the microscope the most beautiful appearance.

The peculiarities of these plants are so remarkable and interesting that they deserve more than a passing notice. They do not grow upright in tufts like the mosses, but have a flat, creeping, lichen-like habit, spreading over rocks and trees in closely-applied circles which radiate from a common centre. The whole typical plant is like a series or necklace of roundish flat scales connected at the edges; several of which branch from a common point in the middle. The leaves, unlike those of the mosses, are entirely destitute of a central nerve, for what is called the nervure in the membraneous or leafy species, is nothing more than the stalk itself, on the edges of which the leaves are fastened together in such a manner as to form apparently a continuous whole. They are disposed either in a spiral which turns from left to right, in which case they are called succubous, or in a spiral which turns from right to left, when they receive the name of incubous leaves. In their shape there is a marvellous diversity; and the arrangement and form of the cells is so exquisitely beautiful in almost all the species, that no more pleasing objects can be mounted for the microscope. In some species they are furnished with radicles or rootlets along the whole length of their under side. Their substance is very loosely cellular, easily reviving, after being dried, by the application of moisture. Their colour varies from a pale white to the darkest green and the deepest and most brilliant red and purple; sea-green, however, being the prevailing hue. The fruit-vessel is as interesting and suggestive of marvellous reflection as that of the urn-mosses. It is generally supported on a very delicate silvery stem; and is at first round, gradually splitting as it becomes ripe into two or four valves, which bear a close resemblance to the calyx or corolla of flowering plants. In the centre of this calyx-like organ may be seen a tuft of delicate straw-coloured hairs, like floss silk, with the spores or seeds in the form of minute yellow dust intermingled. These hairs or filaments are spiral, highly elastic, and hygrometrical, twisting and writhing even upon the field of the microscope; and like the spring-like ring round the fruit-vessel of the fern, serve by their coiling and uncoiling, in certain states of the surrounding atmosphere, to scatter abroad, even to a considerable distance, the powdery seeds imbedded among them. This is a very curious and wonderful piece of mechanism, and highly deserving of microscopical examination.

One genus of this interesting family called Riccia, floats on the surface of stagnant waters, and bears a superficial resemblance to the common duckweed. The fronds are destitute of radicles when growing on the surface of ponds and ditches; but if the water be removed by evaporation or draining, or the plant thrown on the soil at the margin, they become smaller and fasten themselves firmly to the ground by numerous fibrous rootlets; a beautiful example of the ease with which these humble plants accommodate themselves to altered circumstances. They have many air-passages between the cells, which enable them to float on the water. The under surface is covered, to a greater or less extent, with thin scales, which form most beautiful microscopic objects when treated with different chemical tests, from their transparency and variety of colouring. One ally of this genus, called Riella, differs widely from the rest of the tribe in its erect, moss-like habit. It grows on the margins of ponds, streams, and lakes in Algiers and Sardinia, and perfects its fruit when submerged. It is quite a botanical curiosity, presenting a whorled appearance, not unlike the common spiral shells of the sea-shore. Each individual consists of a central stem, round which a distinct leaf or wing is wound in the form of a screw or continuous spiral. On the edge of this wing, towards the summit of the male plant, the antheridia are developed; while in the female the fruit clusters on the stem between the whorls.

The most interesting of all the scale-mosses is the common marchantia or liverwort (*Marchantia polymorpha*, Fig. 3). It is very common, creeping in large, dull,

FIG. 3.—MARCHANTIA POLYMORPHA.

dark-green patches over rocks in very moist and shady situations, such as the banks of a densely-wooded stream in a deep narrow glen, or the sides of rivers and fountains. It may often be seen also on the moist walls of hot-houses, and in the pots and tubs. It adheres closely to rocks, which it sometimes completely covers with its imbricated fronds, by the numerous white downy radicles with which the under-surface is covered. Its fronds are flat, about three inches long, and from half-an-inch to an inch wide, and are variously divided into obtuse lobes. Their texture is membranaceous and strikingly cellular. Their upper surface is most beautifully reticulated and covered with numerous minute lozenge-like scales, with a little dot-like pore or puncture in the centre, analogous to the stomates or breathing-pores of flowering plants. The fructification is very singular, resembling a forest of little mushrooms rising from the leaves; each dividing at the top into eight or ten green rays, and having as many little brown purses placed alternately between them. Each of these purses has a valve which opens generally in July, and contains within it four or five florets, from the centre of which rises a single funnel-shaped filament, covered with a yellow powder affixed to the elaters or elastic spiral hairs previously alluded to. Besides this ordinary male and female stalked receptacle, sterile as well as fertile individuals are provided at all seasons of the year with cup-like bodies, growing on various parts of the upper surface of the frond, always on the mid-rib, and of the same texture as the frond itself. These bodies seem to indicate an approach to the calyx and corolla of the flowering plants. They contain in their interior several lentil-shaped membranaceous bodies of a reticulated structure, equivalent to buds, which frequently throw out rootlets before leaving their receptacles, and striking root on the spots where they happen to fall, in time become perfect fronds. There is no more pleasing and profitable study to the young botanist than the examination of the highly curious structure and complex system of fructification peculiar to this plant. It is interesting also on account of its associations. Under the name of *Hepatica officinarum*, it was employed by the ancient herbalists, from its resemblance to the reticulated structure of the liver, as a cure for all diseases affecting *that* organ. It is still used as a popular remedy for jaundice and other maladies in some parts of England; but its virtues are, in all likelihood, entirely imaginary. Hoffmann and Willemet, in their elaborate treatise upon the uses of lichens, state regarding it, "Cette plante est amère, aromatique, abstersive, vulnéraire, sudorifique, apéritive. On prescrit l'Hépatique en apozème, à la dose d'une poignée pour l'homme, et de deux ou trois pour les animaux." The bruised fronds of some species are singularly fragrant, resembling bergamot.

There is a class of plants whose external appearance and mode of growth would indicate that they belong to the tribe under review, but whose structure and functions are so different, that they are commonly supposed to bear a closer analogy to the ferns. They occupy an intermediate position, and form a connecting link between ferns and mosses; I allude to the Lycopods or club-mosses. They are usually found in bleak, bare, exposed situations in all parts of the world, and sometimes attain a large size; forsaking the creeping habit peculiar to the family, and becoming arborescent in tropical countries, particularly New Zealand, rivalling in rank luxuriance the surrounding trees and shrubs of the forest. The British representatives of the class are comparatively small plants, with the exception, perhaps, of the commonest species (*Lycopodium clavatum*, Fig. 4), which creeps along the ground among the heather on the moorlands, and sends out runners or creeping stems in all directions to the length of several yards, which take a firm hold of the soil by means of long, tough, wiry roots

FIG. 4. LYCOPODIUM CLAVATUM. FIG. 5. LYCOPODIUM SELAGO. FIG. 6. LYCOPODIUM ALPINUM.

on their under-surface. The smallest species is the marsh club-moss (*Lycopodium inundatum*), which grows upright in little tufts at the edge of streamlets, or in marshy hollows among the hills, where it is almost wholly concealed by the surrounding bog-mosses. In this country, the lycopods are all alpine or sub-alpine; one species (Fig. 5) ascending to the highest summits of the British mountains, where it grows in large rigid tufts amid the *débris* of rocks, and another (Fig. 6) trailing in long wreaths over the bare mossy shoulders of the Highland hills, sending up at short intervals from the bare, whitish, procumbent stems, palm-shaped tufts of very hard foliage, very like that of the savine. In other parts of the world, however, they grow on the low grounds in the woods and other warm, humid situations, adding to the picturesqueness and beauty of the sylvan scenery. One species, the Tmesipteris, remarkable for its pendulous habit and very broad leaves, hangs down in long trailing wreaths from the trunks of tree-ferns, in South America and New Zealand. In the little island of St. Paul, isolated from the rest of the world in the Indian Ocean, thousands of miles from any friendly shore, there occurs a beautiful species (*L. cernum*), the presence of which in that remote locality is a puzzle to the student of geographical botany. This island is situated in the temperate zone, while the normal range of this plant is exclusively within the tropics. As, however, the island is volcanic, and contains numerous hot springs, which diffuse a considerable warmth around, this circumstance may account for the presence of the lycopod, especially as it also occurs, far out of its proper range, about the warm springs of the Azores. Luxuriating in beautiful tufts amid the barren tufa of this lonely island, it is a welcome and refreshing sight to the voyager on the way to Australia, tired of the monotony of the sea, and yearning for mother earth. Like himself, a stranger in a strange land, it often reminds the emigrant of the brown moorlands of his native country, where he used to gather the trailing wreaths of the fox-fetters to bind around his cap in the sunny days of youth. One very extraordinary species (*Selaginella convoluta*), which grows in the arid deserts of central South America, among aloes and cactuses, is possessed of remarkable hygrometric properties. In the dry season, when every particle of moisture is extracted from the soil, it detaches itself from its growing place, rolls itself up into a ball, like the young frond of a fern before it is unfolded, and is carried away by the violent equinoctial winds which prevail at the time in these regions, often to very great distances. It remains coiled up in this form for a considerable time; but if carried to a marsh or the margin of a stream, or any other moist place, it begins slowly to unfold, and spreads itself out flatly on the soil like a branch of arbor-vītæ, assumes its former vigour and freshness, takes root, develops its fructification, and casts abroad its seed upon the air. When this new situation is dried up, it resumes its old nomadic habits, and like an adventurous pilgrim takes advantage of the wind to emigrate to a more favourable locality. A singular phenomenon has been observed in a species of selaginella cultivated in Kew gardens, called specifically from this circumstance *mirabilis*. "In the morning the fronds are green, but as the day advances they become pale, recovering gradually their colour by the following day. Dr. Hooker has observed that in their pale condition the endochrome of the cells of the leaves is contracted into a little pellet."

The club-mosses bear in the axils of their leaves minute round or kidney-shaped cases of a bright yellow colour, which form the receptacles of their dust-like seed. Some species have little cone-like spikes at the tips of their branches, under the scales of which, as in the pine tribe, lurk the reproductive embryos. In the common club-moss these spikes are two-pronged, and of a whitish colour, while the seed is highly inflammable, and was formerly employed to produce artificial lightning on the stage, by being blown through a tube and ignited. These seeds originate independently of any reproductive organs or fertilizing influence. Indeed it is these seeds in germination which develop the structure upon which the fertilizing organ, and the organ to be fertilized, are situated. The stems are perennial, and consist of a mass of thick walled, often dotted cells, enclosing one or more bundles of scalariform tissue, which send off branches to every leaf and bud. Among these bundles may be seen elongated cells, distinctly reticulated. This kind of tissue indicates a close relation to the ferns, and justifies the position in which they are usually placed by systematists. New fruit-axils are formed year after year, bearing their new cluster of seeds independent altogether of any fertilizing organs, such as antheridia or archegonia. The club-mosses are all very graceful and beautiful plants. The Spanish moss (*Lycopodium denticulatum*) is a great ornament to conservatories and hot-houses, where it conceals with its luxuriant drapery the mould in the pots, and keeps the roots of the plants moist. Nothing can be lovelier or more elegant than a basket of orchids in full flower, with clusters of this moss drooping in careless grace from its sides. The common club-moss of our moors is often gathered by the peasantry to festoon the ornaments of their mantelpieces; while wreaths of it are collected from the woods of Balmoral, where it grows in abundance, to grace the royal table. All the species of lycopods are possessed of poisonous, or at least questionable properties. The *L. catharticum* has been administered as a strong cathartic. In the Highlands they are employed with alum to fix the native dyes in the manufacture of tartan, while they are said themselves to produce a blue tint.

Lycopods may be said to present the highest type of cryptogamic vegetation, the highest limit capable of being reached by flowerless plants. Indeed, they are said by botanists of the highest reputation to bear a close affinity to coniferous trees, to be, in fact, pine-trees in miniature. This affinity though indicated by very curious resemblances is, however, strictly analogical. The gap between the two great orders of plants is too wide to be overleaped by a sudden transition. There is a resemblance in external form, habit, and fructification; the leaves are in both cases linear; the seeds are in both cases produced from cones or spikes; the formation of the archegonia and embryonic pods of the one, is similar to that of the corpuscles and embryo in the other, but in these points the likeness begins and ends. There is no true homology, but a mere analogy which is often seen to harmonize the most dissimilar works of nature, as if to show that they proceeded from the same creating hand. There may be gradual transition from one class of plants to another, and certain characters may be common to two families; but still there are definite groups in nature, and typical characters belonging to plants, which will for ever keep them distinct and isolated, as illustrations of the infinite variety of the Divine works.

The first pages of the earth's history reveal to us very

extraordinary facts with relation to members and allies of the moss tribe. The club-mosses, in particular, at a former period seem to have played a more important part, or to have found conditions more suitable to their luxuriant development than is the case at the present day. Some of them are stated to have formed lofty trees eighty feet high, with a proportionate diameter of trunk. They are the most ancient of all plants. The oldest land-plant yet known is supposed to be a species of lycopodium closely resembling the common species of our moors. In the upper beds of the Upper Silurian rocks, they are the only terrestrial plants yet found. In the lower Old Red Sandstone they also abounded ; while they occupied a considerable space in the Oolitic vegetation. But it is in the Coal-measures that they seem to have attained their utmost size and luxuriance, sigillaria, stigmaria, lepidodendron, etc., being now considered by competent botanists to be highly-developed lycopodia. Along with ferns, they covered the whole earth from Melville Island in the Arctic regions to the Ultima Thule of the Southern Ocean, with rank majestic forests of a uniform dull green hue. The numerous coal-seams and inflammable shale found in almost every part of the world, form but a small portion of their remains. "Between the time of the ancient lycopodite found in the flagstone of Orkney," says Hugh Miller, "and those of the existing club-moss that now scatters its light spores by millions over the dead and blackened remains of its remote predecessor, many creations must have intervened, and many a prodigy of the vegetable world appeared, especially in the earlier and middle periods,—Sigillaria,

Favularia, Knorria, and Ulodendron, that have had no representatives in the floras of later times ; and yet here, flanking the immense scale at both its ends, do we find plants of so nearly the same form and type that it demands a careful survey to distinguish their points of difference."

# CHAPTER II.

## LICHENS.

"Search out the wisdom of nature: there is depth in all her doings. She hath, on a mighty scale, a general use for all things; yet hath she specially for each its microscopic purpose."—MARTIN F. TUPPER.

To most minds the title of this chapter may suggest no idea of importance. Flowers they love, for they are linked with childhood's recollections of sunshine and mirth, and mingle with the hallowed memories of the dead, and of the scenes amid which they are laid. Ferns they admire as they cluster in the forest shade, gracefully bend down to see their own forms in the mossy spring, or wave from some wild inaccessible crag their delicate fronds in the breeze of summer; and mosses they consider beautiful, as they repose their languid limbs, in the sultry noonday, on the woodland banks wreathed in dreamy-looking shadows, to which these tiny plants lend their all of softness and beauty. But the lowly lichens they pass by with indifference, regarding them only as inorganic discolorations and weather-stains on the trees and rocks where they repose. And yet they too are interesting, both as regards their history and their uses; as interesting as many plants which occupy a far higher position in the ranks of vegetation. Uninviting and apparently lifeless although their external aspect may appear, they are found, when subjected to the microscope, to have their own peculiar beauties and wonders. Simple as is their construction, being entirely composed of an aggregate of minute cells united together in various ways by intercellular matter, and completely destitute of stems, leaves, and all those parts which enter into our ideas of perfect plants, yet by a wonderful compensation they are so extensively diversified in their form and appearance, as to present to the student of nature, a field for his inquiry, as wide and wondrous, as the display of green foliage and blossoms of every hue which glow in the summer sun. To the Pre-Raphaelite landscape painter, intent upon seeking materials for the foregrounds of his sketches, they possess an indescribable interest. Through their instrumentality the miserable hovel, with its rough unmortared walls, becomes a charming and romantic object. The old dyke by the wayside, commonplace and disagreeable although it may look when newly constructed, becomes a pleasing feature in the landscape when garnished with the grey rosettes, eccentric patches, and nebulæ of the lichens; and the rude, rugged rock acquires an additional wildness and picturesqueness through the affluent display of these plants. Along with the wallflower and the ivy, they decorate the mouldering ruin, and harmonize its otherwise haggard and discordant features, by their subdued and varied colouring, with the gentler forms and the softer tone of the scenery around. Thus nature takes back into her bosom the falling works of human skill and power, and luxuriantly adorns them with her living garniture of beauty; and these softening stains with which she touches the rude, stern masses she disjoins, have their value in the composition not simply on account of the pleasure they afford to the eye by the mere tints of a painter's palette, but also and chiefly on account of the meaning they suggest through the eye to the mind as the genuine and expressive colouring of time. To the trees of the forest, lichens impart a singularly aged and venerable appearance which irresistibly commands our homage, and leads our thoughts far back over the dim path of years to the memories of primitive times. So abundant are they in the Highland woods, that every tree is covered with their long white streaming tufts, which look on the green tassel-laden branches, and among the fringy, waving hollows of the pyramid-like foliage, like the snowy blossoms of some unknown fruit-tree. It is impossible to enter a pine forest adorned with a profusion of these curious plants, without admiring the wild and picturesque appearance which it presents. The hoary trees seem like an assembly of aged bearded Druids, metamorphosed by some awful spell while in the act of worshipping their mysterious deity; while the feelings of solemn awe and reverence with which we regard them are deepened and rendered more intense and overpowering by the dread silence, the utter solitude that reigns around—a silence broken only by the low, deep, sybilline sigh of the wind among the tree-tops; the faint crackling sound of the falling pine-cones; or perchance, at rare intervals, the wild, melancholy cries of some little wandering bird afraid to find itself alone in such a dreary place, multiplied with startling distinctness through the forest as they pass along from echo to echo. Perhaps a red-deer stands gazing at you, with large inquiring eyes, at the end of a long vista between the red trunks of the trees; but as you gaze, it glides away into a deeper solitude as noiselessly and as mysteriously as it came; and the very sunbeams, that elsewhere dance and sport with the wavering shadows, and chase each other in long links of golden light over the mossy sward, creep through the dense canopy overhead, and down the lichened trunks slowly and hesitatingly, as though, like children who stand at the mouth of some grim yawning cavern, they longed yet dreaded to enter. How applicable to this weird scene is the graphic description of an American forest, with which Longfellow opens his beautiful poem of "Evangeline"—

> "This is the forest primeval. The murmuring pines and the hemlocks,
> Bearded with moss, and in garments green, indistinct in the twilight,
> Stand like Druids of old, with voices sad and prophetic;
> Stand like harpers hoar, with beards that rest on their bosoms."

We are more indebted to the humble lichens for the charming romance of our sylvan scenery than we imagine; for we are apt to overlook the minute plants by which much of the effect is produced. All who have any taste or poetical feeling whatever, admire the conspicuous beauties of a wood—the clouds of green foliage overhead, the endless ramifications of the branches, the massiveness and elegance of the trunks, and the softness and richness of the grassy carpet underneath; but there are few, comparatively, who pay any attention to those minute varieties of tint and form contributed by the lower orders of vegetation—the starry flower, the plumy fern, or the umbrella-like fungus upon the ground, and the clustered moss and trailing lichen upon the tree; and yet it is with these small and apparently insignificant objects that nature shades the picture, balances and contrasts the colouring, clothes the nakedness, and softens down the irregularities and deformities of the whole scene, which would otherwise be stiff and hard as a forest-piece painted by a Chinese artist.

Lichens are exceedingly diversified in their form, appearance, and texture. Upwards of four hundred and *fifty different* kinds have been found in Great Britain alone, while altogether between two and three thousand species have been discovered in different parts of the world by the zealous researches of naturalists. In their very simplest rudimentary forms, they consist apparently of nothing more than a collection of powdery granules, so minute that the figure of each is scarcely distinguishable, and so dry and utterly destitute of organization that it is difficult to believe that any vitality exists in them. Some of these form ink-like stains on the smooth tops of posts and felled trees; others are sprinkled like flower of brimstone or whiting over shady rocks and withered tufts of moss; while a third species is familiar to every one, as covering with a bright green incrustation the trunks and boughs of trees in the squares and suburbs of smoky towns, where the air is so impure as to forbid the growth of all other vegetation. It also creeps over the grotesque figures and elaborate carving on the roofs and pillars of Roslin Chapel, near Edinburgh, and gives to the whole an exquisitely beautiful and romantic appearance. One species, the *Lepraria Jolithus*, is associated with many a superstitious legend. Linnæus, in his journal of a tour through Œland and East Gothland, thus alludes to it :—" Everywhere near the road I saw stones covered with a blood-red pigment, which on being rubbed turned into a light yellow, and diffused a smell of violets, whence they have obtained the name of violet stones ; though, indeed, the stone itself has no smell at all, but only the moss with which it is dyed." At Holywell, in North Wales, the stones are covered with this curious lichen, which gives them the appearance of being stained with blood ; and of course the peasantry in the neighbourhood allege, that it is the ineffaceable blood which dropped from St. Winnifred's head, when she suffered martyrdom on that sacred spot. A higher order of lichens (*Bæomyces*) is furnished, besides this powdery crust, with solid, fleshy, club-shaped fructification ; while a singularly beautiful genus (*Calicium*), usually of a very vivid yellow colour, spreading in indefinite patches over oaks and firs, is provided with capsules somewhat like those of the mosses. These capsules, though thickly scattered over the crust, are so minute as to be scarcely distinguishable by the naked eye, but under the microscope they present a truly lovely appearance. They are cup or urn-shaped, of a coal-black colour, and supported by a slender stalk about the thickness of a horse-hair. At an early stage they are covered with a very delicate veil, which stretches completely over their mouth ; but this soon vanishes, and exposes to view a mass of black or brown seeds, like the ovule in an acorn, which the slightest touch of the tiniest insect's wing can dislodge, and send away on the breeze in search of a habitat for another colony.

Most of the crustaceous lichens are merely grey filmy patches inseparable from their growing places, indefinitely spreading, or bounded by a narrow line-like border, which always intervenes to separate them when two species closely approximate, and studded all over with black, brown, or red tubercles. The foliaceous species, again, are usually round rosettes of various colours, attached by dense black fibres all over their under-surface, or by a single knot-like root in the centre. Some are dry and membranaceous; while others are gelatinous and pulpy, like aërial sea-weeds left exposed on inland rocks by the retiring waves of an extinct ocean. Some are lobed with woolly veins underneath; and others reticulated above, and furnished with little cavities or holes on the under-surface. The higher orders of lichens, though destitute of anything resembling vascular tissue, exhibit considerable complexity of structure. Some are shrubby, and tufted, with stem and branches, like miniature trees; others bear a strong resemblance to the corallines of our sea-shores; while a third class, "the green-fringed cup-moss with the scarlet tip," as Crabbe calls it, is exceedingly graceful, growing in clusters beside the black peat-moss or under the heather tuft,

> "And, Hebe-like, upholding
> Its cups with dewy offerings to the sun."

As an illustration of the extraordinary appearances which lichens occasionally present, I may describe the *Opegrapha* or written lichen (Fig. 7), perhaps the most curious and remarkable member of this strange tribe. In her cactuses[1] and orchids sportive nature often displays a ludicrous resemblance to insects, birds, animals, and even the "human face and form divine;" but this is one of the few instances in which she has condescended to imitate in her vegetable productions the written language of man. The crust of this curious autograph of nature is a mere white tartareous film of indefinite extent,

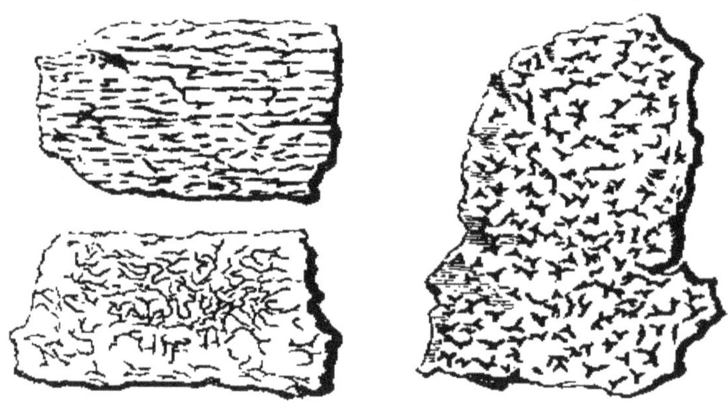

FIG. 7.—OPEGRAPHA SCRIPTA.

sometimes bounded by a faint line of black like a mourning letter. It spreads over the smooth bark of trees, particularly the beech, the hazel, and the oak. On the birch-tree—whose smooth, snow-white, vellum-like bark seems designed by nature for the inscription of lovers' names and magic incantations—it may often be seen covering the whole trunk. The fructification consists of long wavy black lines, sometimes parallel like Runic inscriptions; sometimes arrow-headed, like the cuneiform characters engraved upon the monumental stones of Persepolis and Assyria; and sometimes gathered together

[1] As, for instance, *Cactus senilis*.

in groups and clusters, bearing a strong resemblance to Arabic and Chinese letters.

In that well-known and interesting work, "Travels in Tartary, Thibet, and China," by the French Lazarists Huc and Gabet, there is a long description of a very remarkable phenomenon called the "Tree of Ten Thousand Images," found by them near the town of Koumboum in Thibet. For the sake of those who may not have access to the original work, I shall quote the description entire. "At the foot of the mountain on which the Lamasery stands, and not far from the principal Buddhist temple, is a great square enclosure, formed by brick walls. Upon entering this, we were able to examine at leisure this marvellous tree, some of the branches of which had already manifested themselves above the wall. Our eyes were first directed with earnest curiosity to the leaves, and we were filled with an absolute consternation of astonishment at finding that in point of fact, there were upon each of the leaves well formed Thibetian characters, all of a green colour, some darker, some lighter than the tree itself. Our first impression was a suspicion of fraud on the part of the Lamas; but after a minute examination of every detail, we could not discover the least deception. The characters all appeared to us portions of the leaf itself, equally with its veins and nerves; the position was not the same in all; in one leaf they would be at the top, in another in the middle, in a third at the base or at the side; the younger leaves represented the characters only in a partial state of formation. The bark of the tree, and its branches—which resemble that of the plane-tree—are also covered with these characters. When you remove a piece of old bark, the young bark under it exhibits the indistinct outlines of characters in a germinating state, and what is very singular, these new characters are not unfrequently different from those which they replace. We examined everything with the closest attention, in order to detect some trace of trickery, but we could discern nothing of the sort; and the perspiration actually trickled down our faces under the influence of the sensations which this most amazing spectacle created. More profound intellects than ours may, perhaps, be able to supply a satisfactory explanation of the mysteries of this singular tree; but as to us, we altogether give it up." Botanists whose severe love of truth overcomes in most cases their poetical inclinations, have thrown considerable doubt upon this story, even though related by missionaries of a respectable character. It appears to be in some particulars considerably indebted to an ardent imagination, but it might, nevertheless, be true enough in its main facts. Divested of its apparent embellishments and exaggerations, the tree might be found after all to be only an exotic species of plane or sycamore, covered with immense patches of the written lichen, which—it is well known to botanists—occurs in greater profusion and attains a larger size in tropical than in temperate countries. Many exotic, and one or two European lichens, occur on living leaves. These are principally developed on the upper surface, sometimes only superficially connected with the leaves, which afford them a basis or attachment and growth; and at other times originating like the fungi beneath the true cuticle, forming a carbonaceous, beautifully-sculptured crust, and elegant fructification. The foliage of the Thibetian wonder may, therefore, be indebted for its singular markings to a species of Limboria; and the characters on the bark and branches may have been caused by an unknown opegrapha. In fact, the counterpart of these inscriptions has been discovered by Hooker and Thomson in Khasya, on the leaves of a species of Symplocos.

Let us glance at some of the peculiarities of the lichens, and see if nature has not assigned them a higher and more important commission in her great household, than merely ornamenting old walls and ruins, and covering trees with a shaggy mantle.

Lichens, it has been said, are exceedingly simple in their construction. They are composed of two parts, the nutritive and the reproductive system. The nutritive portion is called the thallus, which, in the typical plant, spreads equally on all sides from the original point of development, in the form of an increasing circle; the circumference of which is often healthy and vigorous while the central parts are decayed or completely wanting. It is composed of two distinct tissues. The lower or medullary portion is composed of spherical cells, filled with a green matter, which seem to be the active, vegetating part of the lichen. These cells frequently accumulate in masses, burst through the layer above them, and appear in the form of a green, tenacious powder on the surface of the plant; while they are capable, if detached from the parent, of continuing the powers of cell-development, and forming the nucleus of new lichens. The external or cortical layer, on the other hand, is supposed by some botanists to serve the same purpose in the economy of the lichen as the bark does in that of the tree, viz., as a protection to the lower, living layer, of the dead cellules of which it actually consists. In some species this outer covering is smooth, and in others covered with small hollows or pits, or with hair or fibres, which serve to fix the plant.

Nature has bestowed upon the lichens a peculiar mode of reproduction, in which there is nothing analogous to that of the higher orders of the vegetable kingdom; and yet they are propagated with as unerring certainty and as great rapidity as the most prolific family of flowers. Every one who has an attentive eye must have often noticed the curious round disks or shields, of a different colour from the rest of the plant, with which their surface is often studded. These are called apothecia, and correspond with the flowers of the higher plants; for in them are lodged the seeds or germs by which the lichens are perpetuated. When examined under the microscope they are found to consist of a number of delicate flask-shaped cells, called thecæ, containing 4, 8, 12, or 16 sporidia, that is, cells of an oval form, with spores or seeds in their interior. The mode in which these spores are ejected affords as wonderful a proof of design as was seen in the case of the ferns and mosses. It is principally in moist or rainy weather that this curious process is performed. When the entire apothecium or shield is wetted, the layer bearing the thecæ or seed-vessels becomes bulged out above, whence arises a pressure on them, which ultimately bursts them at the summit, and causes the expulsion of their contents. Few things can exceed in beauty, as microscopical objects, the sporidia of many of the lichens. Some are bright scarlet, others deep blue, and others green, olive, golden yellow, or brown.

Besides these true organs of fructification, the lichens are furnished with other parts which possess the power of reproduction. A great many species, placed in unfavourable circumstances, seldom or never produce proper receptacles of seed ; but this is no obstacle to their propagation, as their whole surface is covered with collections of free powdery grains, which germinate into new plants wherever they are carried by the winds. There are also present on some lichens spongy excrescences which resemble minute trees ; and one peculiar genus is possessed of tubercles which occur on the back part of the frond, and are lodged in little cups which appear empty as soon as they have fallen out. The recent researches of the French lichenists, Tulasne and Itzigsohn, have discovered another kind of fructification which is very common and exceedingly interesting. This consists of minute, blackish, elevated, somewhat gelatinous points called spermagonia, occurring on various parts of the upper surface of the thallus. These resemble, in external appearance, the tubercular apothecia of the Lecideas ; but their internal structure, as shown in Fig. 8, is quite different. They consist of little cavities or utricles opening on the summit by a tiny orifice, and filled with a thin transparent mucilage, in which is contained a number of linear filaments of extreme tenuity, and somewhat curved, which vibrate slowly in every direction. These curious bodies are supposed to be analogous to the spermatozoids produced in the antheridia of the algæ and mosses, and which seem to perform an essential part in the reproduction of almost all cryptogamic plants. All these kinds of fructification are sometimes found on one plant at the same time, and each of them is capable, under certain conditions, of producing perfect individuals similar to the parent plant. It must not be supposed, however, that they all exercise their functions at one and the same

FIG. 8.—UMBILICARIA POLYMORPHA.

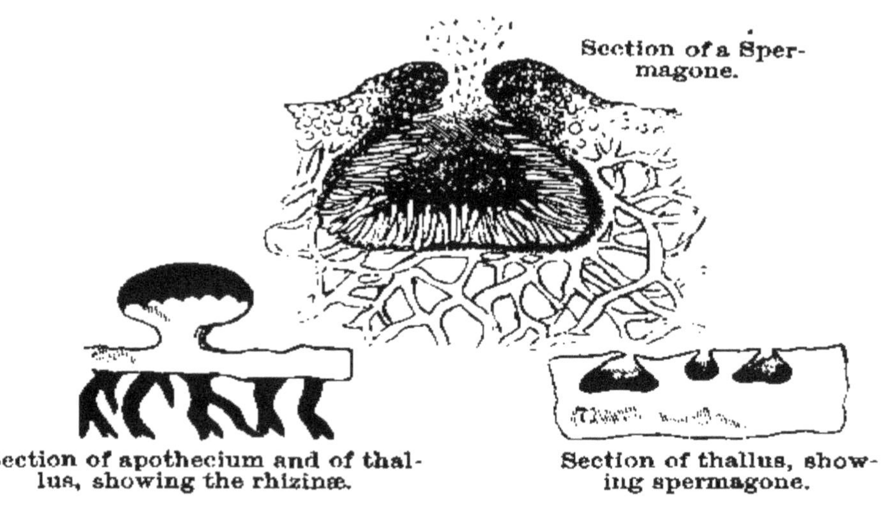


time—for nature is never prodigally wasteful of her resources; but where situation, temperature, or other conditions interrupt propagation by one mode, another is developed more exuberantly than usual to supply its place. If there be not conditions to produce perfect apothecia, there will be soridia, pulvinuli, or cyphellæ instead; and just as the chances of failure are great, so are the modes of reproduction increased: and what an admirable provision is this for the preservation of plants, which would otherwise be speedily exterminated, exposed as they are to the contingencies of being successively scorched, drenched, and frozen on the same naked and barren rocks. And how greatly does it exalt these humble plants in our estimation! Gifted with such powers of reproduction as these we can view the smallest lichen, "not as a single phyton, not as a single frond, but as the aggregate of, it may be, thousands of these, view it occupying as much space, and exercising as great an influence in the economy of nature as the largest forest tree, and rivalling it even in longevity.

Lichens are very slow-growing plants. They spring up somewhat rapidly during the first year or two, as is evinced by the luxurious growth which they form over young fruit-trees and espaliers in gardens; but after a circular frond is formed, they subside into a dormant state, in which they remain unaltered for many years. Mr. Berkeley says that he watched individuals for twenty-five years, which are now much in the same condition as they were when they first attracted his notice. Some of the grey rosettes of Parmelia which occur on walls and rocks, not unfrequently attaining a circumference of many feet, must be very aged, judging by this standard. The foliaceous and shrubby species are the most fugacious, though even these have great powers of longevity. We have no data from which to ascertain the age of tartareous species, which adhere almost inseparably to stones. Some of them are probably as old as any living organisms that exist on earth. The geographical lichen, which often spreads over the whole rocky summit of a mountain in one continuous patch, many separate individuals being absorbed in one, must date from fabulous periods. I have gathered it in this form on the summit of Schiehallion, on smooth quartz rocks, which exhibit here and there the glassy polish and deep striæ or flutings peculiar to glaciated surfaces, as distinct and unchanged by atmospheric disintegration as though the glacier, which had left these unmistakable traces behind it, had only yesterday passed over them. And if these ice-marks can be accepted as an indication of the age of the lichen—the first and sole organic covering of the rock, be it remembered—then in all probability it was in existence during the last great changes of the globe which preceded the creation of the human race. I do not press this point, however, for such a method of computation may be objected to on the score of being inapplicable ; but I think that it is at least as reasonable to believe, that some lichens date their origin as far back as the glacial epoch, as to believe, that there are trees now in existence that were contemporaries of the first generations of men. There are numerous destructive and obstructive causes, fatal to the longevity of trees, which either do not operate at all, or only to a very limited extent in the economy of lichens ; and, indeed, these dry, sapless, dormant plants appear to me to possess the power of living for ever, without exhibiting any symptoms of decay, unless from accidental or extraneous causes.

In their geographical distribution, lichens to a certain extent obey the same laws to which the higher orders of vegetation are subject, being influenced by temperature, altitude, and the geological character of the rocks upon which they are produced ; and thus several species and even genera are necessarily rare and confined to particular localities. It may, however, be said of them in general that they are cosmopolitan, universally distributed over the surface of the globe, and capable of existing in almost every situation, from the calcined plains of burning Africa to the snow-mantled pinnacles of icy Spitzbergen. Placed almost at the lowest scale of organization, they often require nothing more for their conservation, than the moisture of the atmosphere precipitated on naked masses of rock ; and their simple form and structure enable them to resist an amount alike of heat and cold, sufficient to destroy all vitality in more perfectly organized plants. In the Arctic regions—those outer boundaries of the earth, where eternal winter presides—these humble plants constitute by far the largest proportion of the flora, and by their prodigious development, and their wide social distribution, give as marked and peculiar a character to the scenery, as the palms and tree-ferns impart to the landscapes of the tropics. In the southern hemisphere also, lichens almost extend to the pole. They mark the extreme limit at which land vegetation has been found, one shrubby species, with large, deep, chestnut-coloured fructification, called *Usnea fasciata*, having been observed by Lieutenant Kendal on Deception Island, the Ultima Thule of the Antarctic regions. "There was nothing," he says, in his interesting account of his visit to that island, "in the shape of vegetation except a small kind of lichen, whose efforts seemed almost ineffectual to maintain its existence among the scanty soil afforded by the penguin's dung." Dr. Hooker also mentions that on this island, he found a few species of the beautiful pale green *Usnea melaxantha*, looking like a miniature shrubbery on the barren rocks; on another island, a few filmy specks of Lecanora and Lecidea, and five peculiar mosses; but that on Franklin Island, and the islands nearer the Southern Pole, he could not perceive the smallest trace of vegetation, not even a solitary lichen or piece of sea-weed clinging to the rocks. Surrounded by huge precipices of black lava, which seemed to fringe them with mourning, and consisting entirely of jagged rocks, upon which the traces of volcanic fire yet existed, covered only with a little red soil, scorched and sterile, or glittering snow-white patches of fragile shells and coral, ground to dust by the fury of the waves,—these remote islands exhibited an aspect so savage and repulsive, so utterly lonely and lifeless, as to impress with horror the stoutest heart.

> "But here, above, around, below,
> On mountain or in glen,
> Nor tree, nor shrub, nor plant, nor flower,
> Nor aught of vegetative power,
> The weary eye may ken.
> For all is rocks at random thrown,
> Black waves, bare crags, and banks of stone;
> As if were here denied
> The summer's sun, the spring's sweet dew,
> That clothe with many a varied hue,
> The bleakest mountain side."

Strange it seems that, while such extreme destitution, such sublime barrenness, prevails in these southern lands, in the Arctic regions, on the contrary, no spot has yet been discovered wholly destitute of vegetable life. The difference, Mrs. Somerville observes, appears to arise "more from the want of warmth in summer, than from the greater degree of cold in winter." The portion of heat imbibed by the soil, during the short summer of the Arctic regions, is prevented from escaping by the covering of snow which falls in the beginning of winter; and thus the temperature necessary for the scanty vegetation is preserved, till the return of the sun at once converts the Arctic winter into tropical summer, without the intervention of spring. Whereas in the Antarctic regions, the soil, owing to the much smaller quantity of snow that lies on it, is exposed to great alternations of temperature, which no vegetation, however simple and tenacious of life, can long successfully resist.

In the deserts of Asia and Africa, and on the coast of Peru, botanists have wandered for many leagues, without finding any other trace of vegetation, than a species of grey or yellow lichen, growing on the blanched and mouldering bones of animals that had perished by the way. In tropical countries, where there is not too much moisture and shade, the trees are shaggy with lichens; and some of the most magnificent species, both as regards size and colour, have been gathered in the Cinchona forests which clothe the lower slopes of the Andes, and in the warmer and more densely-wooded parts of Australia and New Zealand. The thick impervious forests of Brazil, however, are said to be almost destitute of them; their places on the trunks and boughs of the trees being occupied by endless varieties of ferns, tillandsias, orchids, and other epiphytic plants, which seem to hold a floral revel; the amazing luxuriance of higher vegetable life effectually keeping down and banishing plants of a simpler structure, and of a more sluggish and feeble nature. On the loftiest mountains of the globe they constitute the last remnants of vegetation, the last efforts of expiring nature which fringe around the limits of eternal snow ; and long after the botanist has left behind him the last stunted Alpine flower, blooming like a lone star on a midnight sky, amid the loose crumbling stones of the *moraine ;* long after the last moss has ceased to deck the brown and lifeless ground with a scarce perceptible film of green, his eye, wearied by the universal desolation, rests with peculiar interest and pleasure on the hardy lichens, which clothe every rugged rock that lifts up its head through the avalanche, and which luxuriate amid "the rack of the higher clouds and the howling of glacier winds." On the Alps of Switzerland the last lichens are to be found on the highest summits, attached to projecting rocks, exposed to the scorching heats of summer and the fierce blasts of winter ; and from forty to forty-five kinds have been found in spots, surrounded by extensive masses of snow, between 10,000 and 14,780 feet above the level of the sea. It is interesting to know, that the only plant found by Agassiz near the top of Mont Blanc, was the *Lecidea geographica* (Fig. 9), a very beautiful lichen, which covers the exposed rocks on the sides and summits of all our British hills, with its bright-green map-like patches. This species was also gathered by Dr. Hooker at an elevation of 19,000 feet on the Himalayas, and occupied the last outpost of vegetation which gladdened the eyes of the illustrious Humboldt, when standing within a few hundred feet of the summit of Chimborazo, the highest peak of the Andes. Strange it must have seemed to this enterprising traveller to stand on that elevated spot, and to see around and beneath him an epitome, as it were, of what takes place on a grander scale over the whole globe—a condensed picture of all the climates of the earth from the tropics to the poles, with all their different zones or belts of vegetation. Above towered the inaccessible summit in its everlasting shroud of stainless snow, boldly relieved against the deep cloudless blue of the tropical sky; around him the bare and rugged

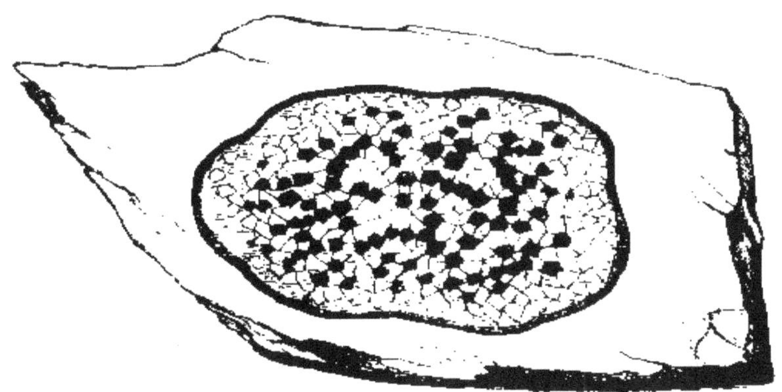

FIG. 9.—LECIDEA GEOGRAPHICA.

trachytic rocks, adorned with the green crust of this beautiful lichen, a few pale tufts of moss, or a solitary flower drooping here and there its frail head from a crevice; immediately beneath him the green grass-clad slopes, variegated with rainbow-coloured flowers and stunted willow-like shrubs; and far down in the valleys at the base, a glowing gorgeous world of tropical luxuriance—palms and bananas and bamboos, dimly revealed through the seething, sweltering vâpours which perpetually surrounded them.

The *Lecidea geographica* affords, I may mention, the most remarkable example of the almost universal diffusion of lichens, being the most Arctic, Antarctic, and Alpine lichen in the world—facing the savage cliffs of Melville Island in the extreme north, clinging to the volcanic rocks of Deception Island in the extreme south, and scaling the towering peak of Kinchin-junga, the most elevated spot on the surface of the earth. A catholic beauty, it is to be found in every zone of altitude and latitude—"a pilgrim bold in Nature's care."

On the British mountains we find lichens in great abundance and luxuriance, in spots which favour their growth by the humidity continually precipitated from the atmosphere. Most of the species found sparingly scattered at the highest elevations, are identical with those found in the greatest profusion covering immense areas on the plains of Lapland, and on the level of the sea-shore in the Arctic regions; the isotherms or lines of equal temperature passing through these points. Similar species are also found all over the world below the level of perpetual snow, which on the Alps is 7000 feet, and on the Andes and Himalayas about 15,000 feet. It is somewhat remarkable that Alpine lichens generally are more or less of a brown or black colour. This peculiarity seems to be owing to the presence of usnine or usnic acid, which in a pure state is of a green colour, as in the lichens which grow in shady forests, but which becomes oxidized, and changes to every shade of brown and black, when exposed to the powerful agencies of light and heat, on the bleak barren rocks on the mountain side and summits. These gloomy lichens, associated as they almost always are with the dusky tufts of that singular genus of mosses the Andreas, give a very marked and peculiar character to many of the Highland mountains, especially to the summit of Ben Nevis, where they creep, in the utmost profusion, over the fragments of abraded rocks which strew the ground on every side, otherwise bare and leafless, as was the world on the first morning of creation, and reminding one of the ruins of some stupendous castle, or the battle-field of the Titans. Some of the Alpine lichens, however, are remarkable for the vividness and brilliancy of their colours. The mountain cup-moss, with its light-green stalk clothed and fillagreed with scales, and emerald cup studded round with rich scarlet knobs, presents no unapt resemblance to a double red daisy. It grows in large clusters on the bare storm-scalped ridges, and forms a kind of miniature flower-garden in the Alpine wilderness. The loveliest, however, of all the mountain lichens is the *Solorina crocea*, which spreads over the loose mould in the clefts of rocks, and on the fragments of comminuted schist on the summits of the highest Highland mountains, forming patches of the most beautiful and vivid green, varied, when the under-side of the lobes is curled up, by reticulations of a very rich orange-saffron colour. This species is not found at a lower elevation than 4000 feet; hence it is unknown in England, Ireland, and Wales, whose highest mountains fall considerably short of this altitude. I have gathered it on Cairngorm, Ben Macdhui and Ben Lawers. In this last locality, which is well known to botanists as exhibiting a perfect garden of rare and beautiful Alpine plants, it grows in greater abundance, I believe, than in any other spot in the Highlands. It occupies the whole ridge of rugged and splintered rocks, marked by the tear and wear of elemental wars during countless ages, which runs along the summit of the hill. The surface of these rocks is covered with masses of sharp abraded stones, interspersed with meagre tufts of grass and moss ; and among these the saffron Solorina luxuriates in large patches. With what delight have I seen this beautiful lichen, beaming out on me from its dreary and desolate home, in the blustering days of early April, when the snow was falling thick around, and the howling wind sweeping by with unobstructed keenness ! With fingers almost benumbed with the cold, I have picked it up to admire its beauty—a beauty, such is the arrogant idea which man entertains of his own importance in the world—which seems utterly thrown away in a spot where human foot and human eye rarely if ever rest. How often among those wildly desolate and pathless solitudes, where one may wander for whole days without catching a glimpse of a single living thing, save perhaps some raven on its way to its nest, leaving behind it the blue sky without speck or cloud, or a ptarmigan scarcely distinguishable from the grey rocks around, winging its slow wheeling flight to the neighbouring hills, and uttering its soft clucking cry ; or when standing on some lofty storm-riven summit, cut off from the rest of creation, by the howling mists that come writhing up from the dark abysses on every side, and as lone as a shipwrecked mariner on some desolate island in the sea, thousands of miles from any shore ; how often amid such dreary scenes does a little wild-flower, or even lowlier fern or lichen, arrest the weary eye by its simple and mute appeal, and awaken thoughts and sympathies which are never felt, or at least allowed their full sway, amid the busy haunts of men. Like the little moss which revived the spirits of the lonely and despairing Park in the African desert, it carries us back to the populous world we had well nigh forgotten, reminds us of the enjoyments and affections of home, and more than all, raises our thoughts to the Maker of the great and the small, who placed it there to cheer by its presence the lonely wilderness, and whose wondrous skill and goodness its every petal, leaf, or frond declares in language, silent and unuttered, yet more eloquent than a thousand words.

The great object which nature intended to subserve by the universal diffusion of the lichens, is obviously that of preparing, by the disintegration of hard and barren rocks, an organic soil in which higher orders of vegetation may exist. Humble and apparently insignificant as they are, it is to them we owe the bright array of vegetable forms, which contribute so largely to the beauty and magnificence of the world we inhabit; they form the first link in the chain of nature by which the whole earth is covered with a robe of vegetation. Their powdery crusts and little coloured cups, drawing their nourishment in most part from the surrounding atmosphere, extend themselves over the naked and desolate rock, and form, by the particles of sand into which they crumble its surface, and their own decaying tissues, a thin layer of mould fit for the reception of the simplest mosses. These, in their turn, add their contribution of withered leaves, and increase the film of soil; others of a larger growth supplying their places, and running themselves the same round of growth and decay. Plants of a higher and yet higher order gradually succeed each other, each series binding together, and preparing for the growth of its own species or of others, the loose and incoherent mass of decaying tissues, sand, and disintegrated soil which the previous occupants had left behind them. At length the rock, once as bleak and desolate as though it had been vomited from the depths of some vast volcano, and on whose surface the smallest wild-flower could not find a resting-place for its tiny root, becomes a verdant meadow fit to support a host of animals; a rich garden of beautiful flowers smiling in the sunshine; or a wide expanse of noble forest waving its billowy foliage in the passing breeze.

> "Seeds to our eye invisible can find
> On the rude rock the bed that fits their kind;
> There in the rugged soil they safely dwell,
> Till showers and snows the subtle atoms swell,
> And spread th' enduring foliage; then we trace
> The freckled flower upon the flinty base;
> These all increase, till in unnoticed years
> The sterile rock as grey with age appears,
> With coats of vegetation thinly spread,
> Coat above coat, the living on the dead;
> These then dissolve to dust, and make a way
> For bolder foliage nursed by their decay."

Precisely the same effects are produced on the newly-formed coral islands of the Pacific. The winds or the waves waft thither the invisible spore of some lichen that may have had its birthplace on the rocks of the far-off Andes; it finds a resting-place, and the few simple circumstances necessary for its development, in some sheltered nook where the dashing waves have ground the coral into glittering sand; and through course of time it assumes a crust-like appearance, puts forth its organs of fructification, and sows around it a colony of similar individuals. These harbour the wind-wafted soil beneath their tiny leaves, and form, by their decomposition, a layer of mould to which new species are day after day adding their decaying tissues, until at last a sufficient soil has been deposited for the growth of the ferns, hibiscus, bread-fruit, and cocoa-nut trees that have been wafted from the neighbouring islands. And thus, through the agency of an all but invisible seed, developed into the lowliest form in which it is possible to conceive that life can be maintained, what was once a barren, solitary islet, where no sounds were heard but the ceaseless dashing of the waves against the snow-white reefs, or the shrill cries of some chance flock of sea-birds, that made it their temporary resting-place during their flight to some happier shore, has become a paradise of bloom and beauty where man takes up his abode, and finds every comfort and luxury that can minister to his simple tastes.

Even on the desolate rocks that jut out from the sides of lofty mountains, where the eagle or the condor builds its eyrie, these humble sappers and miners of the vegetable kingdom are busy, fulfilling the task appointed them in the great household of nature, and forming a layer of soil, which ever and anon, as soon as it is deposited, is carried down by the storm or the stream to fertilize the valleys at the base. Egypt is the gift of the Nile; its rich alluvial soil has been brought down by the swollen waters of the sacred river from the mountains of Abyssinia, where it was formed, perhaps, by the agency of lichens and other Alpine plants, and precipitated in its present form over the barren sands of the Lybian desert. And who knows how much of the tropical fertility and luxuriance of the vast plains, which stretch onwards from the bases of the Andes and the Himalayas, may be owing to countless generations of lichens, working ceaselessly far up on the inaccessible summits, amid the icy rigour and sterility of an Arctic climate. This is not an extravagant supposition; we see every day the wonderful power of little things; and we find that the most gigantic results are often dependent upon agencies minute and insignificant in their individual state, but irresistible in an aggregate of countless myriads. It is a sublime truth, and one worthy of universal acceptation, that even in the smallest and most apparently useless productions, the intelligent eye will often behold some of the most splendid manifestations of God's inscrutable wisdom and gracious goodness. The bleak sterility of these lofty regions, where the lichens perform their untiring operations under circumstances where we should naturally suppose life and organization alike impossible, is yet the means of preserving the fertility of mighty territories which would otherwise become deserts!

The student of nature who has examined these humble plants with sufficient attention, must have been often struck with wonder and admiration at the peculiar fitness which they display for the work to which they have been appointed, as the pioneers or precursors of all other land vegetation. What could be better adapted to withstand the fury of the storms that beat upon their exposed places of growth than the crustaceous, powdery, or leaf-like expansions which they often assume, hard and inseparable almost as a portion of the rock itself? Then their capacity of extracting their nourishment principally from the surrounding atmosphere; the curious property which they possess of continuing for years without undergoing any perceptible change; their strong persistent vitality by which they are able—when scorched by the summer sunshine, deprived of all their juices, and reduced to shapeless, hueless masses, which crumble into powder under the slightest touch of the hand or the foot—to revive again when exposed to the genial influences of the rain, assume their fairest forms and hues, and develop their organs of fructification for the dispersion of their kind; and lastly, the facility with which they can replace portions of their substance that have been torn away by storms, broken by the tread of man, or eaten by animals; all these qualities illustrate the wonderful adaptation, in their structure and habits, to the unfavourable circumstances in which they are often placed. Furnished by such powers as these, wherever they fasten their tiny fangs the process of disintegration commences; and though carried on slowly and imperceptibly, though ages may elapse before any apparent effects have been produced, except the increase of individuals and the more shaggy and picturesque appearance of the rocks, yet the object of that steady, ceaseless labour will one day be accomplished; and it is humiliating to the pride of man to find, that the noble piles of architecture built by him as if for eternity, though apparently as solid as the rock out of which each individual stone had been hewn, and as hard as the famous Roman cement which had resisted the utmost efforts of Goth and Vandal, must yield in the end to the slow but persevering assaults of the most diminutive and contemptible vegetables, and be brought back again by these apparently feeble agents to the bosom of nature, out of which he had reared them with such labour and skill. Here, indeed, we have an illustration of that comprehensive saying of Melanchthon, "The humble ones are the giants of the battle;" here we have sermons in stones, lessons taught us by the lifeless lichens of the permanence of nature, and the never-ceasing change and decadence attendant upon all the works and possessions of man.

The objects which lichens subserve when they are produced on rocks and ruins are thus sufficiently obvious; but it is not so easy to determine their precise use when growing on trees. It has been asserted by some writers that so far from being beneficial, they are absolutely prejudicial to the welfare of the forests in which they abound. Such individuals, however, it is evident, totally misapprehend the nature of these plants, for they extract their nourishment principally from the medium with which they are surrounded, and not from the matrix on which they are developed, or to which they are attached. The fungi are the only plants that are produced from decay and corruption, and maintain their existence by exhausting the vital juices of other plants. That lichens are not injurious to the plants on which they grow, is clearly proved in the case of Peruvian bark; for the specimens which are covered with healthy lichens abound more in the peculiar medicinal principle, and realize a larger price, than those which are bare and destitute of lichens; while, on the other hand, the bark that is covered with the beautiful *Hypochnus rubrocinctus* and other fungi is utterly worthless, as these deadly parasites decompose all the substances upon which they fasten by the absorption of their nutritive matter. There is hardly a tree in the whole world which, at some stage or other of its existence, has not been covered with lichens. I have frequently observed the trees of a whole Highland forest, covered from head to foot with a dense shaggy garment of these plants, and yet maintaining, during the natural term of their existence, a green and healthy appearance. The species that grow upon trees, it must be observed, are generally very different from those which grow upon stones. There is a considerable preponderance of foliaceous and filamentous over crustaceous forms, and these, owing to the looseness of their hold upon the bark, being generally attached only by small roots in their centre, or by a single knot at one of their extremities, do not close up the breathing pores of the tree, or prevent that free circulation of air which is necessary for the healthy performance of all its functions. Indeed, I am disposed to think that lichens are not only harmless, but greatly beneficial to trees; for those who have paid particular attention to pines which grow in open and elevated situations, must have often noticed that, not only is their bark thicker and more rugged on the side most exposed to the prevailing winds and rains, but also that it is more densely covered with shaggy lichens, so as to afford considerable warmth and protection. The colder the climate, and the farther north we proceed, the more densely clothed with this picturesque garment of nature's providing do we find the trees and shrubs, on the same principle, one would imagine, as the hyperborean animals are covered with thick furs. Indeed, so universally are lichens and mosses produced on the north side of trees, that the American backwoods-man, and the Norwegian woodcutter, whose faculties of observation have been keenly educated by nature herself, often employ them as a rude but safe compass to guide them through the intricacies and tangled labyrinths of the primeval forests.

Such are some of the most obvious purposes which these humble plants serve in the economy of nature; let us now direct our attention to a few of the uses to which man has applied them. This is the only point of importance connected with them in the estimation of many—especially of those who gauge the works of the Almighty by a dry utilitarian law—and see no beauty or interest in any object, except in so far as they can find some real or manifest utility in its existence. Judged by this standard, and weighed in the balance with pounds, shillings, and pence, the lichens will not be found wanting. On account of the large quantity of starchy matter which they contain, they often considerably contribute to, and sometimes even entirely form, the diet of man and animals, in those dreary inhospitable regions where the wintry rigour, or the scorching heat of the climate, forbid all other kinds of vegetation to grow. Every one is familiar with the fact that the reindeer moss (*Cladonia rangiferina*, Fig. 10), forms altogether the food of that animal during the prolonged northern winters. This lichen grows sparingly in little tufts among the heather in this country, and sometimes whitens the sides and plateaus of the Highland hills, covering bare and verdureless places where the snow first falls in winter, and lingers longest in summer ; but it is in the vast sandy plains called by the Laplanders tundra, which border the Arctic ocean, that it flourishes in the greatest pro-

FIG. 10.—CLADONIA RANGIFERINA.

fusion and luxuriance. There it completely covers the ground with its snowy tufts, and occupies as conspicuous a place in the economy of nature as the grass in warmer regions. Linnæus says, that no plant flourishes so luxuriantly as this in the pine-forests of Lapland, the surface of the soil being completely carpeted with it for many miles in extent ; and that if by an accident the forests are burnt to the ground, in a very short time the lichens re-appear, and resume all their original vigour. These plains, he adds, which strangers would call an accursed land, are fertile pastures to the Laplander, who, in possession of a tract of such country, deems himself a prosperous man. There vast herds of reindeer roam at will, enjoying themselves where the horse, the camel, and the elephant would perish. The reindeer is the life, hope, and wealth of the inhabitants of those dreary and inclement regions. It draws their burdens with all the patience of the ass, yields its milk with all the docility of the cow, and transports its owner from place to place over the snowy and frozen plains, with all the fleetness of an Arabian horse. Its flesh serves for food ; its tendons for strings to their bows, and its thick-furred skin for comfortable garments and bed-clothes to protect them from the rigours of an Arctic climate. And this useful animal is exclusively dependent upon an humble lichen for its support. What a deep interest therefore invests this otherwise insignificant plant ! That vast numbers of families, living in pastoral simplicity in the cheerless and inhospitable Polar regions, should depend for their subsistence, upon the uncultured and abundant supply of a plant so low in the scale of organization as this, is surely a striking proof of the great importance of even the smallest and meanest objects in nature.

When the ground is covered with hard and frozen snow, so that the reindeer cannot obtain its usual food, it finds a substitute in a very curious lichen called rock-hair (*Alectoria jubata*, Fig. 11), which covers with its beard-like tufts the trunks of almost every tree. In more severe winters, the Laplanders cut down whole forests of the largest trees, that their herds may be enabled to browse at liberty upon the tufts which cover the higher branches. The vast dreary pine-forests of Lapland possess a character which is peculiarly their own, and are perhaps more singular in the eyes of the traveller than any other feature in the landscapes of that remote and desolate region. This character they owe to the immense number of lichens with which they abound. The ground, instead of grass, is carpeted with dense tufts of the reindeer moss, white as a shower of new-fallen snow ; while the trunks and branches of the trees

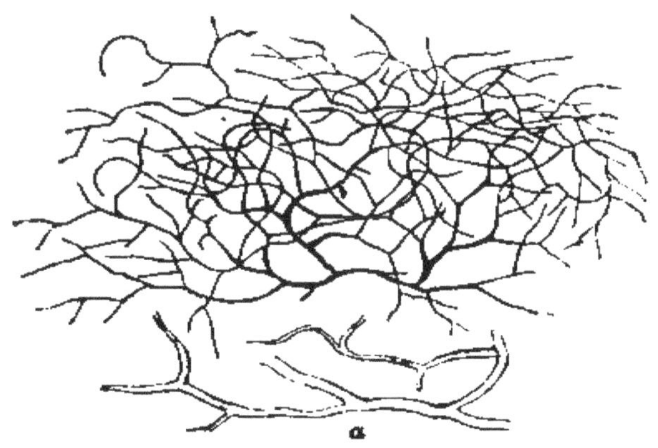


FIG. 11.—ALECTORIA JUBATA.
(a) Enlarged portion.

are swollen far beyond their natural dimensions with huge, dusky, funereal bunches of the rock-hair, hanging down in masses, exhaling a damp earthy smell, like an old cellar, or stretching from tree to tree, in long festoons, waving with every breath of wind, and creating a perpetual melancholy twilight around.

Another beard-like lichen (*Usnea florida*, Fig. 12), often growing along with the rock-hair, is gathered in great quantities in North America, from the pine-forests, and stored up as winter fodder for cattle in inclement seasons. Goats, and especially deer, are fond of it; and in winter, when other food is scarce, they hardly leave a vestige of it on the trees within their reach.

FIG. 12.—USNEA FLORIDA.

The tortoises of the small rocky islands of the Galapagos Archipelago subsist almost entirely upon it.

But it is not to animals alone that lichens furnish a supply of food. Man himself is frequently directly indebted to them for a subsistence. There are few, I presume, who are not acquainted with some particulars regarding the history and uses of that remarkable lichen, sold in chemists' shops under the name of *Cetraria Islandica*, or Iceland moss (Fig. 13). Although in this country it is only used medicinally, as a restorative diet in exhausting diseases, and during convalescence, for which it possesses an immemorial reputation; it forms the

FIG. 13. CETRARIA ISLANDICA.

most important article of food which the natives of Iceland possess. In fact, without it they would as certainly perish, as the favoured inhabitants of Britain without the more highly organized cereal plants, which, year after year, wave in all their golden beauty over the whole land, and are so strikingly suggestive of nature's bounty and munificence. What barley, rye, and oats are to the Indo-Caucasian races of Asia and Western Europe; the olive, the grape, and the fig, to the inhabitants of the Mediterranean districts; the date-palm to the Egyptian and Arabian; rice to the Hindoo; and the tea-plant to the Chinese,—the Iceland moss is to the Laplanders, Icelanders, and Esquimaux.

In Scotland, the Iceland moss grows sparingly on the bare wind-swept sides and summits of the loftiest mountains, but in Iceland it is exceedingly abundant over the whole surface of the country. It attains a large size on the lava of the western coast, and in the extensive desert tracts of Skaptar-fel-Syssel; and numerous parties migrate to these places with all their household effects, during the summer months, in order to collect it, either for exportation to the Danish merchants, or for their own use as an article of common food. These excursions generally take place once every three years, for the lichen requires that time to arrive at maturity, after the spots where it flourishes have been cleared. Olafsen and Povelsen, in their interesting *Travels in Iceland*, observe, that a person can collect four tons in a week, with which, they say, he is better off than with one ton of wheat. We are also informed, in a report on this lichen, published several years ago by the Saxon Government, that the meal obtained from it, when mixed with wheat-flour, produces a greater quantity of bread, though perhaps of a less nutritious quality, than could be manufactured from the latter alone. The extremely bitter taste, however, by which it is characterized,—owing to a peculiar astringent principle in it called cetrarin, which has been procured in a state of purity, in the form of a white powder like magnesia, by Herberger,—has always proved a great drawback to its adoption as an independent article of food, especially in this country. In Iceland and Lapland, however, the inhabitants remove this disagreeable quality by a very simple process. They first chop it to pieces, and macerate it for several days in water mixed with salt of tartar or quick-lime, which it absorbs very freely ; it is then dried and reduced to powder, and mixed with the flour of the common knot-grass, made into a cake or boiled, and eaten with reindeer's milk, and eaten with relish, too, by these poor people, who confess, with a most simple and affecting gratitude, that "a bountiful Providence sends them bread out of the very stones." The powder is not unlike starch in appearance, and possesses some of its properties, for it swells in boiling water, and becomes, on cooling, a fine jelly, which soon hardens into a tough, transparent substance, very pleasant to the taste, especially when flavoured with sugar, milk, a little white wine, or aromatics. It is frequently used for making blanc-mange in this country, for which purpose it is said to be equal, if not superior, to Irish moss or the finest isinglass. The bitter principle is often used for brewing, and in the composition of ship-biscuit, to prevent the attack of worms.

Those who have read the affecting account which Franklin and Richardson give of their expedition to Arctic America, must be familiar with the name of the Tripe de Roche, which occurs on almost every page, and is intimately associated with the fearful sufferings which these brave men endured, a part of which only would have sufficed to unseat the reason of most individuals. During their long and terrible journey from the Coppermine River to Fort Enterprise, one of the stations of the Hudson's Bay Company—a journey to which, I venture

FIG. 14.—GYROPHORA CYLINDRICA.
(*a*) Enlarged portion.

to say, there are few parallels in the annals of human hardship—in the almost total absence of every other kind of salutary food, their lives were supported by a bitter and nauseous lichen, to which the name of Tripe de Roche (*Gyrophora*, Fig. 14) has been given, as if in mockery. I cannot resist the inclination to transcribe from this melancholy narrative a single fragmentary passage, which will give some idea of the fearful condition to which these heroic adventurers in the cause of science were often reduced. I need not preface it by any comment of mine ; it speaks for itself. "Mr. Hood, who was now nearly exhausted, was obliged to walk at a gentle pace in the rear, Dr. Richardson kindly keeping beside him, whilst Franklin led the foremost men, that he might make them halt occasionally till the stragglers came up. Credit, however, one of their most active hunters, became lamentably weak, from the effects of tripe de roche upon his constitution, and Vaillant, from the same cause, was getting daily more emaciated. They only advanced six miles during the day, and at night satisfied the cravings of hunger by a small quantity of tripe de roche, mixed up with some scraps of roasted leather. Having boiled and eaten the remains of their old shoes, and every shred of leather which could be picked up, they set forward at nine, like living skeletons, advancing by inches, as it were, over bleak hills, separated by equally barren valleys, which contained not the slightest trace of vegetation except this eternal tripe de roche." The dreadful uncertainty, that for so many long years, hung over the fate of Franklin and his heroic comrades, has at last been dispelled by the discovery, during M'Clintock's recent search, of a large cairn at Cape Victoria, in King William Land, containing, among other mournfully interesting relics, a journal of one of the officers of the lost expedition, announcing the intelligence of the certain death of its leader on the 11th of June 1847. A short distance beyond this fatal point, two human skeletons were found in the bottom of an abandoned boat, with no food beside them except some tea, chocolate and tripe de roche, on which miserable and unnutritious diet they lingered out their existence in these frightful solitudes, till death mercifully put an end.

to their sufferings. Let us hope that no more valuable lives will be sacrificed to the love of science and adventure in these terrible regions ; the numerous expeditions undertaken in recent times having taught us the limit of human endurance, if they have done nothing else.

The tripe de roche consists of various species of Gyrophora—black, leather-like lichens, studded with small black points like coiled wire buttons, and attached by an umbilical root, or by short strong fibres to rocks on the mountains. Some of them bear no unapt resemblance to a piece of shagreen ; while others appear corroded, like a fragment of burnt skin, as if the rock on which they grew had been subjected to the action of fire. They are found in cold exposed situations on Alpine rocks of granite or micaceous schist, in almost all parts of the world—on the Himalayas and Andes as well as the British mountains ; but it is in the Arctic regions alone that they luxuriate, covering the surface of every rock, to the level of the sea-shore, with a gloomy Plutonian vegetation, that seems like the charred cinders and shrivelled remains of former verdure and beauty. Though they contain a considerable quantity of starch, they are exceedingly bitter and astringent, and produce intolerable griping pains when eaten. No one would have recourse to them for food except in a case of dire necessity. The Canadian hunters who are often reduced to the last extremity, during their long and toilsome excursions in search of furs, through the desolate regions of Arctic America, often allay the pangs of hunger with this nauseous diet. And sometimes in my own wanderings among the almost unknown and unvisited solitudes of the Scottish mountains, when my stock of provisions was exhausted, and a renewal was not to be expected, the nearest shepherd's sheiling being perhaps many miles distant, I have been compelled to satisfy my cravings by eating small portions of the tripe de roche, which I found blackening the dreary rocks around. In such situations, I have felt deeply how weak and helpless is man, when thrown forth from the social scenes and comforts of civilized life, left to his own unaided resources, and exposed to the merciless energies of physical nature, and how, without some ultimate trust in the Almighty source of his being, that being is but as a straw upon a whirlpool.

There are several other species of lichens, which have now and then, on rare occasions, been employed as articles of food. There is a greyish shaggy lichen abundant on pine-trees in the British woods, called Evernia, which is said in ancient times to have rivalled even the Iceland moss for its nutritious qualities. Forskoel says in reference to it in his *Flora Arabica*, "I have heard a great deal about a Schoebean plant unknown to me, without a portion of which, mixed with its contents, no kind of bread is manufactured. Shiploads of it are regularly conveyed to Alexandria from the Grecian Archipelago. A handful of the lichen is inserted in water for two hours, which, when added to the dough, imparts to the bread a peculiar flavour, esteemed delicious by the Turks." It is possessed of a mawkish insipid taste, especially if produced on oaks, somewhat astringent, but not destitute of nutritious qualities.

There is a curious lichen found in some eastern countries called *Lecanora esculenta*, regarding which several strange facts have been related by travellers. Some authors are strongly of opinion, that the manna with which the Israelites were fed in the wilderness may be referred to this lichen. A pamphlet has been published upon the subject by Dr. Arthaud. Such a reference may be supposed by some to militate against the professedly miraculous character of the event. But this objection may be overruled by the consideration, that though the manna was miraculous, in so far as the manner of its conveyance to the Israelites, and the circumstances connected with its gathering, were concerned, it was not miraculous in its origin. The quails were conveyed to their camp by supernatural means, but they were not supernatural in themselves; and, in like manner, the manna was showered down by the direct agency of God, in the very place where, and at the very time that it was required ; but it was not a miraculous substance ; it was not specially created for that purpose. God is sparing, as it were, of His miracles ; and in all His direct interpositions on behalf of His people, we find that He makes use of objects and agencies already existing, causing these to fall in with His intentions, without originating new ones. If this be true ; if the manna was a vegetable product already existing, and not a special creation, there is more likelihood of its being a species of lichen, than any other vegetable matter which commentators have conjectured. The descriptions of Moses apply with greater accuracy to the *Lecanora esculenta*, than to any other substance with which I am acquainted ; while the singular circumstances connected with the history of this lichen, as related from time to time by trustworthy witnesses, renders the supposition of its identity with the manna of the Israelites still more plausible. Showers of this lichen have sometimes fallen several inches thick, having been torn from the spots where it grew, and transported by violent gusts of wind. In 1829, during the war between Persia and Russia, there was a great famine in Oroomiah, south-west of the Caspian Sea. One day, during a violent wind, the surface of the country was covered with a lichen, which fell from the sky in showers. The sheep immediately attacked it, and devoured it eagerly, which suggested to the inhabitants the idea of reducing it to flour, and making bread of it, which was found to be palatable and nourishing. The people affirmed that they had never seen this lichen before or after that time. During the siege of Herat, more recently, the papers mentioned a hail of manna which fell upon the city, and served as food for the inhabitants. A rain of manna occurred so late as April 1846, in the government of Wilna, and formed a layer upon the ground three or four inches in thickness. It was of a greyish-white colour, rather hard, irregular in form, inodorous and insipid. Pallas, the Russian naturalist, observed it on the arid mountains, and the calcareous portions of the Great Desert of Tartary. Mr. Eversham collected it in the steppes of the Kirghiz to the north of the Caspian Sea. It has been seen on the Altai range, in Anatolia, in South America, and recently in Algeria by Dr. Guyon. It occurs in irregular-shaped fragments, varying in size from a pin's-head to a pea or small nut; and when seen in its native sites, is apparently attached to no matrix whatever, and has no fecula in its composition.

In medicine, lichens were at one time very highly esteemed. In the days of Aldrovandus and Paracelsus, who added the study of alchemy and the occult sciences to that of plants, they were extensively employed in the preparation of sympathetic ointments, and in the various distillations connected with the search for the elixir vitæ and the universal solvent and nostrum. Wonderful cures were ascribed to a particular application of them; and in the works of the botanists of the middle ages, we find long and elaborate observations upon the peculiar virtues of species developed upon the oak, the pine, and the beech. The common dog-lichen (*Peltidea canina*)—a species everywhere abundant on moist banks and turfy walls, and easily distinguished by its livid brown wrinkled leaves, and red, nail-like fructification—was formerly employed, at the suggestion of the celebrated Dr. Mead, as a cure for hydrophobia (hence its specific name), and in many instances with success; but whether the cures were effected by an inherent power in the plant itself, or merely by the aid of a strong imagination, may be left an open question. Another species of the same family (*Peltidea apthosa*), with a remarkably vivid green thallus, growing by the side of mountain streams, was in high repute at one time as a powerful anthelmintic, and is still used by the Swedish peasants, when boiled with milk, as a cure for the apthæ or thrush in children. When the primitive principle that "like cures like" formed the basis of all medical treatment, several lichens were employed for the cure of diseases, on account of their fancied resemblance to the organs or parts of the body affected. Among such lichens the species in greatest favour was probably the lung-wort (*Sticta pulmonaria*), which grows in immense shaggy masses on trees and rocks in sub-alpine woods. From the resemblance of its reticulated and lobed upper-surface, usually of a greyish-brown colour, to the human lungs, it was highly recommended as an infallible cure for all diseases of these delicate organs. The beautiful cup-lichen, so abundant on dry moorlands under the shade of the heather, was long a favourite rustic remedy in this country for coughs. Gerarde, the old English herbalist, says: "The powder of this moss given unto small children, in any liquor for certaine daies together, is a most certaine remidy against that perilous maladie called the chin-cough. Albeit the remidy doth require care, and is not to be adventured upon save under the guidance of an experienced gudewife." On account of the intensely bitter principle contained in greater or less degree in all lichens, many species used to be employed in intermittent fevers and agues, as substitutes for Peruvian bark, which was then sold at a price so extravagant, as to be utterly beyond the reach of the poorer classes. For the same reason, they were often administered in the form of powders and decoctions, as tonics to purify the blood and strengthen the system. Their astringent qualities—depending, I may remark, in a great measure upon the kind of tree on which they were produced—were also turned to advantage in the cure of hæmorrhages, fluxes, and ruptures; and Linnæus informs us that the Laplanders fill up their snow-shoes with one species, and apply it to the feet to relieve the excoriations occasioned by long and fatiguing journeys. During one period of medical history, lichens formed the principal drugs in the pharmacopœia, and were prescribed for almost all the ills that flesh is heir to. Superstition had much to do with their popularity in this respect. Their strange shapes, their anomalous character, occupying, as it were, an intermediate position between plants and minerals, between life and death; leading a perpetual mesmerized or suspended existence; the curious situations in which they were found, growing on decaying wood or moist earth, or on the bare rock in weird, lonely spots, where fairies might sport and enchanters weave their unhallowed spells; they were naturally enough supposed by a credulous and ignorant people to be invested with magic qualities. As the knowledge of plants became more generally diffused, they lost much of their mystery, and consequently of their power over disease; and now they have almost entirely disappeared from medical practice. It must not be supposed, however, that they were thus summarily expelled from the schools of medicine, because they were entirely destitute of healing qualities. Some of them have been found, by chemical analysis, to contain principles of great efficacy in certain complaints; but as these principles varied in their strength, according to the circumstances in which the plants were produced, no dependence could be placed upon the action of the doses administered. It is obvious that the chemical qualities of cellular plants, whose construction is so extremely simple, must vary considerably in different individuals and in different situations. The nature of the matrix on which lichens grow, and of the medium which surrounds them, must, to a great extent, determine the presence in them of certain constituents which are extremely volatile, and dependent upon such conditions. The lichen that develops certain qualities when growing on the bark of a tree, will not develop them to the same extent when growing on a rock ; and there will be a similar, if not a greater difference between the qualities of an individual produced in the shade of a dark moist wood, and those of the same plant, scorched by the sunshine and swept by the wind on a bare exposed rock on the hill-side. It was this variable chemical character, and the uncertain medical results connected with it, that banished the lichens from the druggists' shops. The discovery of new and more powerful drugs, obtained from tropical plants stimulated by intense sunshine and highly organized soils, hastened their exile, and effectually closed the door against their return to favour ; while at the same time it greatly diminished the list of native remedies, the products of a cold, moist climate, and of poor and feeble soils. The Iceland moss is the only species of lichen which has retained its place in modern pharmacy, as a tonic and febrifuge in ague ; but it is now principally employed, when added to soups and chocolate, as a palliative to consumption, and as an article of diet in the sick-room, and is being gradually superseded by the more nourishing productions of foreign countries.

It may seem strange that lichens should be employed in perfumery, considering that in themselves they are entirely destitute of odour, but such nevertheless is the case. The ancients appear to have been in the habit of using extensively a species of white filamentous lichen called Usnech, which grew upon trees in the islands of the East Indian Archipelago, St. Helena, and Madagascar, and exhaled, when moistened, an exceedingly agreeable fragrance, somewhat resembling musk or ambergris. This odour it may have derived from the spice trees on which it was produced. Among the Arabian physicians it was once in high repute when macerated in wine, as a cordial and soporific. So late as the seventeenth century, some of the filamentous lichens were sold in the shops of barbers and perfumers under the name of Usnea, and they formed the basis of a celebrated fragrant powder for the toilet, called Corps de Cypre gris or Cyprio, which is still manufactured on a large scale in Rome, and in some other cities of Italy. Their employment for this purpose, however, did not depend upon any peculiar inherent scent, for the species used are perfectly odourless, but upon their aptitude for absorbing and retaining, for almost any length of time, the fragrance communicated to them. Indeed, several of our tree-lichens possess in so remarkable a degree this curious property, that they are still employed in the manufacture of the most valuable and esteemed powder perfumes ; and they might be turned to useful account, by the sanative commission, in imbibing and retaining the noxious vapours from cesspools and over-crowded streets, which are so injurious to the health of the inhabitants of our large cities ; their small bulk and light weight allowing of their being easily removed, when thoroughly saturated with the offensive effluvia.

Various other substances useful in the arts and manufactures are yielded by the lichens. The late Lord Dundonald discovered a method of extracting from a species of white filamentous lichen (*Evernia prunastri*), very frequent upon pines and oaks, a kind of gum which was extensively used in Glasgow during the French war, as an efficient substitute for the expensive Gum Senegal, in calico-printing. When it was the absurd fashion to wear the hair whitened with powder, this same lichen was sometimes pulverized and employed, on account of its cheapness, instead of flour or starch. A species of yellow shrubby lichen, like brass wire (*Borrera flavicans*), found on apple-trees in the south of England, used to be employed in Norway in poisoning wolves, which were at one time a dreadful scourge in the country, ranging the gloomy pine forests in immense herds, committing fearful havoc among the sheep-folds and cattle-sheds, and when rendered desperate by hunger, even attacking travelling parties and the houses of the inhabitants. Dead carcases of sheep, stuffed with a mixture composed of the powder of this lichen and pounded glass, were left exposed in their favourite resorts to be devoured by these ravenous animals, when it never failed to prove fatal. This is the only lichen known to possess poisonous properties; but the deleterious action of the mixture employed, may have depended more upon the attrition of the sharp surfaces of pounded glass, than upon the vegetable powder. Chemists have detected oxalic acid in several species of crustaceous lichens growing on the bark of trees, and distinguished by an intensely bitter taste; and in one or two species in such abundance, that 100 parts yielded 18 of lime, combined with 29·4 of oxalic acid. The oxalate of lime bears the same relation to lichens as carbonate of lime to the corals, and phosphate of lime to the bony structure of the more highly organized animals. On account of this circumstance, some of the crustaceous lichens are extensively employed in France in the manufacture of oxalic acid ; and a considerable proportion of what is now used in this country is derived from this source. In London, various species of tree-lichens are sold for the use of bird-stuffers, who line the inside of their cases, and decorate the miniature trees upon which the birds perch, with their shaggy leaves, so as to give them a more picturesque and natural appearance. The inhabitants of Smoland in Sweden are said to scrape a peculiar species of yellow crustaceous lichen from old pales, walls, and rocks, and mix it with their tallow, to make the beautiful golden candles which they burn on festival days. A wonderful race are these same Smolanders. They are so remarkably industrious and inventive, that they have given rise to a popular proverb in Sweden, "Put a Smolander upon a roof, and he will get a livelihood." "This character," says Frederika Bremer, in her charming work, *The Midnight Sun*, "is strangely imprinted on the remote forest-regions of the country. The forest, which is the countryman's workshop, is his storehouse too. With the various lichens that grow upon the trees and rocks, he cures the virulent diseases with which he is sometimes afflicted, dyes the articles of clothing which he wears, and poisons the noxious and dangerous animals which annoy him. The juniper and cranberry give him their berries, which he brews into drink; he makes a conserve of them, and mixes their juices with his dry salt-meat, and is healthful and cheerful with these and with his labour, of which he makes a pleasure."

If we wish to obtain a true idea of the value and importance of lichens in human economy, we must consider them in perhaps the most singular of their aspects, viz., as dye-stuffs and sources of colouring matter. Many of the tree-lichens, in a moist state, are very showy, yielding in water a coloured infusion corresponding to the hue of their own leaves; but strange to say, these are the least valuable species to the dyer. The lichens which are richest in colorific principles, are crustaceous species

Fig. 15.—Roccella tinctoria.

growing on rocks, and utterly destitute of colour in their natural state; and it is one of the most striking triumphs of chemistry as applied to the arts and manufactures, that by its means some of the finest shades of red, purple, and yellow are extracted from such unlikely substances. The lichen popularly known as orchil (Fig. 15) affords a remarkable illustration of the extent to which colorific principles are developed in these outwardly hueless plants. It derives its generic name Roccella from a Florentine family called Rucellai, whose founder, for a long time a trader in the Levant, discovered in the sixteenth century the art of preparing a most valuable dye from it, by the sale of which he realized in a short time a very large fortune. If, however, we are to believe Tournefort, the preparation of orchil was known to the ancient Greeks; the purple of Amorgos, one of the Cyclades Islands, with which the celebrated tunics of the same name were dyed, being obtained from this lichen. Some authors are of opinion that it was the orchil, and not the little murex, a species of shell-fish found on the coast of Syria and Phœnicia, which supplied the famous Tyrian purple, the exclusive badge of imperial rank referred to in Ezekiel: "Fine linen, with broidered work from Egypt, was that which thou spreadest forth to be thy sail; blue and purple from the isles of Elishah was that which covered thee." The frequent representation of the little shell-fish on the coins dug up among the ruins of Tyre must, however, be regarded as a sufficient refutation of this idea. The secret of the Rucellai was soon divulged, and the manufacture transferred to Holland, where a considerable trade in this lichen is still carried on. The orchil is found in small quantities on rocks by the sea-side in the extreme south of England, and in the Guernsey and Portland Isles. In warm climates, however, it occurs in profusion, especially on the volcanic rocks, and the sea-shores of the Canary and Cape de Verde Islands, in the numerous isles of the Grecian Archipelago, and on the coasts of China and Peru. In the Indian collection of raw vegetable products exhibited in the Crystal Palace of 1851, several specimens of orchil from India, Ceylon, and Socotra were shown; and an explanatory note appended to some from the bare, desolate Gibraltar of the Red Sea, the rock of Aden in Arabia, stated most suggestively—"Abundant, but unknown as an article of commerce." It is probable that it occurs on the maritime rocks of all tropical countries in equal profusion. In appearance this valuable lichen resembles a diminutive leafless shrub, forked, and subdivided into numerous roundish, irregular branches. It is tough and leathery in texture, of a whitish or blue grey colour, and covered with a mealy powder, or scattered warty excrescences. It is imported in the same state in which it was gathered from the volcanic rocks; and those who prepare it for the use of the dyer grind it between stones, so as thoroughly to bruise but not to reduce it to powder, moistening it occasionally with ammonia mixed with quick-lime. By this process it acquires in a few days a purplish-red tinge, and is found to form a confused mass of violet-coloured threads. In this state it is employed to give the English broadcloths that peculiar lustre and purple tint, when viewed in a certain light, which are so much admired. When beaten to a pulp, and dried in little cubes about the size of dice, which have an azure colour with white spots, and an unpleasant odour, the orchil is called litmus. This substance contains, according to Gelis, three colouring principles: one soluble in ether, which is orange-red; one soluble in alcohol, and one in water, both of which have a most beautiful purple tint, which they lose when excluded from the air, and regain when again exposed. On account of its exceeding delicacy, and the ease with which it may be applied, litmus is chemically used as a test of akalinity and acidity in the form of paper saturated with it, preserved in well-closed vessels, and secluded from the influence of light. This paper is turned red by an acid and is restored to its original blue colour by an alkali. The orchil contains certain other substances, called orcine and erythrine, which are perfectly colourless, and contain no nitrogen ; but when exposed to the action of ammonia and common atmospheric air, they yield exquisitely beautiful colouring matters, which crystallize in regular flat quadrangular prisms, have a very sweet flavour, and of which nitrogen is an essential element. In the Canary and Cape de Verde Islands, the orchil was at one time the most important article of commerce ; the annual exportation being valued at from £60,000 to £80,000 ; but so great has been its consumption of late years, that the best quality, which generally sells for £200 a ton, and has in times of scarcity been actually sold for the enormous sum of £1000, or about 9s. a pound, has become exceedingly rare, and what is now commonly imported from other countries is worth little more than £30 the ton.

In this country there are many species of lichens, growing in greater or less abundance, on the mountain rocks, which might be advantageously substituted for the rare and expensive foreign orchils. Many of them have been known to the rural inhabitants from time immemorial. The parti-coloured and often exceedingly beautiful tartans of the Highland clans, used to be dyed with the colouring matter derived from the common grey foliaceous lichens which so plentifully clothe almost every tree and wall ; and many an old woman in the remote parts of Scotland, skilled in the medicinal and dyeing properties of the various plants that grow around her humble home, still prefers the dyes she herself prepares, by simply boiling in water heather twigs, birch leaves, roots of the *ruadh* or yellow bed-straw, or the various species of crotal or lichens, to logwood, madder, indigo, copperas, or any other of the imported dyes of the shops; and the results she produces, by a skilful combination of these simple substances, are really astonishing; many of the stuffs which have undergone her primitive dyeing process, being as brilliant and lasting in colour as those which have been subjected to the various baths of the professed dyer.

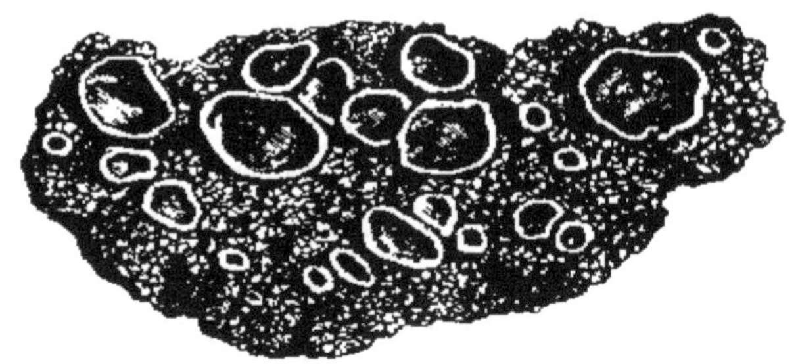

FIG. 16.—LECANORA TARTAREA.

The most useful and best known of our native dye-lichens is the rock-moss or cudbear, Fig. 16 (*Lecanora tartarea*), so called after a Mr. Cuthbert who first brought it into use. It grows in the form of a tartareous granular crust, of a dirty-grey colour, spreading in indefinite patches over the surfaces of mountain rocks, and often enveloping the stems and leaves of mosses and other small plants. It varies in thickness from a scarce perceptible film to a solid mass an inch in diameter, is covered with large irregular shields of a pale flesh colour, and may be easily identified, even without the aid of its characteristic fructification, by a peculiar pungent alkaline smell, which is very disagreeable, especially when the plant is moistened. In the Highland districts, many an industrious peasant used to earn a comfortable living, by collecting this lichen with an iron hoop from the moorland rocks, and sending it to the Glasgow market. The value of this lichen in Scotland is said at one time to have averaged £10 per ton. Hooker states that at Fort-Augustus, in 1807, a person could gain 14s. per week by gathering it, estimating its market price at 3s. 4d. per stone of 22 lbs. It appears also to have been an article of commerce in Derbyshire; the price there given to the collector, who could gather from 20 to 30 pounds per day, being 1d. per pound. This source of remunerative employment in Britain has now ceased, as the lichen is chiefly imported from Norway and Sicily, where it occurs in greater profusion than with us, and is said to contain a larger proportion of colouring matter. The dye produced by the cudbear is quite equal to orchil, and is capable of being so modified as to give any tinge of purple or crimson. It is never employed by itself to give fast colours to cloth, but merely for the purpose of improving the hues already imparted. It is sold to the dyers in the form of a purple powder. Schunk, in his analysis of this plant, discovered a colourless crystalline acid, called erythric acid, which is soluble in alkaline solutions, and converted by them into orcine and carbonic acid, and which, under exposure to the air, acquires first a red and at length a fine deep violet tint.

A species closely connected with the cudbear, and

often growing together with it on the same rock, is very extensively employed in the south of France. This is the famous Perelle d'Auvergne (*Lecanora parella*), which imparts those beautiful and brilliant hues to French ribbons, which are so much admired. The common yellow wall-lichen (*Parmelia parietina*), so abundant everywhere, yields a beautiful golden yellow crystallizable colouring matter called crysophanic acid, which is identical with the yellow colouring matter of rhubarb; and like orchil litmus, it may be used as a test for alkalies, as they invariably change its yellow colour into a vivid red tint. A beautiful and valuable crimson pigment, occasionally employed by artists, is the product of a dark-brown shrubby lichen (*Cornicularia aculeata*), very common on the hills; while the common stone lichen (*Parmelia saxatilis*), which forms grey rosettes on almost every wall, rock, and tree, is still collected abundantly by the Scottish peasantry, under the name of staneraw, to dye woollen stuff of a dirty purple or reddish-brown colour. On the low rocks, on the summits of all the loftiest Highland hills, there is a curious leafy lichen (*Parmelia fahlunensis*), found abundantly, scorched apparently by the sun into a black cinder. Of all lichens, this species, judging from its outward colour and appearance, would seem to be the least capable of yielding colouring matter; and yet when treated in the ordinary way, it yields a brilliant pink, cherry, or claret colour, which in France has been applied to so many useful purposes, that the lichen in consequence has obtained the common name of "Herpette des Tenturiers." But it is needless to enumerate all the different species of lichens, which have been, or are still employed in different parts of the world, in the production of colouring matter. This is the characteristic quality, more or less, of the whole tribe. The whole world may be said to be an open field ; in every clime, in every soil, at almost every elevation, and in all seasons tinctorial species grow, and even luxuriate. It is a matter of surprise in this age of scientific enterprise, considering the tendency everywhere exhibited to multiply the resources of our country, and to find substitutes, in useless and neglected rubbish, for expensive articles employed in the arts and manufactures, that the attention of the commercial and manufacturing public has not been directed to the field of inquiry and research, so promising in rich results, which the dye-lichens present. "The fact that importers or manufacturers," says an esteemed friend, "might find it economical or remunerative to be supplied with substitutes for the Roccellas, which are fast becoming scarce, and consequently expensive, is the most limited view we can take of the advantages of such an investigation. Indirectly a multiplied trade in dye-lichens might scatter the seeds of civilisation, and place the means of a comfortable subsistence at the command of the miserable inhabitants of many a barren island or coast, at present far removed from the great centres of social advancement ; for the dye-lichens will probably be found luxuriantly where no other vegetation can thrive, frequently attaining their highest degree of perfection on the most bleak rocky coasts, or on elevated mountain ranges. It is probable that many rocky isles in the broad Pacific and Atlantic, many hundred miles of desolate sea-coast, and vast extents of mountain districts in Africa, America, Asia, and Australia, which at present yield no products to commerce, and are too barren to support higher vegetation, might furnish an unlimited supply of lichens useful in dyeing. The vast continents of India and neighbouring countries and islands, for instance, already promise valuable results in this respect." The re-introduction of the former trade in cudbear, I may add, would furnish remunerative employment to many of the inhabitants of the Highlands, who have within the last few years been deprived of another source of comfortable subsistence, by the discovery of barilla as a more efficient substitute for the kelp, which they used to gather in immense quantities on the western coasts and islands, and sell to the soap-manufacturers, and who are now compelled by poverty and want of work to leave their native land, and seek their living on foreign shores.

I cannot conclude this chapter more appropriately, than by quoting the following eloquent remarks made by Ruskin, in his last volume of *Modern Painters*, which also apply conjunctly to the subjects of the preceding chapter: "Meek creatures! the first mercy of the earth, veiling with hushed softness its dentless rocks; creatures full of pity covering with strange and tender honour the scarred disgrace of ruin, laying quiet finger on the trembling stones to teach them rest. No words that I know of will say what these mosses are; none are delicate enough, none perfect enough, none rich enough. How is one to tell of the rounded bosses of furred and beaming green, the starred divisions of rubied bloom, fine-filmed as if the rock spirits could spin porphyry as we do glass; the traceries of intricate silver and fringes of amber, lustrous arborescent, burnished through every fibre into fitful brightness, and glossy traverses of silken change, yet all subdued and pensive, and framed for simplest, sweetest offices of grace. They will not be gathered like the flowers, for chaplet or love-token; but of these the wild-bird will make its nest, and the wearied child its pillow. And as the earth's first mercy, so they are its last gift to us. When all other service is vain from plant and tree, the soft mosses and grey lichens take up their watch by the headstone. The woods, the blossoms, the gift-bearing grasses have done their parts for a time; but these do service for ever. Trees for the builder's yard, flowers for the bride's chamber, corn for the granary, moss for the grave."

## CHAPTER III.

### FRESH-WATER ALGÆ.

"Books in the running brooks."

"And plants of fibres fine as silkworm's thread,
Yea, beautiful as mermaid's golden hair
Upon the waves dispread."

SOUTHEY.

"If the Author of Nature be great in great things, he is exceedingly great in small things," was the paradoxical remark of Rousseau, the deep meaning and truthful application of which, the world at the present day is just beginning to perceive. Everywhere, we find that microscopic life performs a work of inconceivable magnitude and importance; that the humblest and meanest organisms, though all unseen and unmarked by the ordinary senses of man, modify, by the mere force of untold numbers, the appearance of the earth, and contribute more to the formation of its grandest features than the great visible agencies around us. It was not, for instance, by Titanic forces that the island world of the Pacific was raised from the immense depths of the ocean, but by zoophytes so minute that the foot-tread of a child could crush thousands of them into atoms. The chalk cliffs of southern England, which form a stupendous barrier to the wild fury of the German and Atlantic oceans; the limestone rocks, of which immense tracts of country are almost entirely composed,—were not formed by the gigantic remains of megatheriums, mastodons, and other extinct monsters, which lived and died amidst the wildest convulsions of a nascent world, but by the shields and shells of inconceivable myriads of organisms, to each individual of which, the stage-plate of the microscope would be as large a field for its gambols, as a whole country would be to one man. It is not by the hurricane or the furious storm that our fairest orchards and most luxuriant fields are laid waste, and converted into wildernesses of skeleton leaves, and blackened and withered stalks, but by the ravages of the tiniest insects, and the minutest and most contemptible fungi.

In these days of popular science, when the most abstruse subjects come to us in forms as light and easy as the whisperings of confidential friends, or the chit-chat of the family circle, no department of natural history is more extensively and successfully studied, than that which relates to the algæ or sea-weeds. And this need not excite surprise, for there is no class of plants more interesting, whether we regard the beauty and splendour of their colours, the elegance and variety of their forms, or the romantic situations in which they occur. The invention of that elegant ornament of the parlour and drawing-room, the aquarium, now so popular, has afforded great facilities for the study of these plants, under conditions and circumstances closely analogous to those of their native haunts; and much insight has in consequence been obtained into their functions and habits, which would otherwise either remain in obscurity, or be revealed only by the "chance fortune of the hour." It would be interesting to state some of the novel facts thus elicited; but I must forbear, as our attention in this chapter, is to be occupied with the history of an important and remarkable division of the algæ called hydrophites, or fresh-water algæ, whose economy is altogether peculiar, and whose forms are widely different from the lovely Plocamiums and Delesserias, which we frequently observe with admiration in our wanderings along the sea-shore.

There is a peculiar charm about the fresh-water algæ, derived from the nature of the element in which they live. Aquatic plants of all kinds are more interesting than land plants. Water is so bright, so pure, so transparent, so fit an emblem of that spiritual element in which our souls should bathe and be strengthened, from which they should drink and be satisfied. It is a perpetual baptism of refreshment to the mind and senses. It idealizes every object in it and around it; the commonest and most vulgar scenes, reflected in its clear mirror, are pictorial and romantic. It is ever varying in its unity, so that the eye never wearies in gazing upon it. All these associations invest the confervæ which flourish in it with a peculiar nameless interest, independent of their own mysteries of structure and function. They mingle, like vegetable lotos-eaters, with the snow-white chalices and broad velvet leaves of the lilies, in the tranquil shallows of the moorland lake; and, with the golden hues of the sunset, and the rosy blush of the heather-hills around, create a scene of enchantment in the clear pellucid depths.

Their dishevelled tresses toss wildly in the foamy rapids of the waterfall, whose misty spray rises to freshen all the scenery around, and whose "sound of many waters" fills the mind with a feeling of animated delight and bounding vivacity. They float in long, graceful wreaths in the streamlet, wherever it clothes a jutting mass of rock with gemmed and sparkling folds of liquid drapery. They lie like motionless clouds in the blue depths of the tranquil linn, that just ripples for pleasure, as it murmurs to itself a sinless secret hidden for ever in its heart. They fringe the pebbly sides of the river, whose deep bulging fulness flows on unceasingly, ever diffusing freshness through the green pastures which it gladdens, and beneath the drooping willows and alders that gratefully murmur over it. They luxuriate in the cold clear springs which form a feature of the most exquisite beauty in the bleak Alpine scenery, gushing up in exposed and rocky spots, and gurgling down the sides of the hills through beds of the softest and most beautiful moss ; not the verdant velvet which covers with a short curling nap the ancient rock and the grey old tree, but long slender plumes waving under the water, and assuming through its mirror a tinge of the brightest golden green. In gathering or admiring these humble plants in such romantic situations, a sense of the beauty of the Greek mythology is awakened in the heart, more vivid and real than is experienced in other circumstances. It seems easy to believe, in quiet far-off scenes where a solitary coot sailing on the water is a considerable interruption to the solitude, and where the link that binds us to the common busy earth is broken and dropped, that the dryads are still hiding among the trees around, and the nymphs gazing upon their own reflected beauty in the limpid waves. The filaments of the confervæ, lying deeper in the fountain than one's own image, look like the green hair of the naiads; and it requires but little exercise of the imagination, to fill up the exquisite forms with their zones of rainbow drops and robes of filmy water-moss, and the beautiful, pure, passionless faces of the invisible bathers to whom the flowing, luxuriant tresses belong.

By the fresh-water confervæ we are brought to the very boundaries of the inscrutable; into those arcana of nature where life, "reduced to its simplest expression, seems invested with a deeper and more thrilling mystery." They are the very lowest in the scale of vegetation, and approximate so closely to certain animals both in form and in vital functions, that the best naturalists are unable to draw the line of distinction between their simplest species and the humblest animal organisms, or, indeed, to determine whether they possess vitality or not. They confound and neutralize the old arbitrary definitions of the three kingdoms of nature. Neither the power of voluntary motion, nor the faculty of sensation can be called the characteristic by which they are separated from animals; nor can mere appearance or ostensible mode of production be regarded as sufficient to distinguish them from minerals. All we can say regarding them, and regarding the animals with which they form connecting links, and into which some even say they are transmuted, being animals at one period of their lives and vegetables at another, is merely that the two lines or systems of life seem to start as it were from a common point at the base ; the inferior forms bearing a certain similarity to each other in structure and functions, which gradually disappears as we ascend the scale of development, until at the summit we behold those vast differences which distinguish an elephant from a palm-tree.

In this class of plants, minute and obscure although they are, the infinite resources of creative power are perhaps more clearly and overwhelmingly revealed to our perceptions, than in even the highest orders of the vegetable kingdom. The most unwearied research, continued for centuries, has not yet assigned limits to that amazing variety which is their most remarkable feature, numbering as they do species that baffle classification, and within which a still more astounding variety of individual types are to be found.

Every one is familiar with that green slimy matter, which during the spring and summer months creams over the surface of the stagnant pool, the half dried-up streamlet, or the wayside ditch ; but there are few who regard it otherwise than as a disagreeable scum or impurity, to which in Scotland the expressive name of *slaak* has been applied. It is in reality, however, an aggregation of plants, perfect in all their parts, and furnished with peculiar organs of nutrition and reproduction. Let us place a small portion of it on a concave glass, containing a drop or two of water sufficient to float it freely, and then place it under the microscope for examination, and what a beautiful spectacle is unfolded to us ! That which to the naked eye appears a mere gelatinous mass of shapeless filth, is found to be composed of a thousand delicate and exquisitely formed threads or filaments, which branch, radiate, and interlace like the most beautiful net-work (Fig. 17). Each of these threads is a transparent tube filled with endochrome, or little green cells, forming different figures, placed at regular intervals, and containing minute germs floating in mucilaginous matter. This internal matter is the fructification. When two filaments approximate, each throws out from one side a small process, which

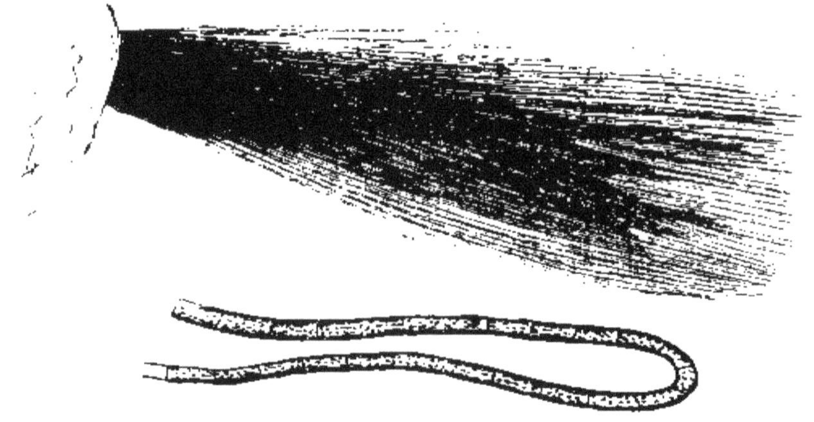

FIG. 17.—CONFERVA RIVULARIS.

unites with a corresponding process from the side of the other ; the two ends of the processes become absorbed, and the interval between the two plants is thus bridged over by a transverse tube. The endochrome of the one cell then passes through the communication thus formed into the other, and the contents of both cells become intimately mixed and form a round mass, which ultimately becomes the seeds or spores by which new plants of the same kind are destined to be produced.

But how is it, it may be asked, that process meets process in two contiguous filaments, and form between them a germinating spore? By what power is a plant given to understand, that a similar plant lies in its immediate neighbourhood, ready to carry on the necessary fructifying process? Certainly we can consider it nothing less than a species of the same indefinable operation, which prompts the bee to construct a cell of an hexagonal form, or a bird to build a nest in the manner peculiar to its species.

We thus find that these obscure plants form no exception to the very general, if not universal law, that each species of living being requires two distinct elements for its perpetuation. Sexual elements have been detected in most of the cryptogamic plants, and in a short time will probably be discovered in all. The power of reproduction by segmentation, or the production of numerous successions of asexual fertile generations, which, in common with many others of the humblest organisms, vegetable and animal, the confervæ possess, is in all cases limited, the species necessarily reverting to sexual admixture for its perpetuation. The germs produced by the conjugation of approximated individuals, when fully ripe, burst the cells in which they are confined, and are consigned to the surrounding water, where they float about, until they meet with some substance to which their mucilage enables them to adhere; and once established in a congenial situation, they spring up into new plants, and extend themselves with amazing rapidity, in a week or two producing thousands and tens of thousands of individuals. Their lives rarely exceed a year in duration, many of them dying in the course of a few months or weeks. They complete the process of reproduction early in spring, and last during the summer, perishing in the autumn, and disappearing altogether in winter. No sooner does the ice, which had bound up the streamlet in its silent fetters, melt under the warm rays of the sun, allowing its water to flow merrily on, and flash and sparkle in the sunbeams, than every stone in its bed, though brown and naked before, is suddenly, as if by magic, invested with a green velvet coating, whose long graceful filaments float freely with the water. Every ditch and marsh, every rivulet of water, every hoof-mark and rut on the road where water has accumulated, is filled with green clouds of these mysterious plants. The purposes which they serve in these situations are sufficiently obvious. Though associated in our minds with stagnation, putrefaction, and malaria, they are the scavengers, the water-filters of nature. Like the flowers and the trees, which on dry land remove the impurities with which the animal world is continually tainting the atmosphere, they purify the waters in which they occur, by assimilating the decaying matter which they contain; while their own tissues form food and shelter to myriads of animalcules, which wander over these—to them—trackless fields and endless mazes, and convert the waste pools and ditches of the wayside into scenes of busy life and enjoyment. This perfect adjustment in the economy of the animal and vegetable kingdoms, whereby the vital functions of each are maintained in the utmost efficiency, is one of the most beautiful and striking phenomena of organic nature.

The largest of the fresh-water algæ is the River Lemania (*Lemania fluviatilis*). It is never found growing in stagnant waters; indeed, it is said to languish and die, when the streams in which it is produced have, by some cause or other, been converted into motionless pools. It loves to grow in clear swift rivers, flowing with a strong current over a rough and rocky bed, and in Alpine streamlets, on the very verge of the numerous cascades which they form during their descent from the hills. It is a matter of surprise how it can sustain the immense force and weight of the impetuous waters, without being uprooted and carried away. Examination will, however, discover that it has been wonderfully provided with means to enable it to brave the dangers to which in such situations it is exposed. Its filaments are elastic, rigid, and bristly, from three to six inches in length, about the size of a hog's bristle, and knotted throughout at equal distances with prominent swelling joints, like those of the bamboo cane. They spring from a tough cartilaginous disk, so firmly applied to the rock as to require a very considerable force to detach it. It is impossible to convey in words, the same strong impression of fitness and perfection of contrivance, which a glance at the plant in its native haunts would produce. It appears one of the most striking examples of that compensatory adaptation of structure to requirements, which we observe more or less in all the lowest plants; in the moss, which, considering its size, adheres with more tenacity to its growing place than the oak of centuries, that strikes out its roots over half an acre of ground; and in the minute crustaceous lichen, apparently as hard as the rock upon which it is produced, over which the devastating storms of the Alpine summit sweep for years without inflicting upon it the slightest injury.

The colour of the Lemania, when fresh, is of a fine deep olive-green; but it changes to black when dried and placed in the herbarium. The dilatations or gouty joints, are owing to the development of the sporules within the fronds; and these may be squeezed out by being compressed between the fingers. The force with which they naturally break through the tough and cartilaginous skin of the frond, in order to form independent individuals, is not the least curious circumstance in the economy of this strange plant. Bory, to whom we are indebted for the name, informs us that the recent filaments of the Lemania, owing to some unascertained gas shut up in the knots, when applied to the flame of a candle explode and extinguish it, while a remarkable movement of retraction is felt by the fingers which hold them.

The confervæ generally grow in single branchless filaments, forming a loose fleecy stratum; but sometimes they are aggregated together into singular forms. There is one species known as the water-net or water flannel, (*Hydrodictyon utriculatum*), which looks more like a piece of green baize manufactured by man, than a production of nature. It forms a beautiful tubular purse or net, with regular polygonal meshes, varying from half a line to half an inch in diameter, grey on the one side, and green on the other. The filaments which compose these meshes are sometimes slender as a horse hair, and sometimes as coarse as a hog's bristle, feeling harsh to the touch when handled. There is no granular fructification within the filaments, consequently the plant is propagated viviparously, each of the articulations giving birth to new filaments, which add new meshes to the net, and, in this singular manner, a single individual often weaves a green net-work covering over the whole surface of a pond. It is not attached to any aquatic plants, but floats freely in the water. It is rare in Scotland and Ireland, but is of common occurrence in ponds and ditches in the middle and south of England.

Another curious conferva, which departs widely from the normal form, is the *Moor Ball* or *Globe Conferva.* It is found occasionally in lakes in North Wales, in Cumberland, and in the Highlands of Scotland. The filaments radiating from a central point form dense round pale-green balls, as if composed of faded silk thread, sometimes four inches in diameter, and having a strong resemblance to the hair balls that are found in the stomachs of goats. They are sometimes employed as pen-wipers in the places where they are found. These balls float freely at a small depth in the water, and are often washed ashore by the waves, where they accumulate in dense masses, and are again covered over with a parasitic confervoid growth.

In ditches by the waysides, may often be seen large dark-green intensely slimy masses of rigid filaments as thick as horse hair. This is the *Zygnema* (Fig. 18), one of the largest and most curious of the confervæ. Under the microscope, the filaments are found joined parallel to each other by transverse tubes, and marked by articulations longer than broad. They are interesting especially as exhibiting the spiral arrangement in their internal granular matter, in some cases like a continued multiplication of the Roman numeral x, and in other cases resembling a series of the letter v; the spiral rings after conjugating producing a dark coloured globule in one of the filaments. The spiral, it may be remarked, is the first regular form which falls under the notice of the unassisted vision, and unites in itself the two principles of unity and variety. In the inner surface of the cell it may be seen first of all; and all the parts of the plant subsequently added, whether microscopic or visible, assume this form. So universal is the spiral tendency

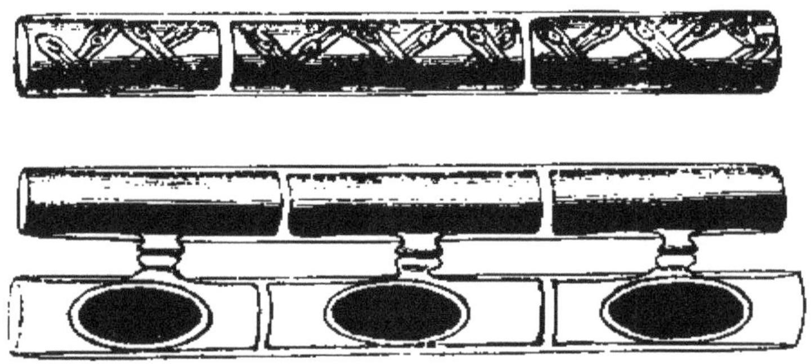

FIG. 18.—ZYGNEMA DECIMINUM.

throughout the vegetable kingdom, that some botanists have asserted it to be a general fact, that, beginning with the cotyledons or seed-lobes, the whole of the appendages of the axes of plants,—leaves, calyx, corolla, stamens, and carpels, form in their normal state an uninterrupted spiral, governed by laws which are nearly constant. It is very interesting to trace in the obscure and humble organisms under consideration, the order and harmony which are so characteristic of the highest works of creation, which are in striking accordance with the native principles of beauty implanted in the human mind, and which proceed, we must believe, from infinite wisdom. The Zygnemas form the principal fresh-water algæ of India, occurring in pools and streams in the central districts, as well as among the Himalayas. They ascend as high as 15,000 feet on these mountains, forming cloudy masses in the ice-cold springs which trickle from the edges of glaciers.

There is a very remarkable class of confervæ called Oscillatoriæ, on account of the singular oscillating motion observed in the filaments by various naturalists, thus connecting them apparently with the animal kingdom;

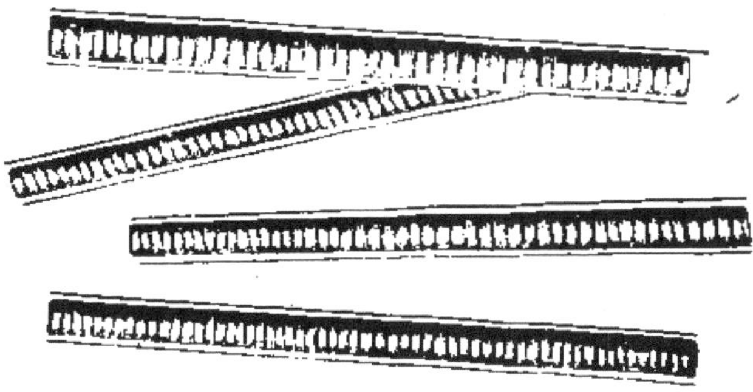

FIG. 19.—OSCILLATORIA NIGRA.

the power of voluntary motion being one of the chief characteristics essentially distinguishing animal from vegetable life. These Oscillatoriæ grow in masses of filaments based on a mucilaginous substance, the remains of old dead individuals deprived of their colour and agglutinated together, the whole emitting a strong odour of sulphuretted hydrogen which is extremely disagreeable, and sometimes causes severe headache. They have been found in a great variety of situations, ascending as high as 17,000 feet, or even 18,000 feet on the Himalayas.

Some species grow in moist, damp places, where they form a thin glossy-black pellicle of indefinite extent over the ground, strongly resembling, when dry, a piece of black satin (Fig. 19). Others are found in ditches and ponds; a third species spreads extensively over damp walls in autumn and winter, a peculiar variety covering the damp walls in the inside of some Suffolk churches with bright sky-blue mould-like patches; a fourth is often found on rotten timber, and trunks of aged trees where rain-water trickles down. They may be found parasitic upon mosses in rapid streams, and forming thick glossy strata of a dull-brown or vivid-green colour, at the bottom of clear, tranquil linns, wherever a film of soil is allowed to accumulate upon the naked slippery rocks. They are found in sulphur springs, forming pale yellow continuous tufts wherever the water retains sensible sulphureous qualities, as if the hepatic gas were necessary to their growth; and in the celebrated warm waters of Bath, a peculiar species grows in broad velvet-like patches of a dark-green colour. Their vitality is so great that they are capable of enduring the extremes of heat and cold, for they have been found on fragments of ice in Melville Island, where the temperature is considerably below zero; and they have been found growing in thermal springs in different parts of the globe, where the heat is sometimes so great that the inhabitants of the surrounding districts dress their food over them, and use them for other economic purposes instead of fire.

A magnificent species forms thick woolly fleeces of a deep red colour, in the central and western districts of India, occurring in great profusion in the hot, sweltering valleys of the great Runjeet, ascending into Nepaul and the lower slopes of the Himalayas. The most singular member of this curious group, however, is the *Trichodesmium erythræum* of Ehrenberg. It occurs in extraordinary profusion in the Red Sea, over the surface of which it spreads for many miles, according to the direction of the wind, in the form of a dark-red shining scum. It is composed of little bundles of filaments marked with striæ, which have been compared to minute fragments of chopped hay. In certain states of the weather it emits a disagreeable, pungent smell, affecting strongly the mucous membrane, and causing violent sneezing and ophthalmia, thus adding to the list of annoyances which render the passage of the Red Sea peculiarly disagreeable to passengers from the West. The habit of this alga is widely different from that of its congeners, and resembles that of the Sargassums or Gulf-weeds, which form extensive floating meadows to the west of the Azores, and are supposed to indicate the site of submerged lands. The name of the Red Sea greatly puzzled the ancients, and has occasioned in later times a display of much superfluous learning to determine whether it was derived from the colour of the water, the reflection of the red coral sand-banks and the neighbouring mountains, or the solar rays struggling through a dense atmosphere. Another conjecture may be hazarded, that it has acquired its denomination from the extreme prevalence and conspicuousness of this red alga in its waters.

The filaments of all the species of Oscillatoria are elastic, simple, exceedingly minute, and mathematically straight. They are distinguished by close parallel rings easily separating from each other. The motion of oscillation, for which all the species are distinguished, is in some remarkably vivid, and would favour the supposition that they are animals and not plants, were it not that their othér characteristics are peculiarly those of vegetables. The filaments continually move from right to left, or from left to right, but in a very irregular manner, some going in one direction and others in another; some being at rest while others are in motion. This lateral oscillation has been attributed to various causes. The majority of naturalists, inclining to the opinion that it is mechanical and not voluntary, have ascribed it to rapidity of growth, which, in such simple plants, is excessive; to the molecular action of light, or to the agitation, by hidden causes, of the water in which the filaments are immersed for inspection. But none of these suppositions afford a satisfactory explanation, as Captain Carmichael ascertained by the following simple contrivance:—He placed a small portion of the stratum of a species of Oscillatoria, composed of a great many individuals united together, in a watch-glass filled with water, and covered it with a thin plate of mica, which effectually excluded the outer air, and kept the water as motionless and fixed as a piece of ice. The glass, with its contents thus arranged, was placed under the microscope, and the oscillation of the filaments was observed most vividly, there being no possibility of disturbance by the agitation of the water, showing clearly that this singular movement was independent of that cause. "The action of light," says this accomplished naturalist, "as a cause of motion, cannot be directly disproved, because we cannot view our specimens in the dark; but indirectly there is nothing easier. If a watch-glass, charged as above, be laid aside for a night, it will be found that by next morning not only a considerable radiation has taken place, but that multitudes of the filaments have entirely escaped from the stratum, both indicating motion independent of light. Rapidity of growth will show itself in a prolongation of the filaments, but will not account for this oscillation to the right and left, and still less for their travelling in the course of a few hours to the distance of ten times their own length from the stratum. This last is a kind of motion unexampled, I believe, in the vegetable kingdom." Many species, it may be remarked, possess at their extremity a tuft of very minute, delicate ciliæ, which possess the power of imparting motion to the filaments on which they are developed. Another strange fact in the economy of these very singular and anomalous plants, is the extremely limited term of their existence. Their cycle of life is often completed in three or four days. The community of individuals associated together in one patch or stratum live for several months; but the individuals themselves die off, and are succeeded by others with a rapidity truly marvellous. The remains of the dead filaments form the bases of the living ones, and thus they go on increasing in depth and breadth until they often cover the whole bed of a streamlet. This peculiarity connects them with the coral-zoophytes, and supplies another link between the animal and vegetable kingdoms.

Several obscure and curious organisms have been included by botanists in this vast and varied order of plants, some of which are supposed to be fungi in an embryonic or imperfectly developed state. They are composed of hyaline or coloured articulated filaments, aggregated together and forming a kind of fibrous crust, sprinkled over with loose granules, which are supposed to be the fructification. The localities where many of them are found prove that they are not genuine algæ. One curious species is found on windows and damp glass in shady places, where it forms round white spots, radiating like a spider's web from a centre, and sprinkled with minute, whitish, powdery particles. Another forms simple, transparent, club-shaped filaments, from a line to an inch in length, on the bodies of fishes and dead flies, found on decaying leaves and weeds in the water. Several species are found in chemical solutions and various infusions, such as distilled rose-water, dissolved muriate of barytes, and gum-dragon. The white flocculent matter often found on the surface of old stale ink, and the yellow hyaline filaments found at the bottom of wine bottles, are referred to this class of plants, to which the generic name of Hygrocrocis has been given, from their byssoid nature, and the situations which they affect. There is one species, the saffron rock byssus (*Chroolepus aureus*), which deserves, on account of its beauty, more than a passing notice. Unlike the other confervoid algæ, which are found in moist situations or in water, it is restricted to the shady side of overhanging cliffs, trunks of trees, leaves and other objects, and never grows in water. It is abundant in the Highlands of Scotland, in deep, leaf-embowered ravines near a mountain-lake or waterfall.

It grows among dense cushions of the beautiful apple and other mosses, to which it affords a fine contrast by its velvety tufts of a deep orange colour, which are rendered especially brilliant by the stray sunbeams that chance to reach their growing-place. In similar localities, and particularly on the micaceous rocks on the Highland mountains, may often be observed its Ethiopian relative, the black rock byssus (*Chroolepus ebeneus*), forming a thin, black, velvety patch of indefinite extent, composed of fine, branched, black hairs, closely matted together, and sometimes sprinkled over with black powder. Few would suspect its vegetable character; indeed, it bears a greater resemblance to a piece of black felt scraped from a hat than to any plant. Both these plants are supposed to be peculiar states of certain lichens, their reproductive bodies being very similar. What a convincing proof do these heterogeneous productions, growing as they do on the most unlikely substances, and in the most unfavourable situations, afford us that the tendency to vegetate is a power restless, perpetual, and universal!

The extraordinary phenomenon of red snow has long been familiarly known to scientific men in this and other countries, and has naturally enough excited the greatest interest. This singular colour in a substance with which we are accustomed to associate ideas of spotless purity and radiant whiteness, has been ascertained to result from an immense aggregation of minute plants belonging to the family now under consideration. They form the species called *Protococcus nivalis* (Fig. 20), in allusion to the extreme primitiveness of its organization, and the peculiar nature of its habitat. If we place a portion of the snow coloured with this plant upon a piece of white paper, and allow it to melt and evaporate, we find a residuum of granules just sufficient to give a faint crimson tinge to the paper. Placed under the microscope these granules resolve themselves into spherical purple cells, from the $\frac{1}{1000}$th to the $\frac{1}{3000}$th part of an inch in diameter. Each of these cells has an opening, surrounded by serrated or indented lines, whose smallest diameter measures only the $\frac{1}{8000}$th part of an inch. The plant, when perfect, bears no inapt resemblance to a red-currant

FIG. 20.—PROTOCOCCUS NIVALIS.

berry; as it decays, the red colouring matter gradually fades into a deep orange, which finally appears to change into a brown hue. The thickness of the wall of the cell does not exceed the $\frac{1}{20000}$th part of an inch. Each one of the cells may be regarded as a distinct individual plant, since it is perfectly independent of others with which it may be aggregated, and performs for and by itself all the functions of growth and reproduction, having a containing membrane which absorbs liquids and gases from the surrounding matrix or elements, a contained fluid of peculiar character formed out of these materials, and a number of excessively minute granules equivalent to spores, or, as some would say, to cellular buds, which are to become the germs of new plants. There is something extremely mysterious in the performance of these widely different functions, by an organism which appears so excessively simple. That one and the same primitive cell should thus minister equally to absorption, nutrition, and reproduction, is an extraordinary illustration of the fact, that the smallest and simplest organized object is in itself, and, for the part it was created to perform in the operations of nature, as admirably adapted as the largest and most complicated.

Saussure, the celebrated geologist, appears to have been the first scientific person who noticed this production, for in his "Voyages dans les Alpes," he states that he found considerable patches of it near the snow-crowned summit of Mont Breven, in Switzerland, so long ago as the year 1760, and afterwards very frequently and in great abundance in his wanderings over the Pennine Alps, and particularly on the Col du Géant on the ascent of Mont Blanc. After this period several eminent botanists collected it in various places; Rammond on the snow-capped peaks of the Pyrenees, and Sommerfeldt on the Doffrefels and other lofty hills in Norway. In March 1808, red or rather rose-coloured snow fell in considerable quantities in the Tyrol, and on the mountains of Carinthia in Illyria; and over Carnia, Cadore, Belluno, and Feltri, to such an extent that the hills were covered with it to the depth of six feet. Ten years later, it is recorded that enormous quantities of the same substance were spread like a bloody pall over the Apennines and the other Italian hills, occasioning no small alarm among the superstitious inhabitants of the surrounding districts, who looked upon it as a dreadful omen of impending calamity, and sought refuge from their fears in various protective ceremonies. Among the Peruvian mountains, Darwin relates that on several patches of snow he found this curious appearance. His attention was called to it by observing the footsteps of the mules stained a pale red, as if their hoofs had been slightly bloody. The snow was coloured only where it had thawed very rapidly, or had been accidentally crushed.[1] It is in the Arctic regions, however, that the red snow is found most frequently, and in the greatest luxuriance. Sir John Ross, during his memorable expedition to these regions in 1808, found on the 16th of June in about latitude 75°, a range of cliffs rising about 800 feet above the level of the sea, and extending eight miles in length, entirely covered with snow, which seemed as though it had been watered by some crimson decoction. Sir W. E. Parry found the same phenomenon, during his heroic attempt to reach the Pole by travelling over the ice in 1827; and ascertained besides, that wherever the surface of the snow-plain, although previously of its ordinary spotless hue, was crushed by the pressure of the sledges and of the footsteps of the party, blood-like stains appeared most visibly; the impressions being sometimes tinged with an orange colour, and sometimes appearing of a pale salmon hue.

Red snow, however, seems by no means peculiar to the

[1] It is a curious circumstance, that Dr. Hooker never met with a single specimen of red snow, during all his wanderings over the lofty snow surfaces of the Sikkim Himalayas, especially as on almost every mountain range elevated above the line of perpetual snow, it has been seen, often in abundance.

Arctic regions, or the highly elevated mountains of the globe. It has been discovered spreading over decayed leaves and mosses on the borders of small lakes, and in water tanks in hot-houses ; and in greater perfection on limestone rocks within reach of the spray of the ocean in Lismore, an island off the coast of Argyleshire. W. H. Harvey, the distinguished Irish botanist, found small patches on micaceous schist near Miltown Malbay, on calcareous rocks at Limerick, and in the neighbourhood of Dublin on granite, with only an occasional supply of moisture. On Ben Nevis and Ben Lawers I have more than once detected specimens, upon the surface of the large masses of unmelted snow, with which the summits of these mountains are sometimes covered even in the depth of summer.

The fact that the red snow is capable of growing in such spots as those in which it has chiefly been found in Britain, namely, on rocks, leaves, and mosses, exposed to occasional or frequent inundations of water, seems to prove that the ice-plains of the Arctic regions, and the snow-crowned sides and summits of the European mountains, are not its natural situations. When, however, its germs have once been deposited in these barren and cheerless localities, the simplicity of its organization, and the consequent strong persistency of the vital principle in it, enable it effectually to resist the cold ; and with that extraordinary power of rapid development which characterizes in a greater or less degree all the members of the family to which it belongs, it forms in a few years, when nourished by the moisture produced by the melting of the icy snow during summer, vast and dense masses, sometimes twelve feet in depth, and extending many miles in length, which afford by their strange contrast to the painful uniformity of the pure and dazzling whiteness all around, a sight more surprising to the Arctic or the Alpine traveller than would be the realization of all the fabled wonders of the Arabian tales.

Another supposed species of Protococcus was discovered by Baron Wrangel in the province of Nerike or Nericia in Sweden, not far from the town of Orebo, and

FIG. 21.—PALMELLA CRUENTA.

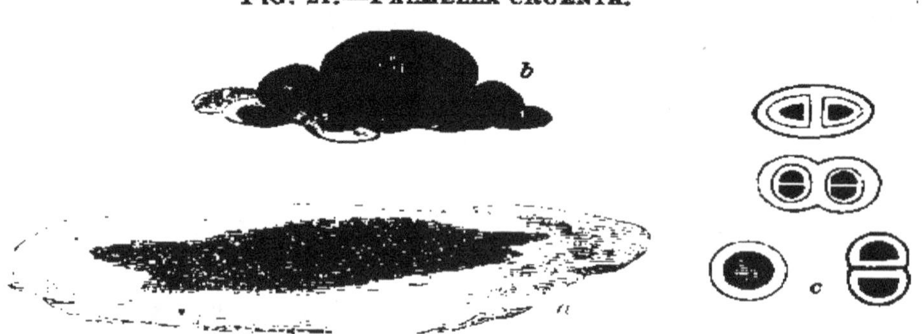

(*a*) Fructification slightly magnified.
(*b*) Fructification much magnified.
(*c*) Fructification highly magnified. Cells dividing into two, and then into four parts, each capable of propagating the plant.

named by him *Lepraria Kermesina.* The same plant was afterwards found by various continental botanists among the fissures of rocks, and on the under surfaces of stones in various localities, and called by them *Protococcus viridis*, or green snow. It was also observed by Martins in similar situations in Spitzbergen. It is now, however, ascertained beyond doubt to be a mere variety of *Protococcus nivalis*, as it is identical with it in every respect save colour ; and this difference is owing to the different nature of the circumstances in which it is developed.

The actinic power of the solar light, aided by some peculiar, and as yet unknown property belonging to the natural whiteness of the snow itself, is highly essential in the production of the beautiful crimson or rose colour, by which the red snow is distinguished ; but this colour, as in the case of the varieties mentioned above, gradually changes to green when secluded from the direct action of light, and developed on dark or opaque objects.

Another extremely curious plant closely allied to the red snow is the *Palmella cruenta* (Fig. 21) or Gory Dew. Like the Protococcus it consists of a number of aggregated globose cells, forming a very thin crust-like frond of a dark blood colour. Each of the cells divides first into two, then into four parts, each capable of propagating the plant. It grows on damp limestone in the open air, or on whitewashed walls, particularly in cellars, and the mouldering rooms of old neglected buildings, and figures largely in the history of the superstitions of the middle ages. Pitarello, a peasant residing at Legnaro, near Padua, observed large patches of it covering the walls of an old and rarely visited room in his house, which so closely resembled huge clots of venous blood, that the greatest curiosity and consternation were excited. The streets of Padua leading to Legnaro were thronged by anxious crowds hastening to inspect the phenomenon, and full of the calamities it foreboded. Many regarded it as a direct judgment of God upon the unhappy peasant, for having forestalled corn during the famine. During the last invasion of epidemic cholera, the same plant was found in abundance, purpling the ground near Oxford, as if red wine or blood had been poured out.

In connexion with the present subject, it may be interesting to glance over the several examples of blood prodigies which history furnishes. The almost unanimous judgment of modern times has stamped these examples as pure fables ; but I think it is easy to account for the presence in them of so much that seems incredible, and to show how that into which the apparently fabulous enters in so large a proportion, can yet be received in the main as true history. Our present investigations will go far to evince that the great bulk of what ancient writers hand down to us as prodigies and miracles, is capable of explanation on grounds intelligible to any ordinary understanding ; and thus that history, so far as these things are concerned, may be true in its narrative of facts, though it be often in error in the view it takes of the nature of the facts narrated. That rivers have run blood, that skies have rained blood, that the very bread in men's houses has been sprinkled with blood, and thus ministered death instead of nourishment to those who have eaten it, and that consecrated wafers and priestly vestments have repeatedly exhibited these horrible appearances,—that all these wonderful things have really happened, we have every reason to believe, from the circumstantial accounts of them given in records purporting to be authentic, received as such by the age that produced them, and preserved and handed down as such to our own times. We believe the facts ; but we do not believe the explanation given of them, or the inferences deduced from them ; our superior scientific knowledge enabling us to account, on natural grounds, for what, in an age of ignorance and superstition, appeared prodigies of fatal presage.

There is an instructive *résumé* of Ehrenberg's paper on this curious subject in *Chambers's Journal*, from which the following paragraph of portents is extracted : —"Appearances of blood flowing from bread when bitten, are recorded as occurring at Tours in 583 ; at Spires in 1104 ; at Namur in 1193 ; at Rochelle in 1163, and at many other places. At Augsburg, in 1199, a person having kept the consecrated wafer in his mouth, brought it at a later period to the priest changed into flesh and blood. Pilgrimages were not unfrequently made to witness bleeding hosts, as that of Doberan in 1201 ; and that of Balitz, near Berlin, which had been sacrilegiously sold by a girl to a Jew. In 1296, the Jews at Rotil, near Frankfort, having been reported to have caused a host to bleed which they had bought, a fanatical persecution of these people took place, whereby 10,000 were said to have been slaughtered. Several Jews were burned at Güstrow, in Mecklenburg, for a similar offence. In 1492, a priest, one Peter Dove, residing in Mecklenburg, sold two hosts to a Jew for the purpose of redeeming a pawn ; and they having pierced them, abundance of blood flowed out. The priest, now tormented with remorse, confessed the transaction, and betrayed the Jews ; twenty of their number were burned on an eminence at Sternberg, since called Judenberg, and at this very Judenberg did the Mecklenburg deputies recently commence their sittings. In 1510, thirty-eight Jews were executed and then burned, for 'having tormented a consecrated host until the blood came.'

The bleeding of the host, produced in consequence of the scepticism of the officiating priest, gave rise to the miracle of Bolsena in 1264, the priest's garment stained with blood being preserved until quite recent times as a relic. This gave rise to the foundation of the festival of the Corpus Christi by Urban IV., although Raphael, painting his celebrated picture in 1512, substitutes Julius II."

Dr. D'Aubigné, in his *History of the Reformation*, thus describes from the writings of Zwingle in a somewhat inflated, but vivid and interesting style, the appearance of a similar phenomenon :—"On the 26th of July, a widow, chancing to be alone in her house, in the village of Castelenschloss, suddenly beholds a frightful spectacle, blood springing from the earth all around her ; she rushes in alarm into the cottage . . . but oh, horrible! blood is flowing everywhere, from the earth, from the wainscot, and from the stones ; it falls in a stream from a basin on a shelf, and even the child's cradle overflows with it. The woman imagines that the invisible hand of an assassin has been at work, and rushes in distraction out of doors, crying, 'Murder, murder!' The villagers and the monks of a neighbouring convent assemble at the noise ; they partly succeed in effacing the bloody stains ; but a little later in the day the other inhabitants of the house, sitting down in terror to eat their evening meal under the projecting eaves, suddenly discover blood bubbling up in a pond, blood flowing from the loft, blood covering all the walls of the house. Blood, blood! everywhere blood! The bailiff of Schenkenberg and the pastor of Dalheim arrive, inquire into the matter, and immediately report it to the Lords of Berne and to Zwingle."

This extraordinary and alarming effusion of blood, along with the previously mentioned instances of bleeding hosts, although plainly exaggerated by the dilated eye of fear, which in those troubled times saw everywhere frightful portents and terrific signs, apparently foreboding the most calamitous events, were no doubt owing to the excessive development, under peculiarly favourable circumstances, of an exceedingly minute alga, bearing a strong superficial resemblance to the red snow plant. This alga was called by Ehrenberg the purple monad, under the impression that it was an animalcule. More accurate researches, however, have since determined its vegetable nature, and it is now called *Palmella prodigiosa,* from the wonderful rapidity with which it develops and extends itself. The body of this curious atom is but from the one three-thousandth, to the one eight-thousandth of a line (twelfth of an inch) in length. In a cubic inch from 46,656,000,000,000 to 884,736,000,000,000 may therefore exist,—a number, of course, utterly beyond the range of human words and conceptions, and which would take many thousands of persons working unceasingly from the creation of man to the present day to count. Like the red-snow plant, it first of all appears in the form of small, bright, red points, like so many coloured minute dew-drops, or the roe of fishes, composed of inconceivable myriads of individuals, which afterwards unite into large red-currant-jelly-like patches, coalescing and penetrating the substances upon which they are produced. Its peculiar habit would seem rather to indicate affinity with the fungi than with the algæ.

The accounts of blood-prodigies found in ancient history, are matched by well-authenticated phenomena which have presented themselves within the memory of many now living. So late as the beginning of this century, the excessive growth of red algæ on the surface of the Elbe made that river for several days seem to run blood; while shortly afterwards some portions of the Nile reddened in the same way, and remained blood-like and putrid for many months. In Silliman's *North American Journal*, there appeared several years ago, a description of an extraordinary fountain of blood discovered in South America. A person approaching the grotto from which the waters flowed observed a disagreeable odour, and when it was reached, he saw several pools of the blood in a state of coagulation. Dogs ate it eagerly. The late Don Raphael Osijo undertook to send some bottles of this singular liquid—rivalling the famous blood of St. Januarius—to London for analysis, but it corrupted within twenty-four hours, bursting the bottles. Before the potato-blight broke out in 1846, red mould spots appeared on wet linen surfaces exposed to the air in bleaching-greens, as well as on household linens kept in damp places in Ireland. In September 1848, Dr. Eckard, of Berlin, while attending a cholera patient, observed the same appearance on a plate of potatoes which had been placed in a cupboard of the patient's house. The potatoes were transmitted for examination to Ehrenberg, who found the colouring matter to consist of extremely minute algæ, or animalcules as he called them, somewhat allied to the *Palmella pro-*

*digiosa.* In the spring of the year 1825, the waters of the Lake of Morat presented an appearance in many places of being coloured with blood, and popular attention was speedily directed to this strange occurrence. M. de Candolle, however, proved that the phenomenon in question was caused by the development of myriads of the purple conferva (*Oscillatoria rubescens*). The phenomenon occurred every spring for several years, when the fishermen of the neighbourhood, more poetical than this class of persons usually are, remarked that "the lake was in flower." M. Montagne records a similar phenomenon in the *Comptes Rendus.* He happened to be at the Château du Parquet in July 1852, when the temperature had been exceedingly high for about ten successive days. This continued warmth of the atmosphere, was probably instrumental in providing the conditions suitable for the development of a red parasite, which attacked all kinds of alimentary substances, and particularly pastry, imparting to them a bright red colour, resembling arterial blood. "The servants," he observes, "much astonished at what they saw, brought us half a fowl roasted the previous evening, which was literally covered with a gelatinous layer of a very intense carmine-red, and only of a bright rose colour where the layer was thinner. A cut melon also presented some traces of it. Some cooked cauliflower which had been thrown away, and which I did not see, also, according to the people of the house, presented the same appearance. Lastly, three days afterwards, the leg of a fowl was also attacked by the same production." From a microscopic examination, M. Montagne concluded it to be the same thing as described by Ehrenberg. The particles of which it is composed have an active molecular motion, and hence Ehrenberg's mistake in supposing it to be an animalcule. Its resemblance to the gelatinous specks which occur on mouldy paste, or raw meat in an incipient state of decomposition, would seem to indicate that it is a fungus allied to the moulds, and not an alga. Its vitality is not impaired by desiccation, even at a high temperature. A portion of paste containing this Palmella was dried in an oven for forty-eight hours, until nearly baked into biscuit, yet fragments of it readily grew when scattered on fresh-made dough.

A red colour, closely resembling blood, not unfrequently astonishes the sailor in some parts of the ocean. Captain Tuckey mentions that the water of the Gulf of California is reddish, whence it is sometimes called the Vermilion Sea. Captain Colnett, in his interesting voyages, states that "the set of the currents on the coast of Chili, may at all times be known by noticing the direction of the beds of small blubber (gelatinous algæ) with which the coast abounds, and from which the water derives a colour like that of blood. I have often been engaged," he adds, "for a whole day in passing through various sets of them." D'Orbigny also remarks that there are immense tracts off the coast of Brazil filled with small animals so numerous as to impart a red colour to the sea; large portions are thus highly coloured, and receive from the sailors the name of the Brazil bank, which extends over a great part of the coast of the country, keeping at nearly the same distance from the shore. Another bank of the same kind occurs near Cape Horn in latitude 57°, and was encountered by Captain Cook during his third voyage. Mr. Scoresby narrates that he noticed in his last expedition to the Arctic regions in 1823, some insulated patches of reddish brown water, which were found to be occasioned by minute algæ; and often too were the floating icebergs tinged with them of a carmine or deep orange hue. Ehrenberg frequently observed in the steppes of Siberia, lakes and other collections of water filled with red algæ. "In a *fen*," he remarks, "with a pool of water, the dark-red blood colour was very striking even at a distance. This colour I found on examination was confined to the slimy surface, which in different places formed a shining skin. The red colour was darkest at the edge of the marsh." How many a wonderful fairy tale has science divested of its gilded ornaments, and converted into hard fact and unvarnished truth! And how many a phenomenon, magnified by the unthinking ignorance and credulity of vulgar superstition into an evidence of supernatural agency, and an omen of future calamity, has the microscope resolved into a mere collection of minute and simple vegetables, or equally harmless animalcules!

There is a startling thought suggested by these accounts of blood-prodigies. Occurring as most of them did before the outbreak of epidemics which they were supposed to herald, they obviously point to the conclusion that they were developed by abnormal conditions of the atmosphere. In ordinary circumstances, but few either of the animals or plants which caused these alarming appearances are produced, and then only in obscure and isolated localities; but their seeds lie around us in immense profusion, waiting but the recurrence of similar atmospheric conditions as existed in former times, to exhibit as extraordinary a development. For all we know there may be existing amongst us the germs of other forms of life, ready to develop themselves into new manifestations of the power and wisdom of God, if it should please Him to adapt the vital envelope of our globe to the uses of other occupants. The present electrical condition of the air is admirably adapted for the healthy development of the forms of life that now exist in it; and so likewise is the water for the organisms that pervade it. But who can tell what species of plants and animals would succeed the present species, were there but the smallest change effected in the proportions of the constituents of these elements? Geology reveals to us the singular fact that, when the air and the water were densely impregnated with carbonic gas during the coal era, an extraordinary development of the humblest forms of animal and plant life was the result. The earth was covered with dense forests of ferns and mosses, and the waters were peopled with myriads of corallines. And were similar conditions of the atmosphere and the water to occur again, or should any change be produced in the existing conditions, the change, while it would prove fatal to the most highly organized of the present race of animals and plants, would stimulate into excessive growth and profusion animals and plants of the simplest construction, which are now kept in check, and occupy but the most obscure and subordinate positions in the ranks of nature's agencies. And if the advent of widespread plagues in the middle ages was heralded by the vast development of the confervæ and infusoria, we are led by a cogent induction to conclude that it is a change of the air and water which breeds the epidemic, and that these are the first growths of that new animal and vegetable kingdom which would succeed the existing forms, if mankind were to be swept away!

The subdivision of the confervæ to which the red snow and the gory dew belong, contains the simplest of all vegetable forms, if, indeed, they be plants at all, occurring in shapeless gelatinous masses of all hues, covering irrigated perpendicular cliffs in dark and shady places, or rocks exposed to the spray of waterfalls, and frequently hanging down in flakes from their surface. Their extreme simplicity is more puzzling to the botanist than any amount of complexity would have been. Their fundamental structure, in almost all cases, appears to be simply a mass of cells variously arranged in a jelly-like polymorphous substance, to which the name of frond has been applied, more for the sake of convenience than from any sense of its propriety; each cell being a distinct individual plant, apparently having no connexion with the other cells to which it is placed in juxtaposition, and performing for and by itself all the processes of nutrition and reproduction. The question naturally arises, whether these obscure and extremely simple organisms which stand at the very lowest extremity of the vegetable kingdom, be really perfect plants, or rather the commencement, the first of the transitional stages of more highly organized plants, unable to develop themselves owing to their being placed in unfavourable circumstances? Some eminent botanists have contended that the spore germs of the lower cryptogamic plants are in all cases precisely the same, developing themselves into different plants according to the medium and the circumstances in which they are placed: becoming palmellas when produced on moist rocks, confervæ in streams, confervoid mosses on shady banks and fields, lichens on dry rocks when stimulated by the action of light, and fungi when produced on decaying substances, and excluded from air and light; and this opinion seems to be strengthened by the fact so well known to botanists, that the permanent organization of the lowest plants is very frequently only the temporary or transitional condition of higher, and that so close is the resemblance between them that without due care in watching the progress of their development, they may easily be set down as distinct species. To this theory of development, however, plausible though it looks, I do not subscribe. Some of these productions may not be autonomous, some may seem to pass into each other by intermediate forms, and may bear a close resemblance to the primordial stages of plants belonging to other tribes; but still there are real species among these lower genera—species which are permanent and do not undergo any further transformation, for in the circumstances in which they are found they can exist and multiply and perfect their fructification independently. Few objects are more beautiful and interesting under the microscope than some of these obscure bodies, and their study is absolutely necessary to the physiologist, if he wishes to obtain a clear insight into the real character and phenomena of growth and reproduction in the higher tribes of plants, and especially the changes which take place during the very early or embryonic condition of the more complicated structures.

The *Nostoc* (Fig. 22), one of the species belonging to this strange class of plants, is interesting on account of the historical associations connected with it. It occurs in the form of a greenish jelly or slimy mass on gravelly soils, rocks, pastures, and roadsides, among grass and moss, especially in moist weather. It is widely distributed, occurring as far south as the Antarctic regions, several species having been found by Dr. Hooker on wet rocks near the sea in Kerguelen's Land. It ranges, on

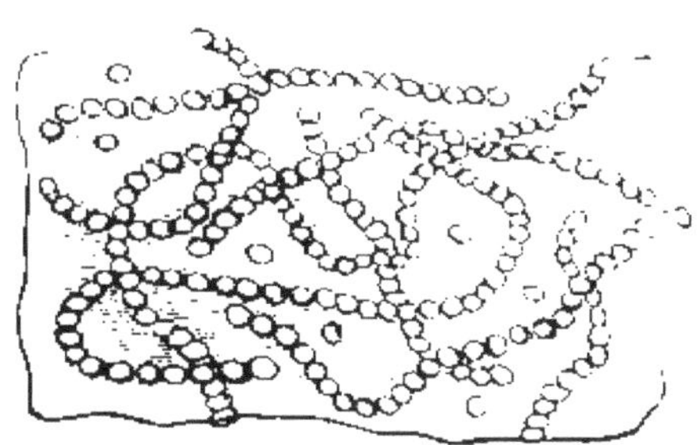

FIG. 22.—NOSTOC COMMUNE.

the other hand, as far north as Baffin's Bay, and the shores of the Polar Ocean, growing on the soft, boggy slopes of the sea-shore, from whence it is drifted about by the wind in detached masses, and forming the only vegetable production of any importance over many square leagues. Dr. Sutherland, in his fascinating journal, relates that it has often been found in great abundance on floating icebergs, and in small depressions in the snow upon the ice, at a distance of ten miles from the land. It affords a welcome food,—far more palatable than the tripe de roche, the only other edible substance which occurs in these inhospitable regions,—consisting as it does of a modification of cellulose, without any deleterious mixture. It affords food and shelter to several species of Poduræ, and an interesting little spider called *Desoria Arctica.* In the warm springs of India the Nostoc frequently occurs, and is successfully employed by the natives as an outward application for scrofulous affections, owing to the presence in it of minute quantities of an alkaline iodide. In China, it is a frequent denizen of ponds and streams, whence it is carefully gathered and dried, to form an ingredient with the famous edible bird's nests, in their rich and nutritious soups. In the salt lakes of Thibet, and the marshes in the woods of New Zealand, it attains frequently gigantic proportions, forming masses of quaking gelatine, many feet in circumference. The vulgar suppose the Nostoc to be the remains of a fallen star, or of a Will-of-the-wisp, and hence they attach many superstitious ideas to it. It derived its name from Paracelsus, the celebrated alchemist, who employed it from its ambiguous character and simple structure in the composition of the universal solvent and the elixir vitæ. We find frequent mention of it in the writings of the alchemists, by whom it was highly esteemed on account of the mysterious virtues which it was supposed to possess.

The structure of this plant, simple as it appears, is very curious and interesting. Examined under the microscope, it is found to consist of a number of slender moniliform threads or necklaces of spores, invested with a firm and copious gelatine, which originated at an early stage from each individual thread, but has now become the common envelope of the whole mass. The plant is propagated by the division of these threads into their individual joints, which burst through the common *jelly*, and become dispersed in the water, where they are endowed with spontaneous motion, enabling them to contend against currents. "These fragmentary threads," says Berkeley, "divide longitudinally and transversely, at last constituting a bundle of new threads, which gradually, by increase of the gelatinous or filamentous elements, assume the normal form of the species."

Another allied species is the mountain dulse of the Scotch (*Palmella montana*), occurring very frequently in patches of a deep but dull purple colour, in moist, stony places, on the mountains of Skye, Arran, and on the west coast of Scotland, where it is used by the Highlanders, when rubbed between their hands in water, as a paste with which to purge their calves. Attached to aquatic plants, and the stones at the bottom of ponds, and in the shallow margins of still lakes, may often be seen a very curious little plant belonging to this tribe, called *Rivularia angulosa*. It closely resembles greengage plums in size, shape, and appearance, and is always found associated in little colonies. It is a simple, roundish mass of gelatine, filled internally with beautiful beaded filaments. The least touch detaches it from its growing-place, when it rises to the surface of the water with the velocity of an air-bubble, and refuses to sink again, floating freely about. The whole genus Rivularia is composed of exceedingly curious plants, most of them occurring in shallow rivulets, and alpine cascades and streamlets, where they adhere, in the form of glossy, bead-like dots of a dark-olive colour, to the stones of the bottom, generally preferring the pure white quartz and the glittering mica schist. The whole plant is not larger than a pin's-head, or a small pea; but it sometimes spreads widely in favourable situations, covering all the stones in the bed of a streamlet, and giving them an appearance, as the little, bustling, transparent waves roll and sparkle over them, as if they were full of eyes. But the most beautiful and interesting of all the members of the gelatinous confervæ is the *Batrachospermum moniliforme* (Fig. 23), which is universally distributed

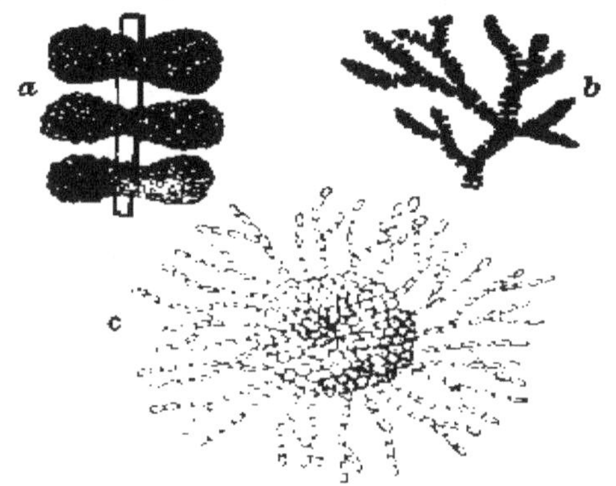


FIG. 23.—BATRACHOSPERMUM MONILIFORME.
(*a*) Magnified. (*b*) Natural size. (*c*) Magnified.

over Britain, and is especially abundant in subalpine streamlets. It is easily known by its growing in clusters composed of branching filaments, which appear even to the naked eye like necklaces or strings of small beads, being strung, as it were, with numerous gelatinous globules placed close beside each other. These branches are so exceedingly flexible that they obey the slightest movement of the water, and it is impossible to express the pleasure which is excited in the mind of the botanist, while contemplating a cluster of this little alga, in those pure, clear, sunny wells, with which he sometimes meets in his wanderings among the hills, springing up far away in lonely spots, where the curlew builds her nest among the rushes, their mossy sides starred with the large, snow-white flowers of the grass of Parnassus, and adorned with the closed hoods and diamond-studded leaves of the sun-dew. Every movement of the tiny fairy exemplifies the curve of beauty, every filament winds ceaselessly and rapidly through a thousand forms of matchless grace. When removed from the water, however, the filaments lose all trace of organization, and slip through the fingers like a piece of jelly or frog-spawn. The Batrachospermum occurs in the Ganges, in North America, Hermite Island near Cape Horn, and New Zealand, and is probably distributed all over the world. "One curious circumstance in this plant is, that the threads of the knot-like masses send decurrent joints down the stem, thus making that compound which was originally simple."

On shady walls and thatched roofs, at the foot of rocks and houses in damp situations, may often be seen a stratum of densely-crowded transparent green leaves, plaited and wrinkled with rounded lobes. This plant, called *Ulva crispa*, is the terrestrial variety of the familiar green laver of the sea-coast. Another species of the same genus (*U. bulbosa*), occasionally fills stagnant pools and ditches of fresh water, with its excessively soft and lubricous masses, appearing as if in a state of fermentation. It is exactly the counterpart of the common sea species. The *Enteromorpha intestinalis*, with which every visitor to the sea-coast is familiar, adding greatly to the beauty of rocky pools, left full by the receding tide, also occurs not unfrequently in fresh-water ponds and stagnant waters in spring and summer. An allied species, *Tetraspora lubrica*, forming irregular masses of considerable extent, and exceedingly lubricous, in gently running water, has its fruit, consisting of minute granules imbedded in the fronds, loosely arranged in fours. The first stages of all these fresh-water representatives of the marine ulvæ, are in all respects simple confervæ ; but the cells at the extremity of the filaments divide, and by repeated division, these filaments are laterally expanded, until they form a plane-leaf-like frond, as in ulva, or close all round after they have expanded, until they produce a tube or sac as in enteromorpha.

One of the most singular of the confervaceous algæ is the *Botrydium granulatum*. It grows on the ground in moist shady situations in spring and autumn, and is perhaps more frequent than is supposed, its minute size causing it to be overlooked. It consists of a number of green vesicles of the size of mustard-seed, aggregated together, and sunk, as it were, into the soil, the whole bearing a close resemblance to a miniature branch of unripe grapes, whence the name. Under the microscope, each vesicle appears filled with a watery fluid containing minute granules, which escape when ripe by an opening at the top ; in dry weather the upper part collapses, sinks in, and becomes cup-shaped. The vesicles are attached to the soil by a tuft of root-like fibres, into which their fluid contents descend when pressed. This singular provision is necessary, as the plant is frequently exposed to dry air, which absorbs the moisture on the surface of its native soil, and would consequently wither it, were it not furnished with radicles, which penetrate beyond the risk of desiccation. There are some very curious and little-known green algæ allied to this plant, which are furnished with similar adaptations, as their fronds are so incrusted with lime as to render nutriment through the surface precarious. They resemble cacti, reticulated corals, flabelliform corallines, little wheels fixed on delicate stems, etc., and are very beautiful in their shapes or in their structure, when divested of the carbonaceous coating in which they are masked. Caulerpa, Halimeda, Acetabularia, etc., are examples of these curious organisms, which might easily be overlooked as corals. They are all natives of warm climates, such as New Zealand and Papua. In pools and ditches of fresh water may often be seen vast masses of the two-pronged filaments of *Vaucheria dichotoma*, each filament being sometimes two feet long, almost rivalling the huge masses of *Cladophora mirabilis*, and the *Conferva melagonium* of the Arctic regions. It differs little from the Botrydium, except that the spherical vesicle of the latter is elongated into a simple or branched thread. Another species is very common on the ground in damp, dark situations, such as the ledges and crevices of cliffs in sub-alpine glens, and is also occasionally observed in gardens on walls or unfrequented walks, creeping over the earth in a very thin intricate fleece of a bright grassy-green colour. The filaments are tubes containing an internal green pulverulent mass like the other confervæ ; but the fructification is developed on the outside in the form of dark green homogeneous vesicles attached to the filaments. The spores of some of the species are furnished with ciliæ, and are in consequence endowed with active motion, while they are vivified by the agency of spermatozoa.

The various species of confervæ are known in country places by the popular name of crow-silks, and are used when dried for stuffing beds, for making wadding for garments, and some of them even for manufacturing paper. Pliny mentions that, in his time, they were in much repute as a healing remedy for fractured limbs. They sometimes abound to such an extent as to be positively injurious to the health of the people. After floods, for instance, when the water stands several days, they sometimes luxuriate so much, as on their subsidence to form a uniform paper-like mass, to which the name of meteoric paper has been given. Till the stratum becomes perfectly dry, which is a slow process, except on the outer surface, the smell is often very disagreeable, and the gas generated from it renders the meadows extremely unwholesome. Every one must have remarked the unpleasant odour exhaled by streamlets when their waters begin to fail in a hot summer, and thus expose the masses of confervæ which they contain. Specimens of the so-called meteoric paper have been preserved in the library of Bernhedin. One side is smooth, and of a brownish-ash colour, the other of a greenish red-brown. One of the pieces preserved was thirty-four feet long and three feet wide. The grey side was the more compact, and much resembled grey blotting-paper. It received its paler hue from the bleaching effect of the sun's rays.

The existence of life within life, or of a flora within the bodies of living animals, is one of the most extraordinary facts which the microscope has revealed to us. Upwards of ten species of entophytes have already been discovered parasitic upon man, two of which belong to the confervæ: the one Lewenhoeck's alga, a minute filamentous plant growing between the interstices of the teeth, and covering the roof of the mouth in abnormal conditions of the body; and the other the *Sarcina ventriculi* of Goodsir, a free unattached plant existing in rare cases in the stomach, and counteracting, by its extreme minuteness and its very rapid reproductive power, the expulsive efforts of that organ. Man, however, is less infested by these entophytes than any other animal, on account of the cooking process to which his food is subjected, which effectually destroys the germs of parasites, and his high degree of organic activity, which is unfavourable to their development. Animals of feeble vitality and sluggish habits, using solid innutritious food difficult of assimilation, and therefore remaining long in the alimentary canal; or animals swallowing their food in large morsels, to which the germs of plants may adhere, are rarely, if ever, free from these entoparasitic plants, which, however, when few in number, or not of excessive size, are quite harmless. They are found principally in those portions of the body which are easy of access from without, such as the stomach and intestinal canal, and where, of course, all the indispensable conditions for the maintenance and reproduction of such life exist. In accounting for their origin the opinion may be hazarded, either that their germs belonged to plants growing externally, and were taken along with the food into the digestive organs, where they commenced as it were a transmuted development under the influence of abnormal conditions, or that they are the natural and normal form of new cryptogamic plants which exist frequently in the open air around us, although from their exceedingly minute size they escape our observation, their primitive structure enabling them to grow indiscriminately in all situations, and even in the most opposite circumstances. Dr. Joseph Leidy, to whom we are indebted for much new and interesting information upon this obscure subject, found the most extensive entoparasitic flora with wonderful uniformity within the intestinal canal of a species of myriapod, and a species of beetle living in decaying stumps of trees. The vegetable forms he discovered in this singular situation are exceedingly curious, and notwithstanding their very subsidiary position as parasites, display as high a degree of organization as any of the larger confervæ which inhabit our streams. They consist, in almost every case, of yellowish or colourless transparent tubes, varying from half a line to two or three lines in length, attached to their growing-place by broad disks, and proceeding in a straight or gently flexuose curved line to the free extremity. They are filled with exceedingly minute, faintly yellowish, oil-like granules, enveloped by much larger globules, arranged like a string of beads along the whole interior. Exceedingly minute and obscure although these organisms are, they present many beautiful instances of means adapted to the end in view in their form. "They are generally fixed upon the mucous membrane of the intestinal canal in which they grow; and from their delicate structure they must be more or less constantly liable to rupture in the peristaltic movements of the bowels, and the passage onwards of the food; but from the spiral arrangement of one species, and the sigmoid flexure of another, these graceful filiform plants may be elongated or stretched onwards for a considerable distance without danger of being torn." The economy of these plants is altogether peculiar; existing as they do under circumstances totally different from those in which all other plants are found, and in this respect strikingly illustrative of the wonderful capacities of vegetable life. That vegetable life can exist within animal life is an extraordinary circumstance; but a circumstance still more extraordinary in connexion with their history is, that many of these entophytes are developed upon entozoa, or animals within animals, and are in their turn the seat of other parasitic entophytes more minute, while even on these parasitic entophytes themselves are produced still more minute forms of vegetation. To exhibit this wonderful chain of life more clearly,—in the intestinal canal of a species of beetle there has been found a parasitic animal; on this animal is found growing a plant; on this plant is growing another plant, and on this second plant a third is developed, the smallest variety of the one being produced upon the largest variety of the other. We have thus within the microscopic compass of a beetle's body, an epitome of what takes place on a large scale throughout the world of sense and sight—life supported by life to the third and the fourth degree. These parasite and parasitic-parasite entophytes sometimes grow with such luxuriance that they completely cover the original plants, and hide their forms from view ; while at other times they are confined to the extremity of the branches, or form concentric circles around their base and middle. They consist of simple or branched filaments, sometimes aggregated into thick radiating tufts, like a thick tassel held upwards, each thread or filament measuring from the $\frac{1}{3000}$th to the $\frac{1}{50}$th of an inch in length, and from the $\frac{1}{30000}$th to the $\frac{1}{25000}$th of an inch in diameter. Some of these seem to be articulated, and to contain spores or germs between the joints ; but owing to their exceedingly minute size, the power of the microscope in its present condition is not sufficient to resolve them into their component parts, and of their processes of growth and propagation we know absolutely nothing. They tremble on the extremest verge of the horizon of human knowledge, like the remotest fixed stars in heaven ; and whatever proof of design they may present in their structure and functions, it is not intended for our ken ; for Nature jealously guards the secrets of her inmost shrine, and forbids her most ardent votary to approach beyond the threshold.

But the most extraordinary of all the members of this numerous and highly varied family of plants are the diatoms or brittle-worts, which form a wonderful microcosm of their own ; an *imperium in imperio.* It is but a few years since the miscroscope has drawn aside the veil which hid them from our view, but our knowledge of them, thanks to the all-absorbing attention with which scientific men have regarded them, is already remarkably extensive and accurate. Though these curious vegetable atoms occupy the lowest place in the scale of vegetation, they are, nevertheless, intensely interesting and suggestive of marvellous thought. They constitute an immense family, the individuals of which are numerous beyond the sands of the sea-shore or the stars of heaven ; ay, even beyond the wildest dreams of the Pantheist. They cannot be reckoned by millions simply, but by hundreds of thousands of millions. There is hardly a spot on the surface of the land, or in the depths of the ocean, where some species or other of them may not be found either in a dead or living state. They inhabit streams, ditches, and stagnant pools ; they clothe the leaves and fringe the stalks of sea-weeds ; and they are found in inconceivable multitudes amid the mud and detritus deposited by rivers at their mouths, and by the accumulation of their exuviæ, year after year, occasion a vast deal of labour and cost to the dredger. The mud of the Nile and the Ganges, which have formed the great deltas of Egypt and Bengal, is full of them. Naturalists, who have explored the virgin forests of the tropics, inform us that the very branches of the trees are covered with vast numbers of them ; and those peculiar organisms which are sometimes found in particular diseased states of the stomach and bladder are referred to them. They have been discovered in the stomach of the oyster, the clam, and the barnacle ; and Dr. Hooker says, in the *Botany of the Antarctic Voyage*, that the stomachs of the salpæ and other molluscous animals, which were washed up in immense masses on the ice, invariably contained several species of diatoms. On the soil of our fields they occur in myriads among guano, the product of those vermiverous shore-birds which inhabit the desolate islands of the South Seas ; and on the tops of the highest British mountains—Ben Lawers, Ben Nevis, and Ben Macdhui—I have repeatedly gathered them in great quantities from the black mud which is generally found under masses of melting snow. The ice-bound seas of the north are peopled by almost nothing else ; along with various species of animalcules, they are the cause of that peculiar olive-green tinge which extends over a portion of the Arctic ocean, amounting to not less than 20,000 square miles, every two miles of which, according to Scoresby's estimate, comprehends 23,888,000,000,000,000,—a number which would have employed 80,000 persons since the creation to reckon ![1] In the Antarctic Ocean, on the other hand, far beyond the limits where even the hardy lichen, moss, and sea-weed refuse to vegetate upon the rocks, and where every circumstance would seem inimical to the growth and propagation of even the simplest plants, they occur in countless myriads on the floating ice, and cover the sea with meadows of a pale-brown hue, extending as far as the eye can reach, and down from the surface of the water to abysses deeper

[1] Scoresby says, "After a long run through water of the common blue colour, the sea became green and less transparent. The colour was nearly grass-green with a shade of black. Sometimes the transition between the green and blue water is progressive, passing through the intermediate shades in the space of ten or twelve miles ; at others it is so sudden that the line of separation is seen like the ripple of a current, and the two qualities of water keep apparently as distinct as the waters of a large muddy river on first entering the sea. In 1817, I fell in with such narrow stripes of various coloured water, that we passed streams of pale-green, olive-green, and transparent blue, in the course of ten minutes' sailing."

than plummet ever sounded. They form an enormous bank, flanking at an average depth of 1800 feet the whole length of Victoria Barrier—a glacier of ice some 400 miles long and 120 broad. And it is extremely probable that they are uniformly dispersed over the whole surface of the ocean; for, owing to their extreme minuteness in their individual state, and the transparency of their tissues, they cannot be perceived by the naked eye unless when accumulated into immense masses and contrasted with opaque substances. The surface of the sea, it has been said, is one wide nursery, its every ripple a cradle, and its bottom one vast cemetery. The floor of the ocean is paved with these organisms; those mysterious submarine plains, where the seer's vision of the "sea of glass" seems realized, where no wind blows, and no storm rages, and no current frets, are covered with their remains, unmixed even with a single particle of sand. The soundings obtained from these silent motionless depths, are as pure and free from the slightest intermixture of other matter, as the new-fallen snow-flake is from the dust of the earth. And as a snow-cloud in a still January evening discharges its wavering flakes upon the earth, so are the waves continually letting fall upon their bed showers of minute diatoms whose term of life had expired, kindly strewing the melancholy wrecks of ships with their fleecy coverings, and protecting by their soft cushions the floor of the deep from the abrasion of the waters.

Humble and minute although these diatoms may be, they are among the oldest of the living inhabitants of the globe, having performed their part in creation long ages before the first parents of the human race were called into existence. The wonderful records which they have left behind them in our rocks carry us back to a period when the world, now so beautiful with its verdant meadows and waving woods, was one dreary pestiferous bog, where calamites, sigillarias, and other gigantic marsh plants formed intricate jungles, in whose damp recesses horrid reptiles roared and wallowed, and made war upon each other. In the waters of the primeval seas they flourished in the greatest profusion, supplying the ultimate food of the pleiosauri, ichthyosauri, and the other huge reptiles with which they swarmed, just as their successors form the basis of subsistence, through an amazing series of links, for those mighty devourers, the whales, the seals, and the walruses of the Arctic and Antarctic oceans. The fiery cataclysms, which extirpated whole races of plants and animals, left these atomies uninjured; the physical changes going on over the whole earth only served to carry them uninjured from one geological epoch to another, until at length we behold in the diatoms of our pools, rivers, and seas, the representatives and exact counterparts of the races that lived and died in those ages of the world, compared with which the antiquity of recorded time is but as yesterday. Step by step, up from the lowest fossiliferous strata, when life was just feebly dawning, when the eye that gazed upon the dreary lifeless scenes which the earth then presented was more rudimentary than that of the mollusc, and the ear that listened to the wild ceaseless moaning of waves, the splintering of rocks, and the roar of volcanoes, was but a mere oolitic vesicle;

through the old red sandstone, with its numerous strange and monstrous fishes ; the carboniferous strata, with their countless forms of gigantic vegetable life ; and the limestone rocks, the graves of whole hecatombs of madrepora,—through all these different geological deposits we can trace the presence of these little plants. Endowed with the power of investing themselves, as if by a mysterious process of electrotype, with the silicious matter held in solution by the waters in which they abound, they are in truth indestructible ; and of their remains, individually so minute that thousands may be contained in a drop, and millions packed together in a cubic inch, deep beds of marl, extensive chains of hills, huge limestone rocks, ay, even whole territories of alluvial soil, have been in a great measure composed.

In Virginia, there are vast beds of silicious marl, composed of the skeletons of countless generations of diatoms ; and it is said that the towns of Richmond and Petersburg, in the same province, are built upon an enormous stratum of these plants, every cubic foot of which contains billions more than the living population of men that throng the streets above them. Extensive tracts covered with similar relics of a former age occur throughout Britain ; the peat mosses of Ireland and the Highlands of Scotland abound with them, and hundreds of species have been found beautifully preserved in the vast amber beds of Prussia. The peculiar white powdery substance known by the name of *Berg mehl*, or mountain meal, found in Swedish Lapland, under beds of decayed moss, and mixed by the inhabitants with their food in times of scarcity, is composed of fossil diatomaceæ, several species of which are still living, and occasionally seen in this country. The *fossil flour* which the Chinese mix with their wheat or rice on similar trying occasions;[1] the unctuous clay which the Otomacs gather on the shores of the Orinoco and Meta, and eat by way of a *bonne bouche* after their regular meals; the yellowish earth called caouac found in Guinea, of which the negroes are passionately fond; the kieselguhr or meerschaum, found in Turkey, and employed in the manufacture of pipes; and the polierschiefer, or polishing slate of Berlin, which supplies the tripoli used for polishing stones and metals, are all found, when subjected to the microscope, to consist almost entirely of the silicious plates of diatomaceæ, united together without any visible cement. The world, it has been well said, is a vast catacomb of diatoms, a grand herbarium in which these most ancient plants have

[1] The following particulars regarding Chinese fossil flour, adapted from Ehrenberg's late great work, *Mikrogeologie*, may be interesting:—

"Various kinds of edible earth were known in China in very ancient times, and it may be presumed that many of them are mixed or pure tripolitan fresh-water bioliths, *i.e.*, species of earths or stones, the elements of which consist chiefly of remnants of microscopic living beings. In the year 1839, Biot read before the Academy of Sciences in Paris a treatise, containing everything that was then known on this subject, to which his son, the Oriental linguist, Biot, furnished translations from Chinese and Japanese works. From Schott, in Berlin, Professor Ehrenberg obtained, in addition, the following information, taken from Chinese sources. The first mention of edible earth dates from the year 744 after Christ, and is contained in the Chinese work, Pen-tsao-kang-mu, where it is called Schimian, Stone-bread, or Mi-anschi, Bread-stone; the article in the Japanese *Encyclopædia*, which Biot has translated, is taken from this work. The Pen-tsao says, according to Schott, that stones contain several substances which are edible, especially a yellow meal and fatty liquid, which is contained in the Yu (a stone), and is therefore called the fat, marrow, or mucilage of the white Yu. An earthy substance, prolonging life, and called Schi-nao, is found in the very smooth stone Hoa-shi, which is supposed to be Steatite, and may perhaps be decomposed Steatite. The Schimian is only used as a substitute for bread in times of scarcity, when it is

been preserved in a state of completeness and accuracy little short of their living perfection, to be to us the unimpeachable records of time, as it were, beyond time, of mountains and shores, rivers and seas, that seem mythical even to the geologist.[1] They were at work in the primeval world long before man was ushered upon the scene, and they are at the present day employed in altering and modifying the grand features of the globe; in producing results which man is as incapable to predict as he is powerless to prevent. Who is there that can gaze upon these wonderful plants, which thus, as it were, "connect the ages and the zones," without a dizzy sense of the infinity and permanence of nature, and the power of Him "whose judgments are unsearchable, and whose ways are past finding out?"

*But* this is not all! Wonderful as it may seem, the

miraculously found in different localities, as is believed. The Imperial annals of the Chinese have always religiously noticed its appearance, but have never given any description of the substance. The Pen-tsao quotes, under the Emperor Hiuan-Tsung of the great dynasty Tang, in the third year Tain-pao (744 after Christ), a spring in Wujin (now Liang-tschen-fu, in the province Kan-su), which ejected stones that could be prepared into bread, and were gathered and consumed by the poor. (Schott.)

"Under the Emperor Hian-Tsung, of the same dynasty, in the ninth year of the period Yuen-ho (809 after Christ), the stones became soft and turned into bread. (Biot.)

"Under the Emperor Tschin-Tsung, of the dynasty Sung, in the fifth year of the period Ta-tschong-Tsiang-fu (1012 after Christ), in the fourth month, there was a famine in Tsy-tschen (now Ki-tschen in Ping-yang-fu, in the province Schan-si), when the mountains of Hiang-ning, a district of the third rank in the same part, produced a mineral fat (Stone-fat) resembling a dough, of which cakes could be made. (Schott.)

"Under Jin-Tsung, in the seventh year of the period Kia-yeu (1062), stone meal was found.

"Under Tschi-Tsung, in the third year of the period Yuen-fong (1080), the stones turned into meal. All these kinds of stone-meal were collected and consumed by the poor. (Biot.)"

[1] As the earliest fossil diatoms yet found, judging from the figures of Ehrenberg, are identical in every point with the great majority of species

very realms of the air are peopled with diatoms. The atmosphere we breathe contains hundreds of species, which float about on every breeze, and are wafted hither and thither. Many of them remain for years in the highest strata of the atmosphere, until carried down in the full capacity of life to the nourishing waters of the stream and the lake, by descending currents of air. They have been found in immense numbers in the impalpably fine dust, which at certain seasons broods like a thick haze over the island of St. Domingo, and occasionally falls in great quantities on the decks of vessels far out on the Atlantic. The sirocco and trade winds convey immense quantities of them for hundreds of miles. Clouds of diatomaceous dust, giving the atmosphere an orange or ochre hue, have repeatedly been observed coming in various directions from the coast of Africa, falling on vessels, and diffusing around a darkness so dense as often to

now living in our waters, and forming deposits which will become rock at some future time; and as some species are peculiar to lakes and rivers, and others to seas and firths, while some affect deep and others shallow water, these tiny plants are capable of furnishing considerable information to the geologist, with regard to the conditions under which raised sea-beaches and fresh-water limestone rocks were originally deposited, and the circumstances which operated in the production of the different strata in which they occur. I may add, as an illustration of the universal diffusion of these plants, the curious fact, that the late Dr. Gregory found numerous most interesting diatomaceous forms in small fragments of soil not exceeding a pinch of snuff, adhering to specimens of exotic plants in herbaria. In every case, without exception, he found these organisms; and in all, the proportion to the whole non-calcareous earthy residue was wonderfully large. The soils in which the most numerous species were found, were respectively obtained from the Sandwich Islands and Lebanon. Many of Ehrenberg's profound observations were made on portions of foreign soil procured in this manner, and his example should stimulate collectors of plants to preserve carefully every vestige of earth adhering to the roots of their exotic specimens, as in this way many new forms may be brought to light, and many rare ones studied in the quiet and leisure of home, without the trouble and fatigue of collecting them in their native localities.

cause them to run ashore. Similar showers are not unfrequent in China, and spread over several provinces at once and far out to sea. They are raised from the Mongolian steppes—regions of sand more than 2000 miles long and 400 broad—and falling into the waters of the Yellow Sea, give it that peculiar tinge from which it derives its name. During the dry season in the lifeless plains of the Orinoco, and the great Amazonian basin, when the soil is parched and triturated by the intense, long-continued drought, dense clouds of diatomaceous dust are raised by the winds and wafted to great distances. These showers happen most frequently in spring and autumn after the equinoxes, but at intervals varying from thirty to fifty days. From the nature of the species wafted by these winds, the region which originally produced them can be ascertained with tolerable accuracy; and hence they afford a clue to those mysteriously wayward aërial currents, and cyclical relations in the upper and lower atmosphere, which have hitherto perplexed meteorologists. It has been observed that these storms, in certain districts, amply compensate for the annoyance they occasion. The soil of the countries most subject to the visitation, when of a compact character, is loosened and lightened by the dust, and at the same time the lighter fertilizing matters carried away by the great rivers are replaced by organic remains, so that an abundant harvest follows the devastations committed by these dust-showers. Nearer home these curious meteoric phenomena have occasionally been observed. Black rain, composed of portions of decayed plants, mixed with the skeletons of diatoms, fell in Ireland in April 1849, over a district of

700 square miles. A great mass of substance remarkably like paper fell during a violent storm in 1687. near the village of Randen in Courland, which excited great curiosity at the time, and was found after the lapse of many years, by the all-penetrating microscope of Ehrenberg, to consist of a compactly matted heap of diatoms and confervæ. Diatoms have even been discovered in the pumice and ashes ejected from the burning craters of volcanoes.

"The dust we tread upon was once alive!" was the exclamation of one great poet; and "How populous, how vital is the grave!" was that of another, but little did either Byron or Young know how extensively true were the words they uttered. The microscope shows us how inconceivably populous is the whole world, when thus the loftiest regions of the atmosphere, and the fathomless depths of the ocean, and the darkest, deepest abysses of the earth, where we should suppose all life impossible, are peopled with myriads upon myriads which the Infinite mind alone can enumerate, of minute vegetable organisms, performing their allotted task in the great workshop of nature, and adding a thousand times more to the mass of materials which compose the crust of the globe, than the bones of elephants and whales!

To the investigation of the diatoms, we must not bring any of our preconceived notions of vegetable forms and structures, for we shall assuredly find them completely overthrown, by the new and strange modes of organization which these minute plants display. Indeed, so peculiar and abnormal are some of these modes, so unlike those of all other plants, that the zoologist and botanist are not yet agreed as to which kingdom of nature—the animal or the vegetable—they ought to be referred; and, accordingly, they have occasionally been classed and figured as plants by one naturalist, and as animals by another. Ehrenberg, the great Prussian naturalist, whose microscopic researches have laid open to us a new and strange world of minute organic existence, and to whose untiring industry and patience we are indebted for the discovery of most of the wonderful atomies under consideration, was from the very first firmly convinced of their animal nature; and the credit attached in this country to his notions, had the effect of turning away the attention of botanists from them; while the zoologists rejected them from their systems as suspicious and anomalous objects; and the mere microscopist regarded them simply as new and strange forms of life, with the contemplation of whose beautiful structure he could agreeably while away a leisure hour. Nor need we wonder at this perplexity, for even at the present day, when the improvement of the microscope has placed peculiar structures, before quite invisible, within view of the observer, and given him the utmost clearness and definition of outline, many objects remain still undecided; and much has yet to be done before we can come to a satisfactory conclusion regarding them, or even venture to pronounce an opinion upon them at all. In external form the diatoms present remarkable similarities to many species of infusorial animalcules, and spontaneous movements long thought peculiar to the animal kingdom, they likewise exhibit. Even chemical analysis itself, that ultimate test before which every doubt and difficulty usually vanish, is of no assistance to us in their determination; for in their elementary composition they are identical with some of the lowest members of the animal kingdom. In these primitive plants and animals, we may fairly enough conclude that the animal and vegetable kingdoms pass into each other; they form the one common base or point from which these two systems of life start, to recede so widely from each other in the large and complicated organizations which stand at the head of both. "From man to the primary animal and vegetable cell," Schmidt justly observes, "there exists no gap in the realization of a general idea upon which nature as a whole is based. There is no abrupt transition from one kingdom to another, but an insensible gradation. Thus the embryo germ of an alga or sea-weed is identical, in elementary composition and form, with that of a medusa or ascidia; in the former we have the higher stage of development of the plant, in the latter the simpler form of the animal."

The forms which the diatomaceæ assume are exceedingly varied and beautiful. Most of them, as already mentioned, are invested with a very thin transparent glass-like pellicle, engraved with median lines and transverse striæ, the patterns of which are wonderfully constant in the same species, and afford admirable tests for the general excellence of the object-glass of the microscope; the distance between the different markings being often the $\frac{1}{30000}$th part of an inch, and some, it is even said, being only the $\frac{1}{130000}$th of an inch separate, requiring for their distinct determination a magnifying power of twelve hundred diameters, and the aid of oblique light. Some species consist of chains of parallelograms (Fig. 24), connected together at one single point, more beautiful in

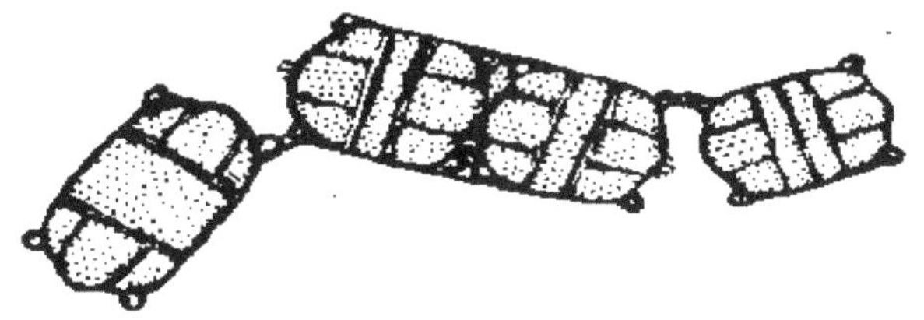

FIG. 24.—DIATOMA BIDDULPHIANA—magnified.

appearance, and more richly and elaborately carved than the costliest bracelet on the arm of a queen. Some resemble miniature flags or fans, adorned with the most exquisite figures; some graceful boats, frosted and granulated, in which a tiny animcule might float over a dew-drop; and some little trees (Fig. 25), covered with variegated leaves, arranged in fan-like clusters, as though intended for microscopic models of a grove of fan-palms. In short, they form circles, triangles, squares, and almost every kind of mathematical figure (Fig. 26), to the utter subversion of all the ideas of vegetable forms which we are accustomed to entertain. They are generally colourless; but some species are of a deep green, or rich brown, or a pale

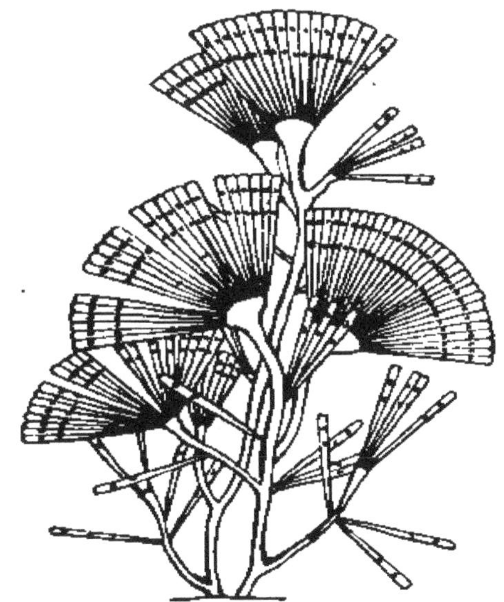

FIG. 25.—EXILARIA FLABELLATA.

yellow or red. They are delicate as hoar-frost, and seem more like the strange vegetation produced on our window-panes on a cold frosty morning, than veritable living plants. These little organisms, we must not forget, exquisitely beautiful and curious in form and structure as we find them under the microscope, appear to the naked eye a mere green or dark-brown film, or indefinite slimy scum, on the leaves of an aquatic moss, or the stalk of a sea-weed !

The propagation of the diatomaceæ is performed in a

FIG. 26.—ACHNANTHES UNIPUNCTATA—slightly and much magnified.

very singular manner. At certain stages of their growth the frustules or fragments of which they are composed, separate in some species into two portions, each of which forms around itself a cell-wall, possessing a form and character precisely similar to those of the original one ; and thus a very material increase in the number of frustules is, through course of time, effected. This process is called fissiparous or merismatic division. In some cases the process of reproduction is performed by the conjugation of two approximated filaments, as was seen in the case of the larger confervæ, the result being the union of their contents by means of interposed tubes, and the subsequent production of a germinating spore ;—thus leaving their vegetable origin no longer a doubtful question. The inconceivable rapidity with which these plants propagate themselves will fully account for their almost universal diffusion, and the enormous accumulation of strata which they form in certain districts. Indeed, so extraordinary are these powers of reproduction, that Ehrenberg describes several species of diatoms, which carry on the process of merismatic division to such an extent, as to produce from a single frustule, invisible to the naked eye, the enormous number of 140,000,000 of distinct individuals, in the short space of four days—a number sufficient to form, by the accumulation of their silicious skeletons, two cubic feet of the Bilin polishing slate.

Such is a brief and imperfect sketch of the history and peculiarities of these wonderful plants. They open up to us the infinitude of microscopic life, reveal a vast and glorious realm of new creative design, whose limits can never be fathomed, and whose mysteries can never be exhausted by man's finite researches. It is not so much what they actually disclose that awes and astonishes us ; but the bewildering boundlessness of the unknown arcana beyond, to which they point. The vast additions which they have made to our knowledge, have only left the immensity of the universe of life greater and more mysterious than before. For it is all but certain, that if our vision could be made more piercing, and our instruments more perfect, while we explored onwards through the successive realms of the invisible towards the inmost shrine of nature, we should find new scenes of wonder and beauty continually unfolding themselves, and new fields of omniscient display constantly revealing to us that God was still before us in all His exhaustless, creative energy, and that we saw but the "hidings of his power."

## CHAPTER IV.

### FUNGI.

"Each step we take is over graves
On which we careless tread;
For ever fresh creative power,
Glows in the quick and dead;
Not dead, the slime that greens the ditch
Is quick, a vital force
Coheres the stone and rolls the star,
Along its life-sprung course."

GOETHE.

NATURE is a perpetually revolving panorama. No sooner does she withdraw one object from our admiring gaze, than she immediately places another as interesting or as beautiful in its room. In watching the progress of vegetation especially, as month after month it expands before us, we are struck with the regularity with which each species of plant visits us in its own appointed time. So remarkably constant are the same plants to their appointed seasons, that their appearance might be regarded as a kind of floral calendar, indicating the various periods of the year. This regularity is not confined to the highest tribes of plants, but is equally observable in the very humblest. The smallest and most obscure tribes have some peculiar functions adapted to each period of the year. Though most of them are perennial, yet they are more luxuriant in some seasons than in others, and are particularly exact and exclusive as to their periods of reproduction. The hard and apparently lifeless lichen remains unchanged upon the rock for years, perhaps as long as the rock itself continues uncrumbled, but every year at the approach of winter, when the moist, stormy weather in which it delights prevails, its dormant suspended life revives, and when all other plants and annuals are hybernating, it begins to exercise the various functions of vitality. The bright silken tufts of the moss continue throughout the whole year to soften the rough harsh aspect of the wall and ruin, and to form velvet pads on the woodland walks to hush the fall of fairy feet, but in spring when "a fuller crimson comes upon the robin's breast, and a young man's fancy lightly turns to thoughts of love," it awakens under the ethereal influence of the universal feeling, clothes itself in its fairest robes, and puts forth its crimson urns, that burn like fairy love-jewels among its emerald leaves. The naiad-like conferværanish from the waters, for nine months in the year, and return to luxuriate in their cool, clear haunts, as duly as the warm breath of April melts away the icy fetters from the rejoicing streams, and once more,

> "Inverted in the tide,
> Stand the grey rocks, and trembling shadows throw,
> And the fair trees look over side by side,
> And see themselves below."

While the approach of autumn is unmistakeably indicated by the springing up of mushrooms in the moist dark recesses of the woods, even when the viewless boundary of summer is not yet past, and the air is still balmy and sunny, and the robe of nature is yet fadelessly green.

Fungi are intimately associated with autumn ; unrobed prophets that see no sad visions themselves, but that bring to us thoughts of change and decay. Indeed, so close is this association that they may be called autumn's peculiar plants. The blue-bell still lingers in the sod, and in the woods a few bright but evanescent and scentless flowers appear, but fungi and fruits form the wreath that encircles the sober and melancholy brow of autumn : fruits the death of flower-life ; fungi the resurrection of plant-death. The seasonal conditions which arrest the further progress of all other vegetation, which cause the leaf to fall, and the flower to wither, and the robe of nature everywhere to change and fade, give birth to new forms of plant-life which flourish and luxuriate amid decay and death. From the relics of the former creations of spring and summer, reduced to chaos, springs up a new creation of organic life, and thus nature is not a mere continuous cycle of birth, maturity, and decay, but rather a constant appearance of old elements in new forms.

This new tribe of plants comes in at a peculiarly seasonable time, when the more aristocratic members of the vegetable kingdom have departed, leaving the favourite haunts of the botanist bare and destitute of interest. Their collection in the field, and the study of their peculiarities in the closet, will furnish ample occupation of a most absorbing and fascinating nature during the whole season, as new facts always connect themselves with new forms. To those who enjoy mysteries and paradoxes there can be no lack of such enjoyment among the fungi. In many respects they are the most mysterious and paradoxical of all plants. In their origin, their shapes, their composition, their rapidity of growth, the brevity of their existence, their modes of reproduction, their inconceivable number and apparent ubiquity, they are widely different from every other kind of vegetation with which we are acquainted. In studying their history we walk amid surprises ; and as we lift each corner of the veil, more and more marvellous are the vistas which reveal themselves.

The first thing that strikes us with wonder, in regard to these anomalous organisms, is their origin. Incapable of deriving the elements of growth from the crude unorganized crust of the earth, they are parasitical upon organic bodies, and are sustained by animal and vegetable substances in a state of decomposition. That living and often nutritious objects should spring from festering masses of corruption and decay; that plants, endowed with all the organs and capacities of life, should start into existence from the dead tree that crumbles into dust at the slightest touch, or draw their nourishment from dried and exhausted animal excretions, which have lain for months under the influence of drenching rains and scorching sunbeams, is indeed a profound mystery of nature. No sooner does the majestic oak yield to the universal law of death, than several minute existences, which had been previously bound up and hid within its own, reveal themselves, seize upon the body with their tiny fangs, fatten and revel upon its decaying tissues, and in a short space of time reduce the patriarch and pride of the forest, which had braved the storms of a thousand years, into a hideous mass of touchwood, or into a heap of black dust! How strikingly do these plants illustrate the great fact, that in nature nothing perishes; that in the wonderful metamorphoses continually going on in the universe there is change, but not loss; that there is no such thing as death, the extinction of one form of existence being only the birth of another! And what a remarkable and obvious proof do they also afford of that other great fact, the law of vicarious sacrifice; a law which permeates and pervades the present system of things, so that if it were to cease, the whole course of the universe would cease likewise. Trace this strange law up through nature, from its lowest to its highest manifestations, and how much that is fitted to astonish and perplex does it suggest! The mountain rock must yield up that mysterious life it has, which keeps its particles together without changing or decaying, and must have its surface crumbled, by the agency of air or water, into dead inert soil, before the plant can grow. "The destruction of the mineral is the life of the vegetable. Again the same process begins on a yet higher stage. The plant decays, and from its dissolving tissues spring forth new forms of vegetable life. The ear of wheat dies, and out of death more abundant life is born. Out of the soil in which deciduous leaves are buried, the young tree shoots vigorously, and strikes its roots deep down into the realm of decay and death. Upon the life of the vegetable world the myriad forms of higher life sustain themselves; still the same law, the sacrifice of life to give life." Further still, the lower animals feed the higher, and man himself is nourished at the expense of the creatures which he uses for food. The child lives upon its parent's life, and one man suffers for another's benefit. In short, the law of vicarious sacrifice is the law of universal life!

In many of their properties, the fungi are closely allied to some members of the animal kingdom. They resemble the flesh of animals, in containing a large proportion of albuminous proximate principles; and they are almost the only plants that contain azote or nitrogen, formerly regarded as one of the principal marks of distinction between plants and animals. This element reveals itself by the strong cadaverous smell, which most of them give out in decaying, and also by the savoury meat-like taste which others of them afford. Unlike other vegetables, they possess the remarkable property of exhaling hydrogen gas; and the great majority of species, like animals, absorb oxygen from the atmosphere, and disengage in return from their surface a large quantity of carbonic acid. By chemical analysis, they are found to contain besides sugar, gum, and resin, a yellow spirit like hartshorn, a yellow empyreumatic oil, and a dry, volatile, crystalline salt, so that their nature is eminently alkaline, like animal substances extremely prone to corruption. Another property they possess, which connects them with animals, is their luminosity, or the evolution of phosphorescent light from the structure of many of them. Some flowers, especially those of an orange colour, such as the marigold and nasturtium, occasionally present a luminous appearance on still warm evenings, the light being either in the form of slight electric sparks, or steadier, like the phosphorescence of the glow-worm. But this quality is very rare among plants, and is almost peculiar to the lowest orders of animals, particularly those which inhabit the ocean. A species of mushroom (*Agaricus olearius*) grows on the olive-tree, which is often luminous at night, and resembles the faint, pale, lambent flickering light emitted by the scales of fish and sea-animals kept in a dark place. A kind of fungus called Rhizomorpha, from its root-like appearance, covers the walls of dark mines with its long, black, branchy, flat fibres, and gives out a remarkably vivid phosphorescent light, almost dazzling the eye of the spectator. In the coal-mines near Dresden, these fungi are said to cover the roof, walls, and pillars, with an interlacing network of beautiful flickering light, like brilliant gems in moonlight, giving the coal-mine the appearance of an enchanted palace on a festival night. Mr. Gardner, in his interesting travels in Brazil, gives the following account of a remarkable phenomenon of this nature:—"One dark night, about the beginning of December, while passing along the streets of the Villa de Natividade, I observed some boys amusing themselves with some luminous object, which I at first supposed to be a kind of large fire-fly; but on making inquiry, I found it to be a beautiful phosphorescent fungus, belonging to the genus *Agaricus*, and was told that it grew abundantly in the neighbourhood on the decaying leaves of a dwarf palm. Next day, I obtained a great many specimens, and found them to vary from one to two and a half inches across. The whole plant gives out at night a bright phosphorescent light, of a pale greenish hue, similar to that emitted by the larger fire-flies, or by those curious soft-bodied, marine animals, the Pyrosomæ. From this circumstance, and from growing on a palm, it is called by the inhabitants, 'Flor-de-Coco.' The light given out by a few of these fungi in a dark room was sufficient to read by. I was not aware at the time I discovered this fungus, that any other species of the same genus exhibited a similar phenomenon; such, however, is the case in the *Agaricus olearius* (mentioned above) of Decandolle; and Mr. Drummond, of Swan River colony in Australia, has given an account of a very large phosphorescent species occasionally found there." This luminous property which so many of the fungi possess, is attributed by some botanists to a slow spontaneous combustion, somewhat similar to what is exhibited by the *Dictamus albus*, which continually gives off from its surface a volatile oil, and inflames upon the application of a match, so that the bush may thus be enveloped in flames and yet not consumed. Other authorities, however, refer the phenomenon to the liberation of phosphorus from some of its combinations in the plant,—which seems to be the most plausible explanation. Superstition and ignorance have magnified this simple appearance of nature into a supernatural manifestation; the *ignis fatuus* occasionally seen in damp old woods, and regarded by the credulous as a sign of approaching death and an omen of evil, being nothing else than the flickering phosphorescence of fungi in a state of decay. It may be remarked in connexion with this luminous property, that many fungi are capable of generating considerable heat. Dutrochet ascertained that the highest temperature produced by any plant, with the exception of the curious cuckoo-pint of our woods, was generated by a species of toadstool called *Boletus æneus.* Such being the curious properties exhibited by these plants, it is not surprising that at one period they should have been suspected to be animal productions, formed by insects for their habitations, somewhat like the coral structures of zoophytes and sponges. Though this view has long been felt to be utterly untenable, inasmuch as they have the growth and texture of plants, and it is well ascertained that they produce, and are produced from seeds like other plants, yet they are evidently one of the links in the chain of nature which unite the vegetable to the animal kingdom, and show how arbitrary and unfounded were the old definitions which served to distinguish them from each other.

Fungi, unlike most plants, are to a great extent insensible to the influence of light. They commonly prefer damp, close, ill-ventilated places, where the light if any, is of a pale, cold, and sickly character. Within the sheltering darkness of dense leafy woods—

> "Some lone Egerian grove,
> Where sacred and o'ergreeting branches shed
> Perpetual eve, and all the cheated hours sing vespers—"

they are to be found crowding together, and are only accidentally found elsewhere. This propensity to avoid the exposed glare of sunlight, and to grow in the darkest shade, seems very paradoxical, when we consider the essential importance of light among the vital agencies. Even the humblest lichen, moss, or conferva, will not develop itself in the same degree of darkness which is essential to the wellbeing of the fungus. All other plants are absolutely dependent upon light for their very existence. Roses, tulips, sun-flowers, wait upon the beams of the sun, and live only in his smiles. They may be supplied with the requisite conditions of heat, air, and moisture, but without light they will wither and die; or, if they do seem to grow, it is only a false, unnatural, and sickly growth, losing their substance instead of increasing it, and weighing less when dried than the dry seed from which this amorphous growth proceeded. Light is not required for the germination of seeds; but if the plant be suffered to grow up in darkness, it merely uses up the store of food contained in the seed, and when that is exhausted its further growth is stopped. It can obtain no new food from without; for it is light alone that can occasion the decomposition of the carbonic acid contained in the vessels of all the parts exposed to its influence, and without this light the plant could not assimilate the carbon to its own use. It is a remarkable fact that the heat of the sun alone will not enable the plant to perform this operation. It must be exposed directly to the light of the sun; and every cloud in the sky, and every shadow from rock or tree that obscures or hides this direct sunlight, retards the vital activity of every plant on which such shadow falls. The particular ray in the sunlight which produces this intense effect upon the organization of plants, has been separated by physiologists. By causing plants to effect the decomposition of carbonic acid in the prismatic spectrum, Professor Draper, to whom we are indebted for this interesting discovery, ascertained that the yellow ray is by far the most effective, and violet, the nearest to darkness, the least so. The sunbeam has recently been divided into actinic, luminous, and calorific rays. The actinic or chemical rays are indispensable to germination; under the influence of the luminous rays, a mantle of green overspreads forest and field, and the woody tissue is formed; while the calorific rays bring forth flowers and fruit. Thus spring, summer, and autumn each enjoy a peculiar influence from the sun; although, probably, in all the three processes, of germination, growth, and fructification, the three forces are concerned, but in modified activity. Even during the day this distinction is observed; in the evening there being less actinic power than in the morning, and at noon more luminous and calorific power. To all these influences of light the fungi are to a great extent insensible. They do not disturb themselves or deign to turn towards the light at all; they continue to shoot out perpendicularly, horizontally, or even reversed, just as the surface from whence they spring happens to be directed. The Geranium growing in the cottage window, yearningly stretches out its tender leaves and blossoms to the smiling sunshine without; and the pea or potato sprouting in a cellar, which has but one north window, half-closed, spreads its cadaverous, blanched, and brittle shoots in the direction of that feeble flicker of light; but the fungus points its stalk and its seed-vessel as readily from as to the light, as unconsciously downwards to the earth, as upwards from it. Give it air, warmth, moisture, and undisturbed quiet, and it can live and luxuriate without light. But this love of seclusion and darkness gives a dull, sober complexion to the whole tribe. In consequence of this habit, they are the most sombre of all plants, the neutral tints prevailing, to the almost total exclusion of the bright vivid hues of the families of flowers. Green, which is the most frequent of all colours, the household dress of our mother earth, predominant not only in trees, herbs, and grasses, but even in ferns, mosses, lichens, and algæ, is almost unknown in the fungi, most of which are of a pale, etiolated, sickly hue.

Another of the remarkable peculiarities of the fungi is the extreme rapidity of their growth, a peculiarity more frequently to be seen among the lowest forms of animal life than among plants. They seem special miracles of nature, rising from the ground, or from the decaying trunk of the tree, full-formed and complete in all their parts in a single night, like Minerva from the head of Jupiter, or the armed soldiers from the dragon's teeth of Cadmus, sown in the furrows of Colchis. It has long been known that the growth of fungi takes place with great rapidity during thundery weather, owing, in all probability, to the nitrogenized products of the rain which then falls. One is surprised after a thunderstorm in the beginning of August, or a day of warm, moist, misty weather, such as often occurs in September, to see in the woods thick clusters of these plants, which had sprung into existence in the short space of twenty-four hours, covering almost every decayed stump and rotten tree. In tropical countries, stimulated by the intense heat and light, the rapidity of vegetable growth is truly astonishing; the stout, woody stem of the bamboo-cane, for instance, shooting up in the dense jungles of India at the rate of an inch per hour. In the Polynesian Islands, so favourable to vegetable life are the climate and soil, that turnip, radish, and mustard-seed when sown show their cotyledon leaves in twenty-four hours; melons, cucumbers, and pumpkins spring up in three days, and peas and beans in four. But swift as is this development of vegetation in highly favourable circumstances, the rapidity of fungoid growth, under ordinary conditions, is still more astonishing. These plants usually form at the rate of twenty thousand new cells every minute. The giant puff-ball (*Bovista gigantea*), occasionally to be seen in fields and plantations, increases from the size of a pea to that of a melon in a single night; while the common stinkhorn (*Phallus impudicus*), has been observed to attain a height of four or five inches in as many hours. Mr. Ward, in his work *On the Growth of Plants in closely-glazed Cases*, says of it: "I had been struck with the published accounts of the extraordinary growth of *Phallus impudicus*. I therefore procured three or four specimens in an undeveloped state, and placed them in a small glazed case. All but one grew during my temporary absence from home. I was determined not to lose sight of the last specimen; and observing one evening that there was a small rent in the volva, indicating the approaching development of the plant, I watched it all night, and at eight in the morning the summit of the pileus began to push through the jelly-like matter with which it was surrounded. In the course of twenty-five minutes it shot up three inches, and attained its full elevation of four inches in one hour and a half. Marvellous are the accounts of the rapid growth of cells in the fungi ; but, in the above instance, it cannot for a moment be imagined that there was any increase in the number of cells, but merely an elongation of the erectile tissue of the plant." The force developed by this rapid growth and increase of the cells of fungi is truly astonishing. Monsieur Bulliard relates that, on placing a fungus within a glass vessel, the plant expanded so rapidly that it shivered the glass to pieces, with an explosive detonation as loud as that of a pistol ; while Dr. Carpenter, in his *Elements of Physiology*, mentions that "in the neighbourhood of Basingstoke, a paving-stone, measuring twenty-one inches square, and weighing eighty-three pounds, was completely raised an inch and a half out of its bed by a mass of toad-stools, of from six to seven inches in diameter ; nearly the whole pavement of the town being heaved up by the same cause." Every one has heard of the portentous growth of fungi in a gentleman's cellar, produced by the decomposing contents of a wine cask, which, being too sweet for immediate use, was allowed to stand unmolested for several years. The door in this case was blocked up and barricaded by the monstrous growth ; and when forcible entrance was obtained, the whole cellar was found completely filled ; the cask which had caused the vegetable revel, drained of its contents, being triumphantly elevated to the roof, as it were, upon the shoulders of the bacchanalian fungi ! Rapidity of growth in fungi is necessarily followed by rapidity of decay. Though some of the larger and more corky species last throughout the summer, autumn, and winter, and a few are perennial, growing on the same trunk for many years, slowly and almost insensibly adding layer to layer, and attaining an enormous size, yet the vast generality of fungi are very fugacious. They are the ephemera of the vegetable kingdom. The entire life of most of the species ranges from four days to a fortnight or a month; while there are numerous microscopic species of the mould family whose lives are so brief and evanescent as scarcely to allow sufficient time to make drawings of their forms. What a contrast there is between the minute Bread-mould at the bottom of the scale, and the gigantic Wellingtonia of the Californian forests at the top! The one during the warm moist weather of summer appears suddenly, as if by magic, on a stale crust laid aside in a dark cupboard, attains its highest development, ripens and scatters its seeds, and perishes in a few days; the other sent forth its embryo shoots in the primeval solitude more than three thousand years ago, and may yet witness the revolution of many centuries ere it begins to decay. The largest stalk of the Bread-mould is no thicker than a pin, and may be half-a-line or the twentieth part of an inch in height; the trunk of the Wellingtonia, like a huge church-tower, rises nearly 300 feet into the sky, and measures upwards of a hundred feet in circumference. Why does this enormous difference exist? Why does the fungus live for a day and the tree for ages? Why does one seed produce a plant that has but a winter's, or at most a summer's growth, and another grow into a plant which endures for more than three thousand years? They are both composed of the same materials —a collection and combination of simple cells; is it difference of form only that gives a longer term of life to the Wellingtonia than to the Bread-mould? We cannot by any search ascertain the source of life in the fresh seed, or account for the decay by which mature development is followed, and there is nothing in the structure of any plant, or indeed of any created thing, out of which the assigned limit of its life could be found. It is an impenetrable mystery, to be referred humbly to the simple exercise of the Creator's will.

Fungi are extremely simple in their organization. They bring us back to first principles, and reveal to us the secret manner in which nature builds up her most complicated vegetable structures. They are composed entirely of cellular tissue, of a definite aggregation of loose, more or less oval, elliptical cells, with cavities between them. These cells in many species may be seen by the naked eye, and consist of little closed sacks of transparent colourless membrane. Here is the starting-point of life. Such cells are the primary germ or element from which every living thing, whether plant or animal, is produced. The whole process of vegetable growth is but a continuous multiplication of these cells; new ones being formed within the old ones when their nutrient matter increases in quantity beyond a certain point, which then dissolve and disappear, while the secondary or daughter cells in their turn produce two, four, eight, or more young cells to occupy their places, and so on till the number of cells becomes multiplied beyond calculation. In the flowering plants the various vessels and organs arise in a *differentiation*, or a setting apart of particular groups of these cells, and altering their forms and contents for the performance of particular functions in the economy of the plant. In the fungi, however, there is little or nothing of this specializing or differentiating process. Their entire structure is uniform; each group of cells is an exact repetition of all the other cells; one part of each is exactly like the rest. There are no special organs or vessels for the performance of the processes of absorption and reproduction, no complicated apparatus of secretion and excretion. There are no leaves, stems, or roots. Every cell is an assimilating surface; the whole plant is a reproductive organ. Every part of the structure performs the functions, which in more complex plants are performed by organs specially set apart.

Owing to this extreme simplicity and unity of structure, they possess a remarkable power of reproducing and repairing such parts of their substance as have been injured. This power, it is well known, is always more active as the organization of the individual, or the part affected, is less complicated; many of the simplest animals, such as the polypes, admitting of being multiplied by mere mechanical division almost to an unlimited extent. It has been often remarked, that in man and the vertebrata generally, the power of regeneration is confined to the replacement of small portions of the simplest texture, although in them the process of renewal is sometimes very extraordinary. The more highly organized structures, such as muscular and nervous substance, cannot be replaced; should they be ruptured, the wound is repaired by the formation of cellular, or some other of the less complex tissues. Every part of the fungus, however, in its structure, is uniform throughout, can be re-formed with equal facility. Even the organs of reproduction, which may be considered its most highly organized parts, can be replaced or repaired if in any way injured. The tubes of the toadstool, and the gills of the mushroom, have been cut out and separated from the living plant by way of experiment, and yet in a brief space of time they have been so carefully reproduced, that no one could possibly tell they had ever been removed. Snails, to whose soft tender lip they form a succulent and agreeable morsel, are continually eating holes into them, but when they are in active growth, they speedily fill them up again with new tissue. Puff-balls growing among grass on the borders of woodlands, and in the open meadows, are frequently very much injured by the scythe of the mower, cut open, and whole parts sliced off, but these wounds speedily heal themselves, and the parts that have been removed are remodelled, without leaving the slightest cicatrice to mark the point of junction or the seat of injury.

Owing likewise to this extreme simplicity of structure, they possess the faculty of almost indefinite expansion, determined only by the amount of pabulum which the decaying substances on which they are produced afford. The limits of some species are strictly marked out, and they rarely exceed them, retaining nearly the same dimensions throughout their whole lives. It is principally the smallest and simplest species which are thus circumscribed; and these make up by their immense profusion for the insignificance of their individual state. The largest and most highly developed species, which are but sparingly produced, frequently attain to almost fabulous dimensions in favourable circumstances. The scaly polyporus (*Polyporus squamosus*), one of the commonest fungi, everywhere to be met with on the decayed trunks of trees, especially the ash, and easily recognised by its brown scaly pileus, and white porous under-side, grows to a larger size than any other species. Instances have been recorded of its measuring seven feet five inches in circumference, and weighing thirty-four pounds avoirdupois, having attained these vast dimensions in the short space of three weeks. The liver fungus (*Fistulina hepatica*) has been found on an ash-pollard weighing nearly thirty pounds. Mr. Badham, in his interesting work on the *Esculent Fungi of Britain*, mentions having seen a fungus in the neighbourhood of Tunbridge Wells which rose nearly a foot from the ground, measured considerably more than two and a half feet across, and weighed from eighteen to twenty pounds. Specimens of agaric and puff-ball may frequently be met with, measuring a foot and a half in diameter, and weighing many pounds.

Although the structure of all fungi is entirely of a loosely cellular nature, yet they exhibit an astonishing variety of consistence. Each genus, and in many instances each species, displays a different texture. They range in substance from a watery pulp or a gelatinous scum to a fleshy, corky, leathery, or even ligneous mass. Some are mere thin fibres of airy cobweb, spreading like a flocculent veil over decaying matter; while others resemble large irregular masses of hard tough wood. Their qualities are also exceedingly various. Like the ferns they all possess a peculiar odour by which they may be easily recognised, although it is somewhat different in different individuals, some smelling strongly of cinnamon and bitter almonds, others of onions and tallow, while others yield an insupportable stench. The fœtid charnel-house smell of the common stinkhorn (*Phallus fœtidus*) may be felt at a distance of several hundred yards, when the wind is blowing in one's direction, and leads infallibly to its detection, when otherwise it might escape observation, covered, as it usually is, with leaves and broken sticks. Like putrid meat it attracts flies, which are always buzzing about its head; and a few individuals are sufficient to make a whole wood intolerable. Bad as this species is, there is another, if possible, in still worse odour—the Clathrus, which happily is not found in this country, although abundant on the Continent. Like the curious leafless Stapelia, it diffuses a most loathsome stench, which is utterly insupportable at close quarters. This, with its putrid, hideous-looking, raw-flesh-like structure, has originated the popular superstition among the peasants of the Landes, that it is capable of producing cancer; and hence they cover it carefully over with leaves and moss when they come across it in the pine-woods, lest by accident some one should touch it, and be infected with the disease. As regards their tastes the fungi are equally diversified, being insipid, acrid, styptic, caustic, or rich and sweet. Some have no taste in the mouth while masticated; but shortly after swallowing, there is a dry, choking, burning sensation experienced at the back of the throat, which lasts for a considerable time.

Variety is the great characteristic of divine workmanship. The forms of nature are infinitely diversified, so as to gratify the eye, and improve the mind by furnishing it with ever new objects of contemplation, and ever fresh incentives to study. The number of species and sub-species, where there is a marked difference, is immense; but when we attempt to search out the varieties of the same species, we find ourselves treading on the confines of infinitude. No two blades of grass from the same root, no two leaves of the same tree, no two flowers of the same plant, are ever found precisely alike in any one particular. So exhaustless are the conceptions of the Divine mind, and so boundless His skill and power, that no two individuals of any created existence have ever been cast in the same mould, or wrought to the same pattern. And yet this endless variety is invariably so constituted as to secure a general uniformity. There appears everywhere a unity of design and composition, amid an almost infinite diversity of forms. Every individual of every species bears the unmistakable mark of a specific uniformity; and every species, however much it may vary in some subsidiary particular, exhibits the broad and palpable character of the genus or the family to which it belongs. This law of variety with general uniformity, displayed among all the members of the vegetable kingdom, as well as in all the works of nature, is if possible still more strikingly manifested among the simplest and least organized plants. It is impossible for us to conceive how simply, by a little change of arrangement, and a little variation in the amount and proportions of materials, such an endless multitude of objects, and such a countless variety, can be produced,—objects, though all composed of the same cellular tissue, the same simple substances, yet so different in appearance and composition as to seem to have little or nothing in common. And yet this is what is presented to us in the great order of plants now under review. Simple and uniform as is their structure, we have seen how extensively diversified they are in their specific qualities. They are no less varying in their forms. It were impossible to give a true comprehensive idea of these varieties without entering into specific details. Upwards of 1400 distinct species have been found and described in Britain alone. In round numbers it may be said that fungi form about a third of the flowerless plants, numbering as they do about 4000 species altogether. To show how numerous and varying are their forms, it may be mentioned that the British species are distributed in 154 genera, an unusually large proportion, only nine species on an average being included in each genus. A large number of these species constitute separately distinct genera. In no family of plants, indeed, are there so many single forms, which, owing to the absence of affinitive characters, cannot be associated together,—so many genera consisting of only one species. While, on the other hand, there are no other plants which have such immense genera, containing, some of them, hundreds of species. The genus Agaricus, for instance, in this country alone has upwards of 450 species, so closely allied to the common mushroom of our tables, that many of them are continually confounded with it, and yet exhibiting specific differences in colour, shape, size, etc., so distinct as to be easily distinguished by an educated eye. The two genera, Sphæria and Peziza—whose ideal forms, in the former case a simple round ball furnished at the apex with a minute orifice, and filled internally with minute flask-shaped seed-vessels ; and in the latter case, a shallow cup or plane disk of gelatinous matter, surrounded with a margin—are so diversified, that in Great Britain there are no less than 200 species of the one, and 106 species of the other. Some of the other genera are also unusually large, showing how rigidly nature's laws of uniformity and variety are adhered to in this class of plants.

The following instances may be brought forward, as illustrations of the remarkable shapes which many of the fungi exhibit. On the trunk of the oak, the ash, the beech, and the chestnut, may occasionally be seen a fungus, so remarkably like a piece of bullock's liver that it may be known from that circumstance alone. This is the *Fistulina hepatica* or liver fungus. Its substance is thick, fleshy, and juicy, of a dark modena red, tinged with vermilion. It is marbled like beet-root, and consists of fibres springing from the base, from which a red pellucid juice like blood slowly exudes. Of all vegetable substances this exhibits the closest resemblance to animal tissue. Even in the minutest particular it seems to be a caricature of nature, a sportive imitation on an unfeeling oak-tree of the largest gland of the animal body. Tennyson might, with more truthfulness, personify an oak thus furnished with a substitute for the seat of passion, than the garrulous individual which adorned the woods of Sumner Chase ! As already mentioned, it sometimes attains an enormous size, hanging down from the trunk of the oak like the liver of one of the geological monsters of the Preadamite world. Like the liver it is also nutritious, and forms a favourite article of food in Austria, though it is somewhat tough and acrid in taste. Another remarkable species of fungus, called Jew's Ears (*Exidium auricula Judæ*) from its close resemblance to the human ear, clings to the trunks of living trees, particularly the elder, throughout the whole autumnal season. It is of a dusky or red-brown colour, like the ear of a North American Indian, and is wrinkled with large swelling veins branching from the middle, where they are strongest, and somewhat convoluted, the upper side covered with a hoary velvet down, the inside smooth and darker coloured. When it grows on a perpendicular stump or tree, it turns upwards. Another remarkable species (*Tremella cerebrina*), occurring occasionally in winter and spring on dead wood and branches in very moist, dark places, exactly resembles the brain of an animal. Its substance is of a dirty-white colour, more or less tinged or streaked with red, like the ramifications of minute blood-vessels. It occurs in scolloped undulating masses, of a tender, gelatinous consistence when young, growing tougher when old. Its congener, the *Tremella mesenterica*—of more frequent occurrence all the year round, particularly on furze—bears a strong resemblance to the human mesentery. It is of a rich orange colour. This extraordinary resemblance which different fungi bear to the different parts of the animal body, served to confirm the opinion of the ancient botanists and herbalists, that they were animal structures, or at least intermediate links between the animal and vegetable kingdoms.

The simplest fungi consist of a few primordial cells, either separate or conjoined, or of cellular, branched filaments or threads, performing the functions of nutrition and reproduction. Between these and the mushroom, which may be regarded as exhibiting the highest development of fungoid life, there are numerous intermediate forms more or less complex. Some resemble minute mussels with their edges upwards; some are shell-shaped, and others shrubby and branched like coral. Some form large round balls, splitting into star-like expanding rays; others are crowned with mitres or peaked caps. Some are cup-shaped, trumpet-shaped, bell-shaped. Some, such as the leaden-coloured Nidularia so frequent in potato-fields, form a nest in which to rear their young. One forms a yellow scum on moss-tufts in woods, which in a few days dries up and becomes converted into a heap of black powder like soot; another forms, on the stems of grass some inches above the soil, a thick white froth, somewhat resembling the salivaceous exudation of the *Cicada spumaria* so frequent in summer woods, and which may easily be supposed of animal origin. Some form beautiful little goblets elevated on slender hair-like stems; while others are only to be seen through a thick red lattice-work which surrounds them. In short, there is almost no end to the vague, indeterminate shapes which this curious tribe exhibits. Nature, in a capricious or sportive mood, seems to have formed them in imitation of the higher objects of creation, as they are her humblest and latest productions. Having such extremely simple and plastic materials to work upon, she seems to have followed the wildest vagaries of fancy in the determination of their shapes, and to have moulded many of them in imitation of the substances upon which they are produced.

Although fungi in general are sober, nun-like plants, preferring quiet quaker colours suitable to the dim secluded places which they usually affect, yet some of them depart widely from this soberness, and exhibit themselves in the most gaudy hues. Some species are of a brilliant scarlet colour; others of a bright orange. Many are yellow, while a few don the imperial purple. In short, they are to be found of every colour, from the purest white to the dingiest black, dark emerald or leaf-green alone excepted. Some are beautifully zoned with iridescent convoluted circles, or broad stripes of different hues. Some shine as if sprinkled with mica; others are smooth as velvet, and soft as kid-leather. Such is a rapid survey of the varied forms, colours, and qualities exhibited by these simple plants; and surely it is sufficient to show us the vast amount of interest connected with them.

Let us take a specimen of one of the most perfectly-formed and highly-developed fungi, the common shaggy mushroom for instance (*Agaricus procerus*, Fig. 27), which is also the most familiar example, and endeavour to point out the peculiarities of its structure. Like all plants, it consists of two distinct parts, the organs of nutrition or vegetation, and the organs of reproduction; the former bearing but a very small proportion in size to the latter. The organs of nutrition or vegetation consist of greyish-white interlacing filaments, forming a flocculent net-like tissue, and penetrating and ramifying through the decaying substances on which the mushroom grows. These filaments are formed of elongated colourless cells. They are developed under ground, and in other plants would be called roots. This part of the fungus is called by botanists mycelium, and is popularly known as the spawn by which the mushroom is frequently propagated. In favourable circumstances this mycelium spreads with great rapidity, sometimes, especially when prevented from developing organs of repro-

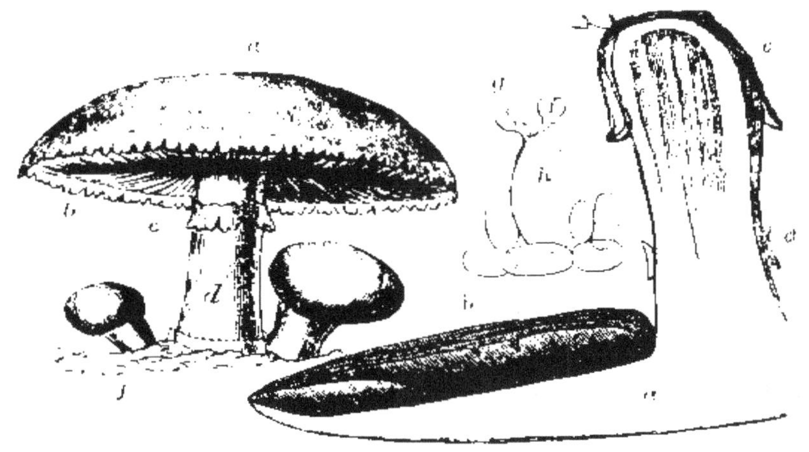

FIG. 27.—PARTS OF MUSHROOM (*Agaricus procerus*).

(*a*) Pileus or Cap. (*b*) Hymenium or Gills. (*c*) Annulus. (*d*) Stipe or Stalk. (*e*) Volva. (*f*) Mycelium or Spawn. (*g*) Spores. (*h*) Basidia.

duction, attaining enormous dimensions. It may be kept dormant, in a dry state, for a long time, ready to grow up into perfect plants when the necessary heat and moisture are applied. When the requisite conditions are present, and the mycelium begins to develop the reproductive tissue, there is formed at first a small round tubercle, in which the rudiments or miniature organs of the future plant may be distinctly traced, just as the future flowers may be traced in the bulb of the hyacinth or the root of the moonwort fern. In this infantile condition, the mushroom is covered completely with a fine silky veil or volva, which afterwards disappears. The tubercle rapidly increases, until at last it produces from its interior a long, thick fleshy stem or stipe, surmounted by a pileus, or round concave cap, similar to that anciently worn by the Scottish peasantry. This is the organ of reproduction, equivalent to the thecæ of mosses and the flowers of phanerogamous plants. This cap is covered with a veil or wrapper, which is ruptured at a certain stage, and retires to form an annulus or ring round the stem. When it is removed from the under side of the pileus, a number of vertical plates or gills is revealed of a pale salmon colour, different from the rest of the plant, and radiating round the cap from a common centre. The whole of this apparatus is called the hymenium. Each of the gills, when examined under the microscope, is found to consist of a number of elongated cells called basidia, united together on both sides of a cellular stratum, and bearing at their summits four minute spores supported on tiny stalks. It is by these spores that the plant is propagated. When a small fragment of a ripe gill is placed on the glass slide of the microscope, in a drop of water, the spores will detach themselves from the gill and float freely on the water; or even if a whole mushroom be laid on a sheet of paper, it will often leave behind its spores in the form of a thin impalpable powder. These spores are so very minute, that many millions of them are required to make a body the size of a pin-head; and they are capable of enduring a temperature at least equal to that of boiling water, as was satisfactorily proved a few years ago when the barrack bread in Paris was affected with mould, which was in active growth almost before the bread was cold. The remarkable elastic force with which many of the fungi eject their seed has often excited attention, and is fully equal to anything of the same kind observed among the flowering plants. In hot-houses, adhering to decaying leaves, may occasionally be seen a curious little plant called *Sphærobolus stellatus* (Fig. 28), which bears no

FIG. 28.—SPHÆROBOLUS STELLATUS.
Natural size and magnified.

inapt resemblance in its shape and functions to a Liliputian mortar. It is of a pale straw-colour, and consists of two coats, both stellated, and separated from each other by a bead of dew exuded by the plant. The rays of the outer case are orange. No sooner is the inner case touched, than it becomes suddenly inverted, and shoots forth, with a loud jerk, a little pellucid ball to a distance of upwards of three feet. This ball or sporangium contains the seeds, and is ejected with a force which, considering the nature and diminutive size of the plant, far exceeds that employed in the projection of a shell from the largest mortar, or a cannon-ball from an Armstrong gun. It is a far more curious and interesting object than the squirting cucumber of which so much is made. Another denizen of the hot-bed (*Peziza vesiculosa*) exhibits somewhat similar properties. When the sun is shining warmly upon its cup, the least agitation raises a visible cloud of sporidia like a thin wreath of vapour. These are beautiful instances of the adaptations, with which nature has provided these lowly plants, for the certain dissemination of their seed.

The mushroom may be regarded as an ideal fungus of the highest type; and consequently the preceding description is only applicable to the class which it represents. There are varieties of structure as there are varieties of form. There are four large sub-orders of fungi in which the organs of fructification are widely different. The first sub-order is called Hymenomycetes, or naked fungi, because the seed-bearing organs are naked, or placed externally. This is the largest, most important, and most highly developed order, containing in this country forty-six genera, and upwards of seven hundred and twenty species. The mushroom, chantarelle, amadou, toadstool, morell, and ergot, are familiar examples of this order. The hymenium assumes various shapes in the different genera. In the mushroom it forms gills, in the toadstool tubes, in the chantarelle veins, in the amadou pores, and in the hydnum spines. Sometimes it is placed on the lower surface of the pileus, as in the mushroom, and at other times it is formed on the upper surface of the cap, as in helvella. The second sub-order, called Gasteromycetes, has the seed-bearing organs enclosed in a membranous covering, like the stomach of an animal, whence the name. This order contains sixty-one genera in this country, and only about three hundred species; one genus alone (Sphæria) containing two hundred species. The stinkhorn, the truffle, the bird's-nest fungus, and the puff-ball, are familiar examples of this order. The third sub-order is called Hyphomycetes, or web-like fungi, because the spores are developed on naked filaments, whose terminal cells are often transformed into a series of spores, like a row of beads. The general appearance of the plants belonging to this order, is that of a quantity of dust-like seeds imbedded in a flaky cottony substance, like a spider's web. The different kinds of common mould, blue, yellow, and green, the grape Oidium, and the red cheese mould, are common examples of this class. It contains only thirty-three British genera, and only about a hundred species, the largest genus containing only nine species. The fourth and last sub-order is called Coniomycetes, or dust fungi, because the spore-cases are produced beneath the epidermis of plants, or the matrix in which they are developed, in the form of a minute collection of dust, entirely destitute of any covering or receptacle, except that which is furnished by the skin of the plant raised around it. This class is the simplest and least organized of the fungi, but it is nevertheless the most destructive of the whole tribe. It contains sixteen genera, and upwards of one hundred and sixty-seven species, three genera alone containing respectively thirty-eight, thirty-one, and sixty-three species. Mildew, smut, bunt, and rust, are *too* familiar examples of this most notorious class.

Such is a brief analysis of the different orders of British fungi, and a general survey of the different kinds of fructification. In regard to the spores themselves, produced by these organs, they are either naked or they are contained in oval cases called thecæ or asci, mixed with peculiar but little-known filaments, to which the provisional name of antheridia has been given, because they are supposed to perform the functions of these organs in the fertilizing of the seed. The Ascomycetes or asci-bearing fungi resemble lichens in every respect, except that they are produced on decaying substances, and are possessed of a mycelium or spawn, peculiarities unknown among the lichens. By some authors, such as Schleiden, they are included among the lichens, notwithstanding these discrepancies. Spores then are produced in the interior of distinct sacs, called thecæ ; or they are developed on the outside of distinct sacs, called basidia ; or they are produced in the midst of a gelatinous mass, without any evident organization, when they are called myxospores.

We have thus seen that all these forms of fungoid life, excessively minute in size and simple in structure although many of them are, yet obey the great law of nature in propagating themselves by seeds or germs. Individuals of the antiquated school of La Marc and Oken, as the author of the *Vestiges of Creation*, have adopted the strange theory that these plants are the productions of spontaneous or equivocal generation, springing up without seed or germ from the soil, or from substances in a state of fermentation. This theory is countenanced and rendered plausible by the almost instantaneous appearance of mildew, dry-rot, mouldiness, and others of the simplest class of fungi on the objects affected, and the strange and almost inaccessible situations in which they are found, as, for instance, in the inside of a large cheese, in the core of an apple, beneath the wrapper with which the careful housewife covers her cherished preserves, and under the epidermis of living plants, localities where it is difficult to conceive how any seed, however minute, could find a lodgment. The nature and habits of these plants are now, however, better understood than they were in the time of La Marc; and no intelligent naturalist will, at the present date, be found to support the theory of spontaneous generation. Enlarged and more accurate researches into the mysteries of nature have established the fact upon a sure and immovable foundation, that a seed is as necessary for the production of the minutest speck of mouldiness which the microscope can reveal to our view, as the acorn is for the germination of the giant oak of the forest, or the date for the growth of the magnificent palm of the desert. It is true that these plants are most frequently found on the products of animal or vegetable decomposition; but they occur in such situations, not because these decaying substances originate them, but just because they afford them the necessary conditions of their growth, their germs having been previously deposited there by pre-existing species. If we sow a quantity of the black dust or spores of the common bread-mould on a stale crust, we shall have a quicker growth and a more abundant crop of fungi than if the crust be left to a natural or chance supply of seeds; just as the farmer has a surer and more plentiful harvest when he deposits a sufficient quantity of seeds in the ground, than when he leaves the chance of a crop to the scattering self-sown wheat of the previous autumn. Indeed, the most prolonged and closest observations, and the most carefully-conducted experiments, have not led to the proof of a single instance of spontaneous or equivocal generation, even of one of the simplest of all living things ; but, on the contrary, they all lead farther and farther from, or entirely disprove it. F. Schulze, of Berlin, performed an experiment to test the possibility of equivocal generation, under the play of the indispensable conditions of life, free from access to any pre-existing vegetable or animal germs. "A glass vessel, half filled with a mixture of various dead vegetable and animal substances in water, was heated to 212° Fahr., so as to destroy any living bodies which might exist within. To the vessel was then adapted a pair of Liebig's bulbs, one of which contained sulphuric acid, the other a solution of potassa, and through these only could the exterior air have access to its interior. The apparatus was then placed in a window, where it received the full influence of light, and the necessary temperature for the production of life. The air within the vessel was daily renewed from May till August, by blowing through the sulphuric acid, from which it could suffer no change, except to be deprived of moisture and organic particles. During all that time not even the simplest animal or vegetable forms were produced ; while in an open vessel, containing the same mixture in the same situation, there were observed on the following day numerous vibrios and monads, and to these were soon added larger animaculæ." This interesting experiment is conclusive of the fact, that, if due care be taken to get quit of the ova of animals and the seeds of minute vegetables from any fluid or other suitable matrix, and at the same time carefully to exclude the further entrance of them through the admitted air, no traces of animal or vegetable life will appear. The presence of mould in such an apparently inexplicable place as the interior of a large cheese, is owing to the exposure of the curd to the air when the cheese was being made, and the consequent deposition upon it of the minute germs of fungi floating around, which afterwards developed themselves when the curd thus impregnated formed the inside of the cheese. It is well known that the exposure of curd for a single day to the atmosphere, will have the effect of producing mouldy cheese.

Countless millions of the subtle seeds of fungi, invisible to the naked eye, and light almost as the particles of vapour around them, are continually floating in the air we breathe, or swimming in the water we drink, or lying amid the impalpable dust and sand of the soil, waiting but the combination of a few simple circumstances, the presence of warmth or moisture, or a suitable matrix, to display their vital energies, and to burst into full, free, independent life. Hundreds of thousands of the minute germs of the various moulds which approach us in our very houses, and fasten upon different articles of domestic use, might be and often are dancing about in the air-currents of our apartments, though totally invisible to us ; but could we sufficiently magnify them, as a sunbeam darted in at our windows and illuminated their bodies, they would appear like so many cannon-balls, moving rapidly up and down, and in every direction. If we venture for a moment to imagine the overwhelming number of seeds which the different species of fungi must disseminate in the course of a single year,— if we consider that each individual of the common puff-ball contains upwards of ten millions of seeds, and these so small as to form a mere cloud when puffed into the air, and that a single filament of the mould which infests our bread and preserves, will produce as many germs as an oak will acorns, so that a piece of decaying matter, not two inches each way, will scatter upon the air at the slightest breath of the summer breeze, or the gentlest touch of the smallest insect's wing, as many seeds, quick with life, as this country will produce of acorns in a twelvemonth ; if we take these things into consideration, it is not too much to suppose that the seeds of fungi must be ubiquitous, and from their excessively minute size penetrate into every place, even into the stomachs and other parts of animals. This circumstance has been made the ground of a belief that malarial and epidemic fevers have their origin in cryptogamic vegetables or spores. Much valuable information has of late years been acquired regarding the habits and mode of propagation of these diseases ; but little as yet has been ascertained regarding their essential nature. The pestilence still "walks in darkness," and neither chemistry nor any other science can tell us what is its essential nature, nor in what its terrible potency consists. If the spores of fungi be really the exciting cause, in predisposing circumstances, of zymotic diseases, these minute bodies conveyed through the air, and introduced into the body in respiration, could easily be detected. The minutest of all known living beings is the *Vibrio lineola* of Müller, measuring only the 36,000th part of an inch, and the smallest known vegetable spore is very much larger than this ; while particles of inorganic matter can be distinguished by the microscope so minute as the 200,000th part of an inch. Be the origin of these diseases however what it may, it is a matter of fact that when cholera last appeared in this country in 1847, an extraordinary quantity of these microscopic spores were found in the air. If they were poisonous, as many of the fungi are, it admits of being suggested at least that those living in places where dense clouds of them were present, being devitalized by other noxious influences, such as vitiated air, defective sewerage, bad water, or an inadequate supply of food, and consequently in a state of body unable to resist the deleterious action of these cryptogamic germs, died from a form of poisoning. These countless myriads, then, of invisible seeds which continually float in our atmosphere, ever ready to alight and spring into life, as the advanced heralds of the plague and the pestilence, may well strike us with astonishment if not with awe. Above us, about us, and in us they roam like vigilant spirits, "seeing that all is right with our physical constitution ; but gladly availing themselves of the slightest flaw to work our destruction."

Although fungi are in an especial manner capable of universal dissemination, yet we find that in their geographical distribution they are as much restricted as other plants. Some representatives of the class are found in every part of the world, and some particular species have the power of indefinite extension and localization, but, as a whole, like the higher cryptogams, they can only spread within certain limited areas. In tropical forests, where the heat fills the stifled and confined air with moisture, where the exuberance of the vegetation excludes the rays of the sun and creates the "dim religious light" which they love, and where, more especially, there is always an immense quantity of decaying organic matter; in such favourable situations we might expect to find them in the greatest quantity and luxuriance. But, strange to say, fungi as a class, are comparatively rare in tropical woods. While every tree has its creeper, and almost every flower its parasite, the plants which, above all others, are most parasitical have very few representatives there; and dead trunks and prostrate boughs, and decaying herbage, rot and crumble away untouched by the ravages of mushroom or mould. Insects in these countries perform the office of fungi in hastening the decomposition of dead matter, and incorporating and deodorizing the decaying particles; and it must be confessed that they perform this duty more speedily and effectually; while, unlike the fungi, they leave no unpleasant traces, no putrifying masses behind when their work is accomplished, and their own turn comes to die. Like some of the epidemic diseases, as, for instance, typhus, with which they are said to be connected, the too high temperature of the tropics seems to offer an effectual barrier to their general distribution in those countries. Their head-quarters seem to be in northern latitudes, where the temperature is mild and genial, and where there is a constant supply of moisture.

Professor Fries of Upsal, the presiding genius of these plants, gathered in Sweden, within a space of ground not exceeding a square furlong, more than two thousand distinct species. "This country," says Berkeley, "with its various soils, large mixed forests, and warm summer temperature, seems to produce more species than any part of the known world; and next in order, perhaps, are the United States, as far as South Carolina, where they absolutely swarm. A moist autumn after a genial summer is most conducive to their growth, but cold, wet summers are seldom productive. The portion of the Himalayas, which lies immediately north of Calcutta, is perhaps almost as prolific in point of individuals as the countries named above, but the number of species on examination proves far less than might at first have been suspected. It is probably not a fifth of what occurs in Sweden. Great Britain, though possessing a considerable list of species, is not abundant in individuals, except as regards a limited number of species. The exuberance even in the most favourable autumn is not to be compared with that of Sweden or many parts of Germany." They are found in the Arctic and Antarctic regions, almost as far as the limits of vegetation. They penetrate to the dreary regions of Greenland and Lapland, supplying the natives with their tinder, and with an excellent styptic for stopping blood and allaying pain; and they announce to the hapless exiles of Siberia, when their gaily-coloured forms spring forth from the crevices of the rocks, and in the dark haunts of the gloomy fir-woods, that the stormy blasts of winter are past, and that the spring and the summer, those short sweet seasons of indescribable beauty and pleasure, are nigh.

Certain genera and species occur only in tropical and sub-tropical regions, having their northern limit in the north of Africa or the coast of the Mediterranean. Several genera and species are confined to New Zealand, others to Ceylon and Java, others to the Cape de Verde Islands and the United States. "In the Sikkim and neighbouring Himalayas we have species of every different climate at different heights. We have below *Polyporus sanguineus* and *xanthopus*, which are peculiar to the hottest parts of the tropics; higher up we have the species of Ceylon and Java; we have then the species of Southern Europe; and finally, the more northern species; or, if we have not the identical species, we have others so nearly allied that it is matter of difficulty to distinguish them. One species occurs as high as 18,000 feet, while others flourished in the warm vale at a comparatively low height above the level of the sea."

But while the fungi are, to a certain extent, restricted in their geographical distribution within certain well-known limits; they are, on the other hand, almost ubiquitous in their choice of habitats. There is hardly a single substance on which some species or other of them may not, under favourable circumstances, be found. As a general rule they all grow on dead and decaying organic matter, on the mouldering trunks and branches of trees and withered plants, and on the bones and droppings of animals. But they are also occasionally found on living trees, and on green leaves, and parts of plants that show no symptoms of decay. A large class called hypodermous or entophytic fungi spring from beneath the cuticle of living plants, and a considerable proportion of our flowering plants are affected with them—a different fungus being developed upon almost every species. Their minute sporules are either directly applied to the plants upon which they are found, entering by the stomata or breathing pores; or they are taken up from the soil by their seeds in the process of germinating, enter into their structure, circulate through their tissues, remaining all the time in a dormant state, until at last, when the part which forms the most suitable nidus for them is developed, they suddenly appear upon it externally in the form of patches or aggregations of black or coloured granules. Many species, contrary to the habits of the race, seem to live on mineral matter. Numerous exotic Polypori, for instance, grow on hard volcanic tufa, without a particle of organic matter. Other fungi are not unfrequently found in this country growing in abundance on the hardest gravel stones, and bare plastered walls destitute of all organic nourishment. Mr. Ivor found a Didymium on a leaden cistern at Kew; another was found by Mr. Sowerby, in the outer gallery of St. Paul's, on cinders; while a still more extraordinary instance is related by Schweinitz of a species of Æthalium vegetating on iron which had been subjected to a red heat a short time before. "A blacksmith," he says, "at Salem, by no means void of sense or cultivation, had thrown on one side a piece of iron which he had just taken from the fire, being called off to some other business. On his return in the morning, he was astonished to see on this very piece, lying over the water in his smith's trough, a quantity of this fungus, of a soft gelatinous consistency. He immediately sent for Schweinitz without moving anything from its place, who was equally astonished to find a distinct species of Æthalium. (This plant forms a yellow mass like curdled egg in tan-pits and hot-houses, cucumber and melon frames, where it is very common and injurious.) The mass of fungi was two feet in length, consisting of a series of many confluent individuals. It had crept from the iron to some adjacent wood; and not, as might be objected, from the wood to the iron. The immense mass had grown in the space of twelve hours." All these curious instances show that fungi do not always derive nutriment from their matrix, and that many of them are essentially meteoric, depending on matter conveyed to them by the surrounding air or moisture. A species of Phycomyces, which bears a strong resemblance to an alga, from its green colour and shining aspect when dry, grows rapidly and in prodigious quantities in soap and candle manufactories, covering walls that are saturated with oil or grease in immense flakes. It is supposed to be a transformation of the common green mould. Some species, such as the truffle, are subterranean, vegetating in the absence of all the external stimulants upon which other plants depend, being apparently attached to the roots of trees, often at a considerable distance underground. Some species are found, as already mentioned, in the coal mines of Dresden. A peculiar fungus (*Racodium cellare*), like a bacchanalian gnome, is found on casks and bottles, and hanging down from the roof in close cellars. It grows in great abundance in the London docks. The dim vaults, with their vistas of casks, extending in the darkness farther than eye can reach, are festooned with this fungoid cobweb hanging from the roof like a soft and comfortable form of stalactite, in the strangest forms and in immense masses. It begins as an incrustation resembling white cotton wool forming on the brickwork of the vault, and as it grows, descending in irregular shapes, hanging down a foot or two in length, and changing to a dingy brown colour, very like a mouse-skin. The men who live in the place are proud of this extraordinary fungus, which carries out the convivial aspect imparted by the wine casks; it is never interfered with, and they point out any larger mass than usual with some complacency.

As a singular instance of the ease with which these plants can accommodate themselves to surrounding circumstances, it may be mentioned that several species of fungi called *snow moulds*, somewhat allied to the common moulds of our cupboards, are found growing on the barren and unpropitious snow. One of these, called Chionype, was first discovered in the north of Iceland; but two other species have since occurred in Germany in great abundance. The Chionype is developed on the snow in clear weather, when the sun has power enough to melt the upper crust, without the existence of a general thaw; and in all probability springs from the droppings or the urine of animals decomposed in the snow. It spreads over the surface of the snow in shining fleecy patches, dotted with red or green particles. When the snow melts, it is left behind upon the underlying grass in the form of a cobweb stratum, which in a few days disappears. Another species of snow-mould recently discovered in Germany, and described by Professor Unger, under the significant name of *Lanosa nivalis*—unlike the former, grows underneath the snow, and in certain seasons is extremely destructive to the grass upon which it is developed. "The years in which it is most injurious are those when a deep snow sets in without any previous frost, when it sometimes destroys whole crops of corn; and this is so well known to the farmer, that in such seasons it is customary in certain districts to plough up the hard frozen surface of the snow, occasionally during the winter. The plant is of a very simple structure, consisting of merely branched or jointed threads, whose ultimate lateral branches at length assume a red tinge, and separate at the articulations, producing oblong spores. It forms white patches a foot or more in diameter, made up of a number of smaller circular patches; and when the snow melts on the approach of spring, these assume here and there a red tint, as if dusted with red powder, in consequence of the ripening of the spores. The snow is scarcely melted when the whole disappears, leaving behind a withered plot, which, according to the greater or less vigour or duration of the parasite, is either completely barren, or but slowly resumes its verdure. In some years the mould is so abundant that the crops are completely destroyed, and there is no other remedy than to sow them again."

Not content with preying upon dead organic matter, or growing plants, some fungi also attack living animals. In this country there are several species of Sphæria and Isaria which grow in garden soil on the larvæ and pupæ of insects; while others are parasitic on the *Elaphomyces gra-*

*nulatus* and *muricatus* in pine woods. In New Zealand, a remarkable group of fungi called *Sphæria Robertsii* grows from the head of the caterpillar of the *Hepialus virescens*, a species of moth, when it buries itself among the moss in the woods to undergo its metamorphosis. In appearance it is a somewhat crooked, long, slender stalk terminating in the spike-like fructification. Its growth destroys the caterpillar ; a striking proof that a retrogade step is sometimes to be found in the animal kingdom—the grub instead of developing itself into a beautiful butterfly being replaced by a nauseous fungus. It is so common and prominent a species in New Zealand, that it has a name in the native language, and is associated with some of the ancient Maori superstitions. In the West Indies, wasps called by the inhabitants *Guêpes végétantes*, may often be seen flying about with fungoid plants as long and nearly as bulky as their own bodies growing upon them ; while in this country itself, it is by no means rare to see a humble-bee, or a common blue-bottle fly, that had been killed by the growth of a club-shaped Sphæria from its body, from half an inch to an inch in length, of a sienna brown or lemon colour. Flies are usually attacked by a fungoid disease about the end of autumn, when the cold damp weather which then prevails has reduced the vitality of their bodies to the lowest point, and rendered them incapable of resisting external agencies. At this time they forsake their accustomed haunts in the open air, congregating within doors for warmth and shelter, and may be seen in considerable numbers adhering to window sills, walls, and various articles of furniture in our rooms. In a few days they die, but strange to say their appearance is so little altered, that it is impossible without actual examination to tell that they are dead. When dying in the ordinary way, they always draw up their legs, and cross them beneath their bodies; but when they perish of this disease, the legs are stretched out supporting their bodies, and retaining them in their natural position. The proboscis is protruded, as if in the act of imbibing nourishment, and their whole appearance is that of vigorous healthy flies that have alighted for a moment, and may be expected in the next to take wing and fly away. The only difference observed is a whitish halo, like a sprinkling of flour, about three inches in circumference, which surrounds them, and consists of the minute dust-like spores shed by the fungus that has attacked them. When more attentively examined, however, the abdomen is seen to be much swollen, the rings composing it being separated from each other by interspaces, occupied with white prominent zones of vegetable growth. The body is a mere empty shell, reduced by the slightest touch to a dry friable powder, and lined with a thin, white, felt-like layer of mycelium, the entire viscera and all the juices being consumed by the voracious fungus. This disease has been long familiar to naturalists, but owing to the imperfection of their microscopes, its real nature was not ascertained until a comparatively recent period. It was first accurately determined by De Geer about the end of last century; and a minute and graphic description is given of it by Goethe, who suffered nothing worthy of notice, however minute, or apparently far removed from his own sphere, to escape his observation. This, and all other vegetable parasites attacking insects, seem to be one of the powerful and efficient checks provided by nature for restraining within due limits the increase of creatures, which, owing to their extraordinary fecundity, rapid development, and unbounded rapacity, would otherwise prove a terrible scourge.

The insect Sphærias are found in different countries. In Australia, where a gigantic species occurs on an enormous larva frequently found beside the banks of the Murrambidgee, in North America, and in China, these deadly parasites are developed upon insects of different tribes. They form a favourite medicine in China, where a bundle of the fungi, with the caterpillars attached to them, is placed in the stomach of a duck, which is then roasted and eaten by the patient as a cure for internal complaints. There is a peculiar disease called muscardine, affecting the silk-worm in Syria and China, before they have woven their cocoons, which sometimes proves fatal to thousands of these delicate creatures. It not unfrequently happens that the silk-grower loses his whole stock of worms from this cause alone. This disease is caused by the mould-like filaments of the *Botrytis bassiana.* These filaments grow with great rapidity within the body of the animal they attack, not only at the expense of its nutritive fluids, but after its death; all the interior soft tissues appear to be converted into a solid mass of mycelium, from which arise one or more aërial receptacles of the spores. It sometimes happens that the caterpillar is only partially affected by this fungoid growth, or only to such an extent as not to destroy the organs immediately essential to its life, in which case it may pass through its metamorphosis into the imago state, and become a butterfly or a moth, with the lower portion of its body filled with a mass of fungoid substance as above described.

But it is not only insects, and other creatures of inferior organization in the larva state, that are thus subject to the attacks of parasitic fungi. They even enter the water—an element in which they are seldom found, and where they always refuse to develop themselves normally—and prey upon gold fishes and other scaly tenants of the deep. The *Achyla prolifera* is one of the most remarkable of these fungi. Every one who has kept gold-fishes must be familiar with this great enemy of his favourites. It consists of numerous transparent threads of extreme fineness, packed together as closely as the pile of velvet, adhering to the surface of the fishes, and covering them as it were with a whitish slime. This appearance is generally regarded as a kind of decay or consumption in the animals themselves, and not as an external clothing of parasitic plants. It is, however, a true vegetable growth, as is evident when it is placed under the microscope, for the unassisted eye can perceive nothing of its true structure; each filament being terminated by a pear-shaped ball, about the $\frac{1}{1200}$th of an inch in diameter, and consisting of a single cell filled with a mucilaginous fluid, in which float the reproductive granules. "The contents of this cell are seen to be in constant motion from the earliest stage of their existence; but as they advance to maturity, the mucilage disappears, and the motion of the granules becomes more rapid and violent, till ultimately they burst their way through the cell, and are transferred to the water, there to perform their circle of being, and to give birth to new granules. All this takes place with such amazing rapidity, that one hour or two suffices for the complete development and escape of the spores; so that we need not wonder when we are told that, once established, the *Achyla prolifera* will often complete the destruction of a healthy gold-fish in less than twelve hours."

The most protean of all the fungi, both in appearance and choice of growing-place, is the group to which the common familiar name of *mould* has been given. There are no less than three different genera and numerous species included under this one name. There is the white or blue mould, forming the genus *Aspergillus* (Fig. 29), from the resemblance of its fructification to the aspergillus or brush used for sprinkling holy water in Roman Catholic countries, which is of frequent occurrence on decaying substances of all kinds, and gives a white and downy, or a blue-grey and powdery aspect to the objects on which it grows. There is next the green mould, forming the genus Penicillium (Fig. 30), extremely common on all sorts of decaying bodies, and presenting a close resemblance in appearance to the former genus, with this difference, that its spore-bearing stem divides into numerous branches like a miniature tree, bearing spores

FIG. 29.—ASPERGILLUS GLAUCUS.

not in regular rows, but like leaves or fruit in irregular clusters on each branch, whereas the stem of the aspergillus is unbranched, and bears on its summit many

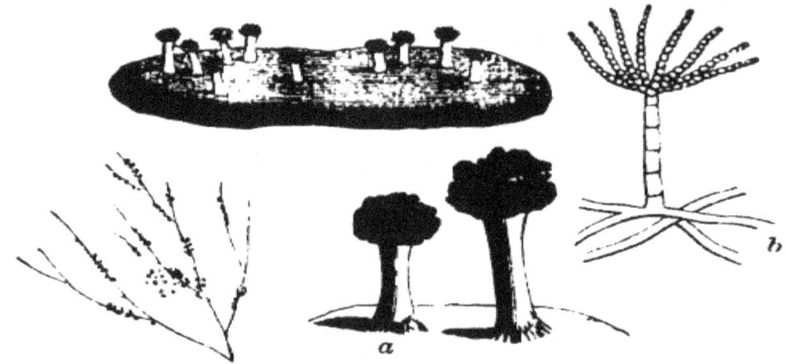

FIG. 30.—(*a*) PENICILLIUM CRUSTACEUM. (*b*) ASPERGILLUS CANDIDUS.

rows of spores, which are placed in linear order like necklaces, and joined to the stem like a bundle of hairs on a brush. The third kind of mould included in this group forms the genus *Mucor* (Fig. 31), or yellow

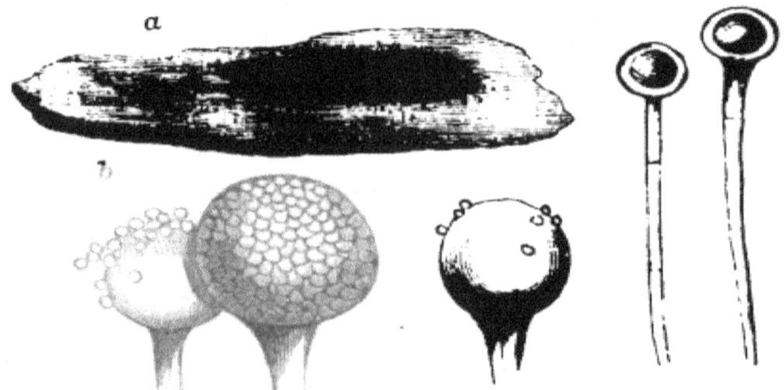

FIG. 31.—MUCOR MUCEDO.
(*a*) Natural size. (*b*) Highly magnified.

mould, also extremely common. It differs from the two preceding kinds in having its spores, instead of being exposed naked to the air like them, enclosed in a rounded membranous case, bursting irregularly as the spores arrive at maturity, which then present themselves like so many dusty particles congregated round a central nucleus. Being so minute, the slightest touch, or the gentlest breath of air, is sufficient to scatter them in thousands, and thus they increase with amazing rapidity. The trivial names of blue, green, and yellow mould, it may be remarked, are of no specific significance, as all these colours are common to the species in the different genera, and occur even in the same species in various stages of its growth. In fact, it is by their different fructification under the microscope alone that the different genera can be recognised, as their mycelium or spawn is precisely similar, and to the naked eye the appearance they present on the different substances which they affect is identical.

Though generically and specifically distinct, as we have thus seen, yet, for the sake of convenience, adopting the popular notion and considering them all as one plant, we find that this mould is not only universally distributed, where fungi are at all capable of growing, but that it is also remarkably indifferent as to its selection of habitats, assuming different appearances in different situations, some of which are exceedingly puzzling to the botanist. Usually mould is found on pots of jam, on decaying succulent fruits, on bread when kept too long in a warm and damp situation, on clothes and other articles of common wear; but it is sometimes found in strangely different situations, where it presents the most incongruous forms. The fungi which are produced on animal tissues, more especially in certain diseased conditions of the skin or the mucous membranes, and the presence of which, in such cases, seems to cause an alteration in the phenomena of disease, have been recently ascertained by careful experiments to belong to this group. There are no less than nine entophytes parasitic upon man; and these are all now referred to some species or other of mould in different stages of development. Several French surgeons narrate cases, in which, on removing bandages from sore surfaces, they have found them covered with a collection of white flocculent filaments forming a web-like tissue. These mycodermata, as they are called, of ulcerated and mucous surfaces, are nothing else than the undeveloped spawn, or mycelium of some species of Penicillium. There is a curious endemic disease that occurs in Poland and the adjoining countries, said to be of Asiatic origin, and to have first appeared in Europe in the thirteenth century, in which the hairs get matted together, and become endowed individually with the most exquisitely painful sensibility. This fearful disease, to which the name of *Plica polonica* has been given, is owing to the development of a species of mould on the head. The allied disease known by the name of *mentagra* affecting the beard of men; the *sordes* on the teeth, occurring in persons affected with low typhoid fever; the *aptha* or *thrush*, as the white spots like curdled milk, which cover the mucous membrane of the mouth and palate of children, are called; the disease called *tinea* or *scald-head*, so frequent on the heads of infants; all these diseases, as well as the mouldiness found in the air-cells of the eider duck, are different forms of this plastic and ubiquitous mould. The vegetable vesicles or aggregations of small rounded cells found in these different diseases of the human body, have been carefully removed and placed in saccharine matter, on fruits or in syrup, in favourable circumstances, supplied with the requisite conditions of warmth and moisture, and attentively watched, when, in the course of a few days or weeks, they were all found to develop themselves, some into the common blue mould, and others into the common green mould. These experiments render it extremely probable, that there is no fungus found infesting any part of the human body, or any part of the economy of other animals, however different or abnormal the appearance it may present, which is not referrible to one or other of the common genera of mould, Penicillium, Aspergillus, and Mucor!

But perhaps the most extraordinary and abnormal forms of mould are those which it assumes in liquids. Fungi, as a class, are entirely confined to solid substances; but there are very few fluids containing saccharine matter in which this all-pervading mould does not occur. Wine, cider, tinctures, syrups, vinegar, catsup, not unfrequently become mothery, that is, present the appearance of fibres or flocculent threads running through them. Every one is familiar with the tough mass that is so often brought up on the point of the pen from the ink-holder. This flocculent matter is the undeveloped mycelium of the green or blue mould. While growing in decomposing liquids, it loses all resemblance to the same plant when growing on decaying fruits and dead organic matter exposed to the air, and becomes a soft, slimy, and somewhat gelatinous body, such as is often found in the bottoms of empty wine-bottles. This slimy mass is no other than the famous vinegar-plant, which a few years ago aroused the attention of domestic circles and scientific bodies, and was extensively diffused as a useful article in the manufacture of vinegar in private families. The report, circulated at the time, of its being an importation from India or South America, has thus been found destitute of foundation, for whatever may have been the history of the first or individual specimens, and though the growth of the plant might go on more rapidly in a warm than in a temperate climate, yet it is evidently a genuine native production, capable of being originated and multiplied indefinitely in this country. This extraordinary substance, familiar, no doubt, to many of my readers, may be described as a tough, gelatinous mass of a pale brownish colour, bearing a close resemblance to a piece of boiled tripe. It is usually placed in a small jar containing a solution of sugar or treacle; and after being allowed to remain in a warm situation for a month or six weeks, the solution is found to be converted into vinegar, this change being due to a kind of fermentation caused by the plant. The solution necessarily causes the vinegar to be of a syrupy nature, but not to such an extent as to communicate a flavour to it; when evaporated to dryness, a large quantity of saccharine matter is left. Dr. Lindley, and most other botanists, are strongly of opinion that this so-called vinegar-plant is an abnormal form of the common *Penicillium glaucum* or blue mould. In fact, it is merely the spawn or mycelium of that plant, increased to an extraordinary extent and closely interlaced together, owing to the absence of the usual spore-bearing stalks, which, as already remarked, are never formed in fungi growing in fluids. Whenever the vinegar is allowed to evaporate, and the mycelium in consequence becomes free from saturation, it produces the usual fructification, and presents the common appearance of mould. Other fungi besides the blue mould may assume the same remarkable form when placed under similar conditions, and all of them may have the power of producing vinegar. Indeed, it should not be so great a matter of surprise, that fungi should assume such extraordinary appearances, when prevented from developing their usual organs of fructification ; for do we not find even among the flowering plants, which are not nearly so plastic, or so susceptible to external influences, very singular changes effected in their structure and conformation, by being kept in a barren and undeveloped state ? The tree mignonette is a familiar instance of the change effected in the structure of an annual plant, by being kept from flowering during the natural period, and placed in favourable circumstances ; and still more surprising illustrations will occur to the florist and botanist. It is worthy of remark that the vinegar-plant, when well supplied with food in an acetous solution, divides at a certain stage of its growth into two distinct layers, which in course of time would again increase in size and divide, and so on, each layer being capable of removal to a separate jar for the production of vinegar. This remarkable mode of propagation by dividing into separate laminæ, which has been taken advantage of in spreading specimens of the plant among different individuals, resembles the separation of buds in the medusæ, and the merismatic mode of division by which the diatoms, and many others of the lowest class of algæ, extend themselves indefinitely ;—thus showing the close and intimate connexion subsisting between plants that in other circumstances are widely different, when placed under similar conditions. Such instances as these may be regarded as circumstantial evidence in favour of Darwin's famous theory of the origin of species by natural selection, that is, that all existing plants have descended from three or four progenitors, or even from one primordial form into which life was first breathed by the Creator ; the vast modification which these plants now exhibit being mainly the result of a process of natural selection carried on during vast geological periods and epochs of time. No human intellect, however, unaided by revelation, is at present able to make such conclusions as these matters of positive proof or positive refutation. They must remain a question of opinion, in the discussion of which peculiarities of mind and education must largely operate as biassing influences ; a kind of Penelope's web, which, however skilfully woven by one, will be ruthlessly unwoven by another, until a more solid and enduring fabric has been put together in the loom by some more competent artist.

A still more striking form of the protean mould under consideration, is that which occurs in the fermenting of yeast and other substances. It may surprise many to be told that yeast is merely an undeveloped condition of the common mould which they see on their bread and cheese. Fermentation is in one sense a chemical process, forming the first step towards dissolution, or that re-arrangement of old elements which is necessary to form new compounds ; but, strange to say, the action is also vegetative. The whole mass of fermenting matter gradually assumes the condition of active vegetative growth. The germs of the mould, which had been incorporated in the material, begin to live and expand, each bearing a distinct plant, giving rise either by gemmation or nucleation to new plants indefinitely, until the entire fermenting principle is exhausted. The form which the *Torula cervisiæ* or yeast-plant assumes is that of a number of small vesicles, containing others still smaller in their interior, strung together in a moniliform or necklace manner. By the time that five or six vesicles are strung together, the fermentation is sufficiently advanced, and the manufacturer checks it. The vegetation is then suspended, and the groups of vesicles separate into individuals, the mass of which thus constitutes the yeast. The cells of the yeast-plant are globular at first, but they soon change, while the fermenting principle is being used up, into the oval form ; when the sugar is still more exhausted, they become linear and filamentous, advancing to the primary stage of mycelium ; until finally when the whole fermenting matter is absorbed and evaporated, they develop into the normal crust and organs of fructification of the common Penicillium or blue mould.

In all saccharine fluids undergoing the alcoholic and even the acetous fermentation, these minute torulæ or yeast-cells make their appearance ; the azote or nitrogen contained in them exercising what is called a catalytic action, that is combining with the carbon and oxygen in the fluid, and causing thereby the alcohol to be disengaged. The question here arises whether the fungus produces the fermentation, or the fermentation the fungus. The following judicious remarks, from the pen of a well-known writer upon the subject in the *Cornhill Magazine*, may determine the matter. "If the force given out by the liquid in fermenting be the cause of the growth of the plant, yeast should never be formed unless fermentation is going on. If on the other hand the growth of the plant be (as has been supposed by some) the cause of the decomposition, then fermentation should never occur unless that growth takes place. But it is well known that the yeast-plant is never developed except during fermentation, while fermentation will take place, although more slowly, without any formation of yeast. It follows, therefore, that the growth depends on the decomposition, and not the decomposition upon the growth. But fermentation is excited by the addition of yeast, and proceeds more successfully in proportion to the rapidity with which the yeast cells are developed. Why should this be if the formation of the living cells is only the effect, and not the cause of fermentation? The intimate connexion of growth and decay explains this fact. The yeast excites fermentation because it is itself exceedingly prone to decompose; more prone than the liquid to which it is added. And in decomposing, it communicates the impulse of its own change to the matter around it, so disturbing the equilibrium of the elements, and bringing about, in a few hours, chemical changes that would otherwise have occupied a much longer time. And this more active decomposition in the fermenting fluid reacts again upon the cells of the yeast, and produces in them a rapid growth and multiplication. They afford the outlet, as it were, for the force given out by the chemical changes to which they have furnished the stimulus."

It is a remarkable fact that we owe beer, wine, and spirits, to the agency of the minute undeveloped cells of the common mould, which in other forms is so destructive and offensive to us!

For what purpose, it may be asked by the incurious or the credulous, were plants so excessively numerous, and so universally distributed, created?—for to many individuals they are such objects of prejudice and disgust, that their real importance as useful productions is little appreciated. We do not know indeed *all* the wise purposes which He who created nothing in vain intended them to serve in the economy of nature; but we are acquainted with some of them, and these are so obvious, so vastly important, and reveal such numerous and striking instances of adaptation of means to ends, that we cannot but lament that such ignorance and prejudice regarding them should exist in this country. There is no elementary and self-subsistent organic matter in nature, as Buffon erroneously taught, and the health and wellbeing of man himself may more or less immediately depend upon the important offices which these despised productions were created to perform. Appearing as they do in those months of the year when the flowers are fading, the leaves falling, and all nature yielding herself up as the passive victim of decay and death, they are obviously intended to remove those decomposing tissues which would otherwise pour volumes of noxious vapour into the atmosphere, and render it unfit to support life; to call back into the great vortex, the ceaseless round of existence, those fugitive particles of effete matter which had served their appointed purpose in one form of organization, and were fast hastening down, by a process of decomposition, to join the atoms of the inorganic world of chaos and death. Every decaying leaf of the wood and the field has its own fungoid parasite, which gradually reduces it to a state fitted to minister to the necessities of next year's vegetation ; and thus, through the agency of little insignificant patches of mouldy, rusty tissue, the "carrion in the sun converts itself into trees and flowers."

In the economy of man, fungi have been applied to many useful purposes. A few are endowed with valuable medicinal properties, and still hold their ground, notwithstanding the vast improvement effected in the nature and choice of drugs in recent times. From their chemical constituents, the medical uses of the fungi are probably of far greater importance than their present very limited application might lead us to suppose ; and in all likelihood, if they were more studied, many of the active species might afford valuable remedies. As it is, however, one species at least is a highly powerful and invaluable medicine. The ergot of rye is an important article in the Materia Medica, as it has been found capable of exerting a very powerful and specific action upon the womb, and is administered in small doses in certain extreme cases. This remedy has been principally used in America, although of late it has been successfully employed in France and in this country. Dufresnoy is said to have used *Agaricus emeticus* with success in the early stage of consumption ; and the sweet-scented Polyporus has been much vaunted for its surprising effects in the treatment of the same disease, but it has now fallen entirely into disuse. A species of Polyporus growing upon the birch is used, when dried and pounded, as an ingredient in snuff, by the Ostyacks on the Obi. *Lysurus mokusin* is used by the Chinese as a remedy in gangrenous ulcers, but its virtues are probably fabulous. In Lapland, the common amadou (*Polyporus fomentarius*), when beaten out into thin pieces, is employed to remove pain by simply laying a piece of it on the part affected, and igniting it. Like the soft contents of puff-balls, it is used occasionally to stanch blood in wounds. When steeped in saltpetre, and cut into thin slices, it forms most excellent tinder, and is so employed in many parts of Germany and England. In Lapland, it is considered an indispensable article in domestic economy, Linnæus relating that he saw it hung up for various purposes on the walls of every cottage he entered.

Many of the fungi are possessed of highly poisonous properties, and serious, and even fatal accidents occur occasionally in this country, and more frequently in France, from an incautious use of them. Sometimes this arises from confounding the edible with the poisonous species ; but even the edible kinds to some people act always as poisons, and there is reason to believe that the best and safest mushrooms, if taken in considerable quantity for any length of time, induce in many individuals a habit of body which may be pronounced a poisoned one. Upon what their poisonous properties depend is not known. Two active substances have been recognised in them. When distilled with water they yield a fugacious acrid principle, dispelled in the act of drying, or by immersion in acids, alkalies, or alcohol. When extracted by water and alcohol, a brown, solid substance called amanitine is obtained, which is more fixed, and resists such processes. The specific action of these two constituents of the poisonous fungi upon the human frame, has not as yet been investigated. They sometimes act like narcotics, producing comatose and other affections of the nervous system, and at other times their action is of an irritant nature, more approaching that of arsenic. Some act as anæsthetics, giving complete insensibility to pain ; while, unlike chloroform and ether, the individual under their influence remains conscious all the time. The common puff-ball deprives the patient of speech, motion, and sensibility to pain, while he is still conscious of everything that happens around him ; thus realizing "that night-mare of our dreams in which we lie stretched on the funeral bier, sensible to the weeping of friends, aware of the last screw being fixed in the coffin, and the last clod clapped down upon us in the churchyard, and are yet unable to move a hand or a lip for our own deliverance." When slowly burnt, this fungus has long been employed for stupifying bees, and thús robbing their hives of the honey with impunity. Experiments, with the same species, have also recently been made on dogs, cats, and rabbits, and similar effects have invariably been found to ensue. When the fumes of the burning fungus are slowly inhaled, they gradually produce all the symptoms of intoxication, followed first by drowsiness, and then by perfect insensibility to pain, terminating, if the inhalation be continued, in vomiting, convulsions, and ultimately in death.

The qualities of fungi seem to vary with the climate

in which they have grown ; for many species which in this country are considered highly poisonous, on account of their intensely acrid qualities, and avoided as such, are eaten with impunity on the Continent. Mr. Berkeley mentions his having been informed by a gentleman of great acuteness and observation, that in some town of Poland, where he was detained as a prisoner, he amused himself with collecting and drying the various fungi that grew within its walls, amongst which were many reputed dangerous, and that to his great surprise his whole collection was devoured by the soldiers. It is well known, indeed, that even the esculent fungi of this country are not always safe to eat ; the qualities sometimes varying very considerably according to the nature of the situations in which they occur. The common edible mushroom of this country has sometimes proved fatal on the Continent, so much so that it is invariably excluded from the Italian markets as most pernicious. The most useful and innocent species become poisonous when growing in damp, dark localities, such as old decaying forests and cellars, where there is little circulation of pure air. The late Professor Burnett, in his *Outlines of Botany*, very judiciously remarks, that "in certain situations, truffles, morells, and common mushrooms are nearly flavourless, while in others their grateful tastes and smells are highly developed ; and in a similar way certain fungi, which are eatable in one country or when gathered from one situation, are deleterious when growing in another ; this difference depending upon the greater or less quantity of poisonous matter formed, the production of which may be favoured or suppressed by external physical circumstances, just from the same cause as celery is said to be poisonous, and sea-kale and asparagus not eatable when growing wild ; but which become bland and esculent when chance or culture, by excluding light, prevents the formation of their acrid principle."

The intoxicating Siberian fungus or fly agaric (*Agaricus muscarius*, Fig. 32), may be adduced as an illustration of the remarkable effects produced by some species of fungi, when growing in foreign countries. We have no experience as yet, in this part of Europe, of any effects so extraordinary being produced by any of our native fungi, or even by the same species when growing in the British woods. It is acknowledged to be one of the most poisonous species in this country ; but it does not exhibit its curious properties to the same extent here, as it does beyond the Ural Mountains. In European Russia, and Siberia, this fungus is to the inhabitants what opium and hemp are to the natives of India and China ; cocoa to the Peruvians ; and tobacco to the inhabitants of Europe and North America. The craving for narcotic

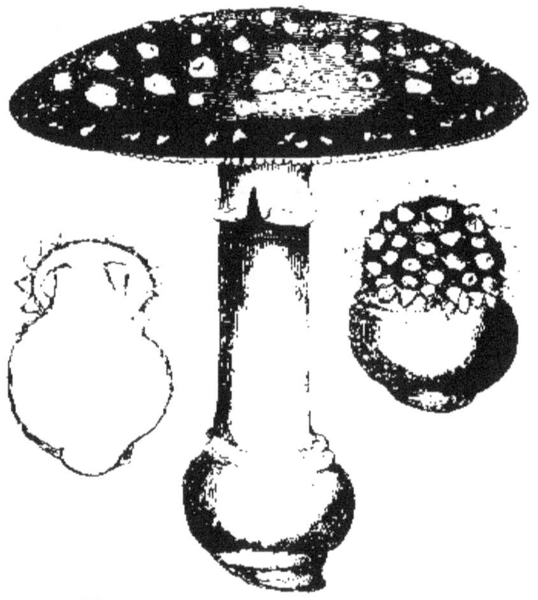

FIG. 32.—AGARICUS MUSCARIUS.

indulgences, so natural to the human race, has, among the Kamtschatkans and Koriacs, found its gratification in an object so low in the scale of nature as a common toad-stool. These races are so dreadfully degraded, that they personify this fungus under the name of Mocho Moro, as one of their household deities, somewhat like the Goddess Siva of the Hindu Thugs; if they are urged by its effects to commit suicide, murder, or some other dreadful crime, they pretend to obey its commands; and, to qualify themselves for premeditated assassination, they have recourse to additional doses of this intoxicating product of decay and corruption.

This plant, around which such a dark and melancholy interest gathers on account of its debasing associations, is by no means rare in this country; in fact, it appears to be very generally distributed throughout the whole of the temperate zone. In the Highlands of Scotland, and the sub-alpine districts of England, it is very common and abundant, particularly in woods of fir and birch, where its tall white stem and rich orange scarlet cap, studded with white scaly warts, frequently of portly dimensions, form a beautiful contrast to the green carpet of moss from which it springs, and the draperies of green foliage that overshadow it. It is exceedingly abundant in some parts of Kamtschatka and the northern districts of Siberia; the ground, in nearly every wood and thicket, being almost concealed by its scarlet sheen. By the natives it is collected during the brief summer months, which in that climate are intensely hot. Sometimes it is plucked up by the roots, and hung up in the air outside their dwellings to dry, and sometimes it is allowed to wither and die untouched in the place where it grows, in which case its narcotic properties are better preserved than when it is gathered and artificially dried. When steeped in the expressed juice of the native whortleberry, it forms a very strong intoxicating kind of wine, which is much relished. But the more common way of using the fungus is to roll it up like a bolus, and swallow it without chewing, which, it is said, would disorder the stomach. Dr. Greville gives some curious particulars regarding this fungus in the fourth volume of the *Wernerian Transactions.* He says: "One large or two small fungi are a common dose to produce a pleasant intoxication for a whole day, particularly if water be drunk after it, which augments the narcotic action. The desired effect comes on from one to two hours after taking the fungus. Giddiness and drunkenness follow in the same manner as from wine or spirits. Cheerfulness is first produced, the face becomes flushed, involuntary words and actions follow, and sometimes at last entire loss of consciousness. It renders some remarkably active, and proves highly stimulant to muscular exertion. By too large a dose violent spasmodic effects are produced. So exciting is it to the nervous system of some individuals, as to produce effects which are very ludicrous. A talkative person cannot keep silence or secrets, one fond of music is perpetually singing, and if a person under its influence wishes to step over a straw or small stick, he takes a stride or a jump sufficient to clear the trunk of a tree." The intoxication produced by this fungus sometimes amounts to absolute delirium, and not unfrequently terminates in convulsions, coma, and death ; and it is a most remarkable fact that it communicates its narcotic properties to the fluids of the debauchee, which, in consequence, are carefully preserved and eagerly consumed during the winter months, when the season of the plant is over, and the stock of dried specimens is exhausted. Thus a whole village is intoxicated through the medium of one man, and one fungus serves to prolong these most fearful and disgusting orgies for many days at a time. It is a singular circumstance that the very same erroneous impressions as to size and distance produced by this plant, are also created by the haschisch of India, and are frequently noticed among idiots and lunatics. It is not improbable that many poor half-demented creatures, particularly if old and ugly, have suffered martyrdom at the stake during the witch-mania of Scotland owing to this natural defect, inability to step over a straw being considered the conclusive test of familiarity with evil spirits !

It is curious to observe how the effects produced by various species of poisonous fungi, should be so very like in many particulars to those produced by alcoholic liquors. The effects in both cases may perhaps be traced to the same cause. Alcohol is the product of fermentation or corruption arrested at a certain stage ; and fungi may also be said to be the products of decaying organic matter, similarly arrested at a certain stage, and embodied in a new form of vegetable growth, the decomposing process in their food being an organizing process in them, or in other words, the force given off in the decomposition of their matrix becoming their "vital force ;" and hence it is but reasonable to expect, when their origin is identical, that their effects should be similar. Into the secrets of nature's laboratory, however, we are not permitted to pry too closely, and "no admittance even on business" is written in large letters above the portals!

Passing from the consideration of the noxious properties of fungi, they exhibit themselves to us now in a more interesting and pleasing aspect as edible substances. In common with several other classes of plants which have the reputation of being poisonous, and yet contain several esculent species invaluable to man, the fungi, although considered as a class dangerous and unwholesome, yet yield in many instances a large and varied supply of palatable and nutritious food. In this world the bitter and the sweet, life and death, are closely mixed up together, and frequently flow from one another; the carrot belongs to the same tribe as the deadly hemlock, the potato is closely allied to the poisonous night-shade; the arrow-root is the innocent product of the fearful woorari poison; and the common edible mushroom, esteemed by rich and poor as a delicious esculent, belongs to an immense family, most of which are suspicious, if not absolutely poisonous, productions. No country is perhaps richer in edible fungi than Great Britain; but such is the extent of wilful ignorance and silly prejudice regarding them, arising from their cold, moist, clammy nature, and the disagreeable situations in which they often grow, that this savoury and important food is year after year allowed to perish ungathered in the woods and fields. Mr. Badham, in his excellent work on the esculent fungi of this country, remarks regarding this culpable neglect: "I have myself witnessed whole hundred-weights of rich wholesome food rotting under trees; woods teeming with food, and not one hand to gather it; and this perhaps in the midst of potato blight, poverty, and all manner of privations, and public prayers against imminent famine. I have indeed been grieved to see pounds innumerable of extempore beefsteaks growing on our oaks in the shape of *Fistulina hepatica; Agaricus fusipes* to pickle in clusters under them; puff-balls, which some of our friends have not inaptly compared to sweetbread, for the rich delicacy of their unassisted flavour; *Hydna* as good as oysters, which they somewhat resemble in taste; *Agaricus deliciosus*, reminding us of tender lamb-kidneys; the beautiful yellow chantarelle, growing by the bushel, and no basket but our own to pick them up; the sweet nutty-flavoured *Boletus*, in vain calling himself *edulis* where there are none to believe him; the dainty Orcella, the *Agaricus heterophyllus*, which tastes like the craw-fish when grilled; the *Agaricus ruber* and *Agaricus virescens*, to cook in any way, and equally good in all; these are among the most conspicuous of the edible funguses."

There are at least thirty kinds of esculent fungi in Great Britain which may be safely used at table, and are as good, if not better than the common mushroom, which appears to be the only species whose merits are at all appreciated. *Agaricus Georgii*, so called from its usually appearing in this country so early as St. George's day—about the beginning of May—though generally rejected by housekeepers in the country as unwholesome, is frequently sold in London, under the name of Whitecaps. The flavour, however, is far inferior to that of the common mushrooms; its smell is strong and unpleasant, and it is little fit for making ketchup, having but a small quantity of juice, and that not of a good colour. It grows to an enormous size, frequently attaining forty inches in circumference, and weighing many pounds. It is easily known by its white pileus and gills, slightly stained with yellow when bruised. In France it is known from its white colour as the *Boule-de-neige.* There is another fungus frequently sold in Covent Garden market under the name of Blewitts, whose taste is very agreeable. This is the *Agaricus personatus*, occurring abundantly in old pastures during the winter months, and often growing gregariously in large rings. It is easily known by its pale bistre or purple-lilac colour, and its rather overpowering odour. Every one is familiar with the common champignon or Scotch bonnets, which form those sour ringlets in the grassy meadows popularly called fairy rings, strangely attributed by some authors to the effects of electricity, and by others, more poetically and quite as truly, ascribed to the fairies as the traces of their moonlight revels. This curious fungus, the *Agaricus oreades* of botanists, though tough and strongly tasted, is sometimes used as an article of food in this country, but too frequently very different and poisonous fungi are gathered under the name. It is almost always gregarious, growing in a centrifugal manner, increasing its circle year by year, while the individuals in the centre decay, and impart by their decay to the grass at the edge a more vivid green than that of the rest of the meadow. Some of the species mentioned in the paragraph quoted from Badham are rather suspicious objects of food, and although they may sometimes be taken with impunity, it is best, as a general rule to avoid them. The *Agaricus ruber*, for instance, is a remarkably beautiful and tempting-looking fungus, having a rich orange or a rose-red cap and snowy gills, but its taste is hot and acrid like that of the mezereon or the cuckoo-pint. Though excellent for food, if properly prepared, it is pronounced by Trattinick to be very unwholesome in a raw state; and M. Roques' account of it is even more unfavourable. The same objection applies to the *Agaricus deliciosus*, said by Badham to remind him of tender lamb-kidneys. The odour and taste of this Agaric are agreeable; but from the account of it given by M. Roques, it would appear that, however delicious, it is not always to be eaten with impunity. These two last mentioned fungi belong to a very remarkable group of the genus Agaricus, called *Galorrheus*, from the milky juice which every part of them exudes when bruised or broken. This milk is like that of the Euphorbia or spurge when pierced, and like it too is frequently extremely acrid, causing irritation and slight inflammation in the parts with which it comes in contact. It is generally white, like cow's milk, but in some species is variously coloured, being of a bright orange in *Agaricus deliciosus*. Like the milk in the laticiferous vessels of the flowering-plants, such as lettuce, dandelion, chicory, and celandine, it exhibits singular movements under the microscope. Minute molecules are observed to move about in it with extreme rapidity, exactly like those observable in gamboge mixed with water. These may be phytozoa, being connected in some mysterious manner with the reproduction of the plant. It is sufficient to mention that this singular group of Agarics contains some of the most poisonous and deadly of all fungi, and that all the species are possessed more or less of the same acrid and narcotic properties, to justify caution in the use of the two members of the group quoted by Badham as esculent, however bland and agreeable they may sometimes be found. With regard to the other species mentioned by this author, they may be used with perfect safety, having stood the test of a pretty long and general experience. Of the *Boletus edulis*, common in woods and pastures all summer and autumn, and easily known by its broad, smooth, dark umber cap, and white tubes and fawn-coloured stipe, Mr. Berkeley observes :—"Though neglected in this country, it appears to be a most valuable article of food. It resembles very much in taste the common mushroom, and is quite as delicate, and might be used with much advantage, as it abounds in seasons when a mushroom is scarcely to be found. Like that, it can be cultivated, but by a much more simple process, as it is merely necessary to moisten the ground under oak-trees with water in which a quantity has been allowed to ferment. The only precaution requisite is to fence in the portion of ground destined for its production, as deer and pigs are very fond of it. This method is said to be infallible, and is practised in France in the Département des Landes."

Next to the common mushroom, the morell (*Morchella esculenta*, Fig. 33) is everywhere esteemed as a valuable and delightful article of food, and as a condiment to heighten the flavour of ragouts. It is unfortunately by no means common in this country. It grows usually in woods, orchards, and cinder-walks in spring and early summer. It presents a singular and easily-identified appearance. It consists of a hollow stem from one to three inches high, surmounted by a round or conical, hollow olive-coloured cap about the size of an egg, with its surface ribbed or latticed with irregular sinuses. Its whole substance is wax-like and friable. We are informed by Gleditch that morells grow in the

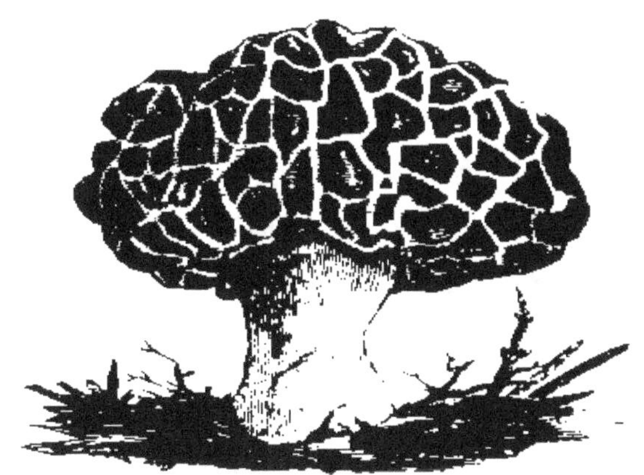

FIG. 33.—MORCHELLA ESCULENTA.
Reduced half size.

woods of Germany, in the greatest profusion in those places where charcoal has been made. Hence those who collect them to sell, receiving a hint how to encourage their growth, have been accustomed to make fires in certain spots in the woods, in order to obtain a more plentiful crop. This strange method of cultivating morells being, however, sometimes attended with dreadful consequences, large woods and plantations being destroyed, the magistrates interposed and put an end to the practice. A nearly allied species, called *Helvella crispa*, is also highly esteemed in some quarters as an agreeable esculent, though hardly known in this country. It is a remarkable-looking fungus, occasionally occurring in woods in autumn. The stem is from three to five inches high, snowy-white, irregular, hollow, deeply furrowed, often full of holes or sinuses like the fluted trunk of the yarroura or paddle-wood of the Indians. The cap is deflexed, and commonly divided into curled or folded lobes which adhere to the stem, but it is extremely irregular and variable, and has neither gills nor pores. Its substance is wax-like and extremely friable, the surface being soft like satin.

The most valuable, however, of all the esculent fungi is probably the truffle (*Tuber cibarium*, Fig. 34). This curious subterranean puff-ball, for such it is, is so local and scarce that it is very little known except amongst wealthy and titled families in this country, seldom appearing at common tables; and probably the greater part of what is sold is imported. It is very rare in Scotland, but exceedingly abundant in some parts of England. It is usually found in beech-woods, growing in clusters half a foot or a foot beneath the soil. In appearance it is a rounded, rough, irregular nodule like a potato; at first white, afterwards black, cracked like a pine-apple, or a pine cone, into

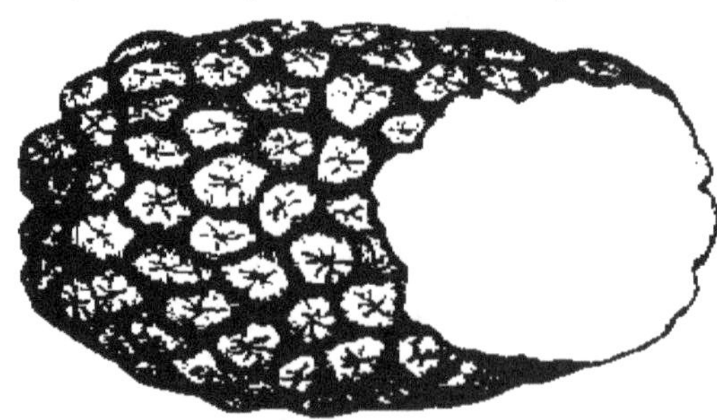

FIG. 34.—TUBER CIBARIUM.

small pyramidal or polyhedrous warts. The internal substance is solid, of a dirty white or pale brown colour, grained like a nutmeg, with darker serpentine lines. The white portions are considered by botanists to be homologous to the mycelium or spawn of other fungi, as their structure is decidedly filamentous; while the veins are the reproductive parts, containing in their cellular tissue minute oval capsules, with two globular, yellowish, warted seeds in their interior. This curious structure, having all the parts of nutrition and reproduction enclosed internally, instead of externally as in other fungi, reminds one of the flower of the fig, which, it is well known, is fixed upon the inside of the receptacle that constitutes the fruit. The truffles of Great Britain seldom exceed three or four ounces in weight; but in Italy and Germany they have occasionally been found weighing eight and even fourteen pounds. They are received at our tables either fresh, and roasted like potatoes, or dried and sliced into ragouts. They are esteemed for their delicious taste, and are much sought for as a luxury, being hunted by dogs trained for the purpose. Pigs are very fond of them, and advantage is taken of their instinctive knowledge of the spots where they are found, and their natural propensity to dig them up, to gather a more plentiful supply than could be obtained by a chance search. Nees von Essenbeck relates an instance of a poor crippled boy who could detect the hiding-places of truffles with more certainty even than the best dogs, and thus earned a comfortable livelihood. They have been successfully cultivated by Bornholz. They are found in dry and light calcareous soil in woods throughout the whole of Europe, as well as in Japan, India, Africa, and New Zealand. "In some parts of France, as in Poitou," says Berkeley, "it is simply necessary, in order to their supply, to enclose a spot on the calcareous downs, sowing it with acorns. As soon as the saplings attain a growth of a few years, the truffles appear, and a harvest is obtained for many years successively without further trouble."

Such is a brief description of almost all the edible fungi known or used in this country; and the fatal mistakes which have been sometimes made, by confounding some of them with nearly allied species of a highly poisonous character, have made them less popular than they deserve, and increased the national disinclination to the use of any fungus save the common mushroom. On the Continent, however, fungi afford not merely a flavouring for a delicate dish, or a pleasant sauce or pickle, but the staple food of thousands of the people; indeed, for several months in the year, especially in Poland and Russia, they constitute not only the staple, but the sole food of the peasantry, and from this circumstance they are called by enthusiastic writers "the manna of the poor." To many who are not reduced by necessity to use them as food, they form a valuable source of income by collecting them for the market. Scarcely any of the four or five hundred species belonging to the genus Agaricus is rejected by the inhabitants of northern Europe, with the exception of the dung and fly Agaric, whose loathsome and poisonous properties are such as to deter the most devoted mycophagist from their use. Even species which are elsewhere universally avoided as poisonous, acrid, or disagreeable, are eaten in these countries with impunity and relish, their noxious properties, if not neutralized by soil and climate, being removed by a process of drying, or pickling in salt and vinegar. M. Roques, in his *Histoire des Champignons*, gives an extremely interesting account of a large variety of fungi which may be used as food. The golmelle of Lorraine (*Agaricus rubescens*); the jozollo of Italy (*Agaricus eburneus*); the verdette and mouceron of the French (*Agaricus virescens* and *prunulus*); the Nagelschwämme of Austria (*Agaricus esculentus*), and the Ziegenbart, and gombas, and Brat-bülz of Germany (*Clavaria coralloides*, and *Boletus bovinus*), abundantly evince the great regard entertained on the Continent for species which, year after year, are suffered to perish unknown and ungathered in this country. The common mushroom is consumed in enormous quantities in Paris, where its flavour is far superior to ours. All the specimens that appear in the market are reared in the catacombs. By some European nations the edible species are eaten raw and uncooked, as they are considered to be more wholesome and nutritious in their natural state. Schwaegrichen informs us, that in consequence of seeing the peasants about Nuremberg eating raw mushrooms, seasoned with anise and carraway-seed, along with their black bread, he resolved to try their effect himself, and that during several weeks he ate nothing but bread and raw fungi, as *Boletus edulis*, *Agaricus campestris*, *Agaricus procerus*, etc., and drank nothing but water, when, instead of finding his health affected, he rather experienced an increase of strength. Many species of fungi have been used for food from time immemorial in China, whose thrifty inhabitants make the most of the productions of their native soil, and easily find substitutes among the cellular plants when their usual food fails them in a season of famine. In India and Africa, likewise, the few edible species that occur have always been highly esteemed; our common ketchup, it may be remarked, being an Indian invention. A kind of fungus called *Mylitta Australis*, which grows on the trunks of trees in Van Diemen's Land, and resembles, when dry, hard compacted lumps of sago, is so frequently used by the aborigines that it is called "native bread;" while in the wild and desolate island of Tierra del Fuego, the inhabitants subsist, during several months, in a great measure, upon a bright-yellow latticed fungus, growing in great abundance on the evergreen beech-trees, and called *Cyttaria Darwinii* after the accomplished naturalist of the "Beagle," and the author of *The Origin of Species.* In New Zealand, the gelatinous volva of a species of Phallus called *Ileodictyon*, is eaten by the natives under the name of thunder-dirt. It has an execrable taste and loathsome smell, in common with the rest of its allies, though its jelly-like consistence would seem to indicate nutritive qualities. Where fungi form the staple or the sole food of the people, it shows that the land is unproductive, or the inhabitants extremely depressed by other causes. In this state the New Zealanders were found by the first emigrants from this country, convulsed and nearly extirpated by intestine wars, and the odious practice of cannibalism, subsisting precariously upon fern roots and fungi, the spontaneous produce of the soil. The land produced no mammal larger than a rat, and yielded neither fruits nor flowers;

ferns and other cryptogamia being the sole vegetation. Since then, however, under the protection of the English Government, and by the aid of British skill and resources, the country has been converted into a luxuriant and fertile garden. The flowerless land can boast of many-coloured gems and delicious fruits amidst the sombre foliage. The soil abundantly rewards the farmer's toil; whilst its green swards make it valuable in the graziers' eyes. The present Maori war shows the high appreciation in which the aborigines hold the advantages of civilisation, and the just value they attach to the possessions which they formerly parted with for a mere trifle, and reveals a striking contrast between their present condition and their savage state less than fifty years ago, when they roamed naked through the waste jungles, and fed upon fern roots and fungi, varied too often by a cannibal feast.

Fungi are to a certain extent capable of artificial propagation, vast quantities of the higher kinds being constantly cultivated for the table. In Italy, a species of Agaric is raised from the grounds of coffee; and a kind of Polyporus, which is greatly relished, is grown simply by singeing the stumps of cob-nut trees, and placing them in a moist, dark cellar. There is a curious production called the fungus-stone, or *Pietra funghaia*,—supposed to be a species of truffle, but in reality nothing more than the spawn or mycelium of *Polyporus tuberaster*, traversing masses of earth which it collects about it in a compact form,—constantly employed for the propagation of that favourite fungus, whose stem and pileus it readily produces when supplied with the requisite conditions of moisture and temperature. The cultivation of the common mushroom is too well known to require comment. Though considered a somewhat precarious crop, it is in the power of almost everybody to grow it, and when carefully conducted it yields a profitable return. This well-known species has almost entirely superseded the wild variety which is now very rarely to be met with in our woods; as is the case with all the animals and plants which man takes under his care and protection. Mushroom spawn is sold by nurserymen in cakes, and for use is broken into pieces of about two ounces weight. When placed either in a cellar, out-house, or shed, where the covering is effective, in a bed of soil well worked into a compost by the droppings of horses and the parings of their hoofs, and allowed to heat to the temperature of new milk, it is certain to produce a plentiful crop. "The common bunt is propagated with certainty by simply rubbing the grains of wheat with the spores; and the rust of the rose (*Coleosporium pingue*) may be communicated to trees hitherto unaffected by watering the ground with a decoction of infected leaves. Finally, the disease of the silkworm and several epizoic fungi are readily propagated by inoculation; while many species of moulds are capable of cultivation in the house, by simply sowing their seed on rice paste, or any other convenient matter."

Fungi afford a remarkable illustration of the fact almost universally observed, that agencies which are generally beneficial sometimes prove destructive. While performing their office as the scavengers of nature, these plants sometimes carry their operations too far, and by their rapid increase, and their devastating effects on the fruits of the earth, cause incalculable damage. Some of the most destructive diseases of the cereal crops are caused by the ravages of microscopic fungi, which attack respectively the flower, the grain, the leaves, the chaff, and the straw. Those who have seen corn-fields in July, when the flower is bursting *through the sheath, must* have often noticed several *greyish-black heads* appearing here and there among the verdant stalks. In some fields these are few and far between; in others they are more numerous, almost every alternate stalk presenting this amorphous appearance. When one of the heads thus affected is pulled and examined, every chaffy scale is found to be filled with a firm black matter, like soot agglutinated by moisture. This strange phenomenon is attributed to the state of the air, to the condition of the seed, or to the character of the soil; but there are few comparatively who are aware of its vegetable origin,—who know that it is owing to the development of minute parasitic fungi, favoured of course by unhealthy conditions of the atmosphere and the soil. To botanists it is known under the name of

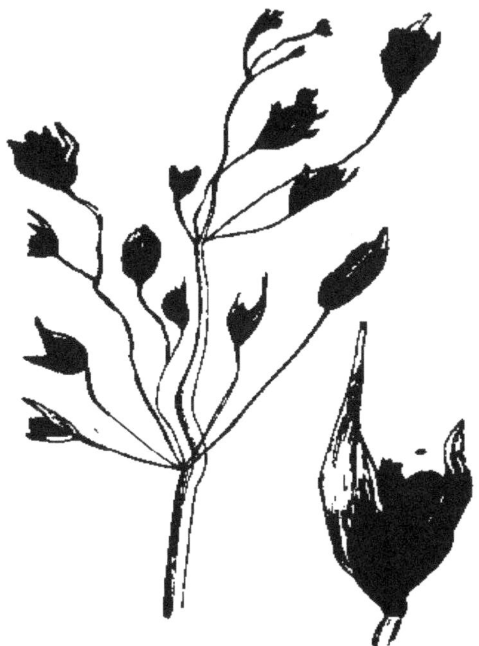

FIG. 35.—UREDO SEGETUM.

*Uredo segetum* (Fig. 35), and by farmers it is familiarly called smut or dust-brand. It is more frequent in corn than in any other of the cereal crops. Examined under the microscope each grain is found to be converted into a vast number of minute round balls or sporules of a deep brownish-black colour. Bauer says that in the 16,000th part of a square inch he counted forty-nine of those sporules, so that four millions of them may exist in a single grain of corn. On the grains of wheat an equally common but still more injurious fungus is developed called bunt (*Uredo caries*, Fig. 36). In this disease the seeds retain their original form and appearance, but the inside is completely converted into one mass of black sporidia, of a much larger size than the sporules of the preceding species, and containing granules within them. The ears thus infected are completely spoiled, and give out an exceedingly fœtid odour when crushed. Every farmer

FIG. 36.—UREDO CARIES. Spores and Mycelium highly magnified.

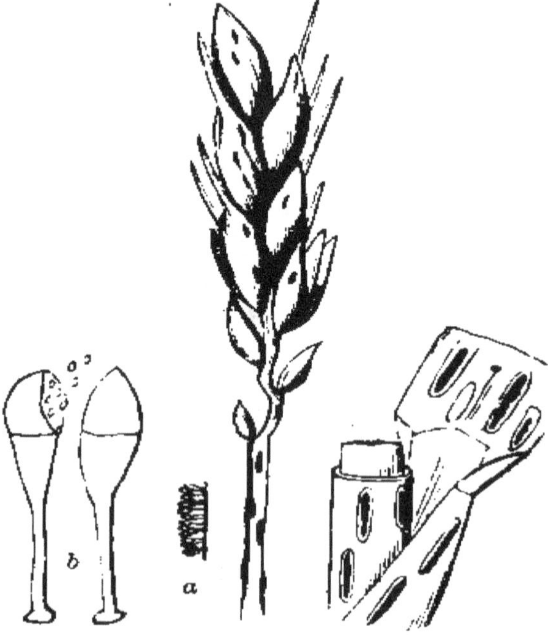


FIG. 37.—PUCCINIA GRAMINIS. (a) Slightly magnified. (b) Sporidia, highly magnified.

has painful knowledge of the disease called mildew (*Puccinia Graminis*, Fig. 37). It attacks the leaves and culms of corn, as well as many of the grasses employed in hay-making, and proves most injurious when developed to a great extent, as is often the case when severe frost immediately succeeds copious and continuous rain in autumn. It appears on the diseased leaves in pale whitish spots, which speedily diffuse themselves, and become confluent, until the whole plant is covered. These whitish spots, under the microscope, are found to consist of a number of filaments aggregated together, on each of which are situated two or three small cells, at first green, then black; the upper one being filled with a large quantity of minute spores. Another parasitic fungus, to which the name of mildew has been sometimes applied, is frequently developed in the same situations, but it is not nearly so injurious as the true mildew. It is known as rust (*Uredo rubigo*, Fig. 38), and consists of yellow oval spots scattered on the parts affected. The spores, which are of a red-brown colour, and exceedingly numerous and minute, are very easily dispersed.

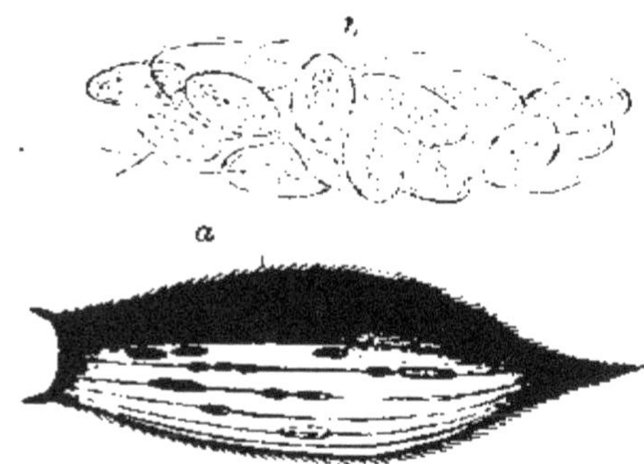


FIG. 38.—UREDO RUBIGO.
(*a*) Diseased chaff-scale. (*b*) Spores.

One of the most remarkable diseases affecting the cereals is ergot. Though found in various kinds of grasses, such as Agrostis, Festuca, Elymus, and Dactylis, this disease is most frequently produced in rye, and hence it is commonly known as ergot of rye. It is not very common, although diffused in greater or less abundance throughout the whole of Great Britain; but in the zone where rye is the prevailing grain, comprehending all the countries bordering on the Baltic, the north of Germany, and part of Siberia, it occurs in great abundance, and is often a cause of much distress. It is owing to the growth of a fungus called *Spermoedia clavus*, which converts the ovary of the grain into an elongated cylindrical excrescence, a little curved, and somewhat resembling a horn or spur projecting from the chaff, and hence the rye thus affected is called in common language spurred-rye. The grain when attacked becomes first soft and pulpy, afterwards it hardens and elongates gradually. It is first of a red or violet colour, afterwards lead-coloured, and finally black with a white interior. Generally only two or three grains in a spike are affected, whose nutritious part is thus completely destroyed, and converted into a highly injurious substance. When rye is extensively cultivated, grains thus diseased often compose a considerable part of the bread produced, and thus not unfrequently give rise to one of the most fearful and distressing diseases with which the human frame is affected. Those who live upon it are afflicted with general weakness, and a sense as if insects were creeping over the skin, then the extremities become cold and insensible; next, excruciating pains are felt; and, lastly, there is dry gangrene, and the fingers and toes drop off. Strange to say, however, the children in some parts of the north of Europe eat with impunity immense quantities of this diseased rye, under the name of St. John's Bread. This is an extraordinary instance of the uncertain effects of the same species of fungi upon the human constitution, and the wide differences they exhibit in their qualities in different countries.

Such are some of the most destructive diseases of the cereal crops; and they show to us in a most striking manner how the welfare, nay the very existence of man himself, may be endangered by the growth of the minutest and humblest plants. It is not difficult to imagine the fearful consequences that would ensue, were these plants to spread universally over all the cereal crops, and convert their nutritious substances into black rottenness and ashes. Not all the vast revenues and resources of England would avail to avert the dreadful results. All the other riches in the world, failing the riches of our golden harvest-fields, were as worthless as the false notes of the forger. How precarious then is the independence of the most independent! As we approach the season of harvest, we are within a month or two of absolute starvation. Were the rust, or the mildew, or the smut to blight our fields; were each spore of the many millions which each individual of these plants disseminates, to germinate and become fertile on the grains on which it alighted, the scourge would be more terrible than the bloodiest and most devastating campaign; the rich and the poor, the nobleman and the beggar, the Queen and her subjects, would alike be swept into a common ruin. But the covenant promise made to Noah endures from age to age, and from year to year, in all its integrity, even in the most unpropitious circumstances; and that kind and watchful Providence, which supplies the large family of mankind with its daily bread, arrests the development and dispersion of these vegetable epidemics, and leaves us even in the worst seasons a reasonable supply of the first necessary of life, thus presenting a sublime fact upon which faith, which is better than independence, can rest in peace!

The failure of the potato crop, which several years ago came like one of those sudden and unexpected hurricanes of the tropics, carrying death and desolation in their train, is doubtless vivid in the recollection of all. This root, from its extraordinary productiveness, with little labour or exertion of any kind, became gradually a substitute in whole districts, especially in Ireland and the Highlands of Scotland, for the older cereal crops, as the staple food of the people; so that when a blight fell upon it, and the crop everywhere completely failed, hundreds of thousands were deprived of their sole means of subsistence, famine and its consequent malignant fevers rapidly spread throughout the land, and the social and agricultural system based upon this uncertain and narrow foundation was convulsed and completely broken up. Various attempts have been made to account for this melancholy failure. Some have attributed it to the attacks of the *Aphis rapæ*, a most rapacious and prolific insect; others to unfavourable atmospheric conditions; and a third class to the growth of minute parasitic fungi or mould. The truth in all likelihood lies in a combination of the two last opinions; the one being the predisposing cause, and the other the consequent effect. A minute fungus, called *Botrytis infestans* (Fig. 39), consisting of grey interwoven filaments, bearing a jointed stalk which branches at the top, each division carrying a rounded spore, appears to be almost invariably connected with the disease, and is found on the decaying plants ; the growth of the fungus being probably aided by some predisposition in the state of the vegetable, induced by the soil or the atmosphere. The epidemic was not confined to the potatoes grown in this country, but seems to have prevailed throughout the world, attacking indiscriminately all the cultivated varieties, as well as the wild plants in their original centre of distribution, the lower mountain plateaus on the western coast of South

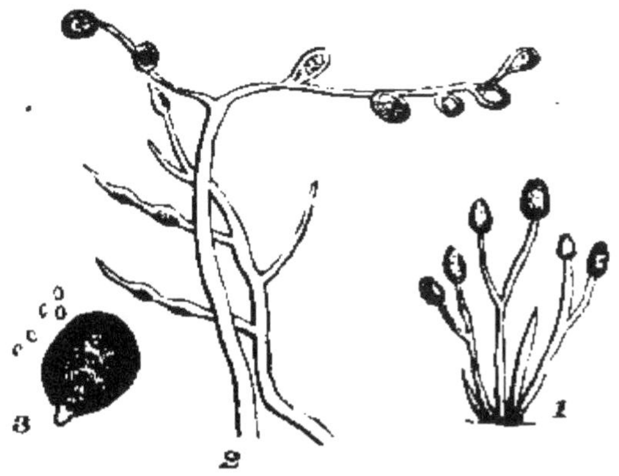


FIG. 89.—BOTRYTIS INFESTANS.
(1.) Young plants ; (2.) Full grown ; (3.) Spore.—All magnified.

America. This singular fact, while it shows that neither the soil, climate, nor mode of farming in this country was the sole cause, clearly establishes the vegetable origin of the disease. It may be remarked that the potato is commonly attacked after the tubers have been formed, and have attained a considerable size. The leaves are usually the first parts affected, becoming tinged with a bluish-brown spot on the under side ; and from thence it spreads rapidly down the stem, till in a very short time the whole of the plant above ground is destroyed and rotten. The disease still spreads its ravages, until ultimately it reaches the tubers, the substance of which, when affected, speedily turns brown, emits a very peculiar and unpleasant odour, and soon decays to a fetid watery matter. The filaments of the fungus are frequently seen ramifying through their cellular tissue. No certain preventive of this destructive murrain has yet been discovered, notwithstanding the many plans proposed, which fail as often as they succeed. The cause, though still in operation, however, seems of

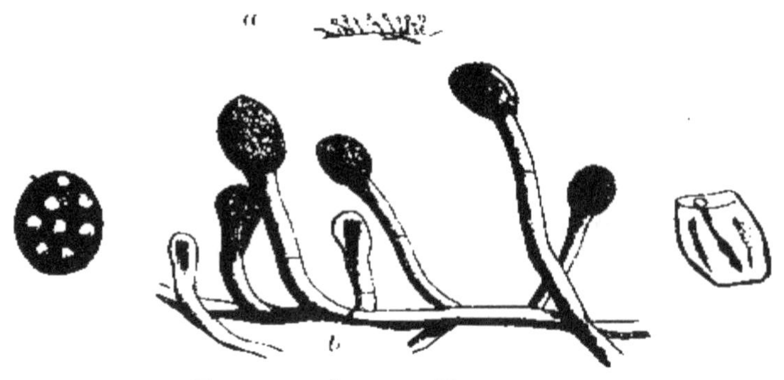

FIG. 40.—OIDIUM TUCKERI.

(*a*) Natural size. (*b*) Magnified.

late years to have somewhat abated in virulence, so that there is yet some chance of again rearing successfully this most useful and important esculent. A somewhat similar disease, it may be added, affects beet-root, spinach, peas, and other garden vegetables.

There is a peculiar disease which has of late years proved most destructive to the vine on the Continent, produced by the attack of a minute fungus, called the grape oidium (*Oidium Tuckeri*, Fig. 40). It affects the leaves and stem indiscriminately; but its favourite growing-places appear to be the grapes, whose succulent saccharine juices supply it with abundant nutriment. It shows itself principally upon the young grape when about the size of a pea. The slightest injury from a touch or an insect, affords it a basis of propagation, and once established, it increases with amazing rapidity, frequently blasting the hopes of the grape-harvest over many districts. Its effect upon the grape is to absorb the juices of the superficial cells of the cuticle, which consequently cease to expand with the pulp of the fruit; it then bursts, dries up, and is finally destroyed. To the naked eye the plant appears a mere effused, indefinite, white patch; under the microscope it resolves itself into a collection of little, downy heaps, with egg-like sporidia arising from the necklace joints of the threads.

The following report of its devastating effects may be interesting:—"In 1847, the spores of this oidium reached France, and were found in the forcing-houses of Versailles, and other places near Paris. The disease soon reached the trellised vines, and destroyed the grapes out of doors in the neighbourhood, and continued to extend from place to place; but, until 1850, it was chiefly observed in vineries, which lost from this cause, season after season, the whole of their crops. Unhappily in 1851, it was found to have extended to the south and south-west of France and Italy, and the grapes were so affected that they either decayed, or the wine made from them was detestable. In 1852, the *Oidium Tuckeri* re-appeared in France with increased and fatal energy; it crossed the Mediterranean to Algeria, has shown itself in Syria and Asia Minor, attacked the muscat grapes at Malaga, injured the vines in the Balearic Islands, utterly destroyed the vintage in Madeira, greatly injured it in the Greek Islands, and destroyed the currants in Zante and Cephalonia, rendering them almost unfit for use, and so diminished the supply that 500 gatherers did the ordinary work of 8000! But it is in France that its frightful ravages are chiefly to be regarded as a national calamity, where the produce of the soil in wine is said to exceed 500 millions of hectolitres; two-fifths of the usual quantity of wine made there has been destroyed, and what has been made is bad. The vineyards of the Médoc, in 1851, were untouched, and the cultivators laughed at the existence of the oidium; but last year the disease showed itself everywhere in the Gironde, even to the borders of the Médoc, with serious injury. The eastern Pyrenees were all deplorably affected, and at Frontignan and Lunel the vineyards were abandoned in despair. Thousands of labourers were thrown out of employ, and the distress was awful. Wine, in France, is the common drink of the peasant; upon this, his bread, and some legumes, he labours; but the wine, bad as it is, has risen to double, and, in the countries most injured, treble its ordinary price." Strange to say, "the vine mildew does not occur in the United States on native vines, but only on those which are imported; and the American varieties cultivated in Switzerland and elsewhere are uniformly exempt."

A very familiar example of an oidium occurs on decaying oranges, commencing at first in minute, distinct, pulverulent spots, which speedily become confluent, and of a deep greenish-grey tinge. This genus of fungi is very destructive to fruits of all kinds ; and one species commits great ravages on peach-trees, peas, and cabbages. The *blanc de rosier*, which infests rose-bushes, is also an ally of this destructive corps. The year 1854 proved most disastrous to the hop-growers in many districts, owing to the ravages of an oidium. The lover of fruit may have often noticed thin concentric, cream-coloured, or fawn-coloured patches on the skin of apples, pears, and plums, producing very rapid decay. These patches are caused by *Oidium fructigenum*, which, when it has once obtained possession of a tree, spreads with fatal rapidity, destroying the fruit while still hanging on the branches.

All the mildews and blights hitherto described are light-coloured ; but there is another class of fungi equally destructive, called black mildews. They are caused principally by species of Antennaria and allied genera, which form thick, black, felt-like patches on leaves, disfiguring trees, and injuring them fatally, by closing up their pores, and preventing the free admission of the air ; as also by depriving them of the full, direct light of the sun. They are principally developed on those leaves which had previously been covered with the honey-dew of the aphides or plant-lice ; and as these little creatures cluster together and impair the vitality of whole trees and forests, it may easily be seen how extensive are the ravages of the fungi which are thus developed. In the Azores the orange-groves have suffered dreadfully from this cause ; while in Ceylon the coffee-plantations, and in the south of Europe the olive-trees, have sustained of late years immense damage from an unusual development of black mildews. Few objects, it may be remarked, are more beautiful under the microscope than the wheel-shaped, ray-like processes which radiate from the seed-bearing organs. These sporiferous bodies sometimes contain a perfect miniature plant or embryo, similar to that of flowering plants, which waits only circumstances favourable for its expansion. Another allied species, called *Fusarium mori*, is produced in such abundance on the leaves of the mulberry, in Syria and China, as materially to diminish the supply of food provided for the silk-worm.

But it is not only in food and luxuries that man

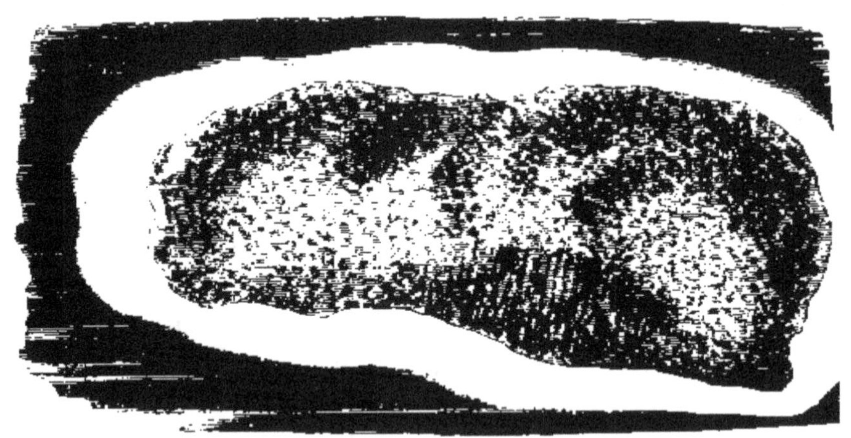

FIG. 41.—MERULIUS LACHRYMANS.

suffers from the ravages of fungi ; he also suffers in his property. Builders have painful knowledge of one or two species, known under the common name of dry-rot. This most destructive plague is usually caused in this country by the *Merulius lachrymans* (Fig. 41). It occurs on the inside of wainscoting, in the hollow trunks of trees, in the timber of ships, and in the floors and beams of buildings in moist, warm situations, where there is not a free circulation of air. It appears at first in round, white, cottony patches, from one to eight inches broad, which afterwards develop over their whole surface a number of fine, yellow, orange, or reddish-brown irregular folds, most frequently so arranged as to have the appearance of pores, and distilling drops of moisture when perfect ; whence its specific name. In the mature state it produces an immense number of minute, rusty sporules, which alight and speedily vegetate in the circumjacent timber, however sound and dry it may appear, destroying its elasticity and toughness, and rendering it incapable of resisting any pressure, until gradually it crumbles into dry, brown dust. This insidious disease, once established, spreads with amazing rapidity, destroying some of the best and most solid-looking houses in a few years. The ships in the Crimea suffered more from this cause than from the ravages of fire, or the shot and shells of the enemy. So virulent is its nature, that it extends from the woodwork of a house even to the walls themselves, and by penetrating their interstices, crumbles them into pieces. "I knew," says Professor Burnett, "a house into which the rot gained admittance, and which, during the four years we rented it, had the parlours twice wainscoted, and a new flight of stairs, the dry-rot having rendered it unsafe to go from the ground floor to the bed-rooms. Every precaution was taken to remove the decaying timbers when the new work was done ; yet the dry-rot so rapidly gained strength that the house was ultimately pulled down. Some of my books which suffered least, and which I still retain, bear mournful impressions of its ruthless hand; others were so much affected that the leaves resemble tinder, and when the volumes were opened, fell out in dust or fragments." There are no means of restoring to a sound state timber thus decayed; and the dry-rot can only be cured or prevented from spreading by removing the affected parts, clearing away all the fungi, and destroying —by a strong solution of iron, copper, or zinc—the vegetative sporules with which the stones upon which the timbers rest may have been impregnated. Many practical persons have written upon this disease; and the remedies proposed are as numerous as their authors. But the only certain preventives of the evil seem to be the removal of the decaying and contagious matter, the impregnation of the surrounding wood with a strong solution of corrosive sublimate, or the white of an egg, and the admission of a free current of air. Much also may be done by cutting timber, destined for building purposes, in winter, when fungi are usually dormant or dead, and properly seasoning it by steeping it in water for some time, and then thoroughly drying it before it is used. Houses, in order to be free from this plague, should be built in dry, open, and airy situations, and efficiently ventilated throughout every part, especially of the wood-work; when these conditions are observed, this evil will disappear.

In concluding this notice of the destructive fungi, mention may be made of a peculiar form of Penicillium or mould, which is almost invariably present in the solution of copper employed in the process of electrotyping. It proves an intolerable nuisance, inasmuch as it is often invested with a silver coat, and injures the beauty and the finish of the articles which are subjected to the process. It is extraordinary that the poisonous nature of the solution does not destroy it ; but it has been often observed that various species of mould luxuriate in solutions of arsenic, opium, and other poisonous chemical substances, which would prove instantly fatal to all other plants.

It is worthy of remark that the destructive effects of all these parasitic fungi may, in most circumstances, be easily neutralized or prevented by a little intelligent forethought, care, and industry; and providing incentives as they do to the exercise of these qualities, they compensate morally in some measure for the physical evils they occasion. Certain conditions are necessary for their development, and it is to obviating and removing these, that the builder and the farmer must look for exemption from the destructive vegetable diseases that affect their properties. It has been ascertained, for instance, that rust and blight arise from the over-manuring of fields; the grain gorged with too copious a supply of nutritious juices, being brought into a favourable condition for the development of the dormant seeds of fungi which the wind may have wafted to it. The tendency in corn to form these diseases therefore may be destroyed by steeping the seed before sowing in a corrosive solution or in brine ; but the same end may be secured in a dry season, and on a favourable soil, by moderate manuring, or by a free use of saline manures.

With regard to the mildew in wheat, it has been suggested by Mr. Tycho Wing, as a remedy, to allow no reeds or loose grass to remain in the ditches, but to clear everything away, and to consume it at once. "As the species which attacks reeds and grass is to all appearance the same with that of the wheat, the disease may be propagated in the spring from such outliers. For the same reason, it is desirable that the stubble should not be left on the land too long, and, indeed, long mowing must be better than reaping." The various mildews that appear on the grape and other fruits and useful plants, may easily be prevented from developing themselves by the application, at an early stage, of powdered sulphur, which, combining as it does with the oxygen of the atmosphere, forms sulphuric acid, the only chemical poison destructive to moulds and mildews.

Fungi, owing to their cellular and perishable nature, do not usually occur in a fossil state. Some slight traces of them, however, now and then occur among the relics of a former state of things. Species of mould have occasionally been found in the amber beds of the tertiary formation—having been deposited and developed on the resinous juices of the amber pines, just as filaments of mould are often seen at the present day adhering to the gum of apricot and cherry trees. These tiny plants, identical as they are with the common green and blue moulds that infest our cupboards, leave us no room to doubt that fungi were as prevalent and destructive in former epochs as they are now. M. Goeppert, who has examined minutely the amber of various lands, has detected in it, besides moulds, fragments of mosses, hepaticæ, and lichens, perfectly preserved, as in a mummy case,—the sole insignificant relics of that vast array of cryptogamic plants, which preserved the balance between the animal and the vegetable kingdoms of the ancient world. Nature, by this curious process of embalming, has perpetuated that which a breath of wind was sufficient to destroy, and moulded into a geologic specimen what a finger's touch would fade. While rocks and forests have been destroyed, without leaving a recognisable trace of their existence behind, the most delicate and fugacious organisms have been handed down to us in the most beautiful preservation from the remote post-pliocene period—the temporal and fragile thus transformed into the eternal.

There is a curious association connected with one of the lowest species of fungi, which shows in a very striking manner the importance of the smallest objects, and their claim to a closer attention than we are accustomed to give them. During the voyage of Captain Penny in search of Sir John Franklin, two pieces of floating drift-wood were picked up in the Arctic regions, beyond the utmost wanderings of the Esquimaux, which, from several unusual appearances presented by them, excited more interest than such a trivial incident in ordinary circumstances would deserve. The one was found in Robert's Bay, off Hamilton's Island, lat. 76° 2′ north, long. 76° west, in the supposed route of the Erebus and Terror through Wellington Channel, and was evidently a fragment of wrought elm plank which had formed part of a ship's timbers. It exhibited three kinds of surface; one that had been planed and painted with pitch, one merely roughly sawn, and the third split with an axe. The other piece of drift-wood was picked up by Mr. Goodsir, on the north side of Cornwallis Island, in lat. 75° 36′ north, and long. 96° west. It was a branch of white spruce, very much bleached in some places, and in others charred and blackened as if it had been used for firewood. On both these fragments of wood traces of minute microscopic vegetation were observed, which, it was hoped, if properly investigated, would throw some indirect light upon the mysterious fate of the missing expedition, by indicating the probable course pursued, and the approximate date. For this purpose they were submitted to the Rev. Mr. Berkeley, who examined them microscopically with the most minute attention, and sent a report to the Admiralty upon the subject, which is published in detail in "Sutherland's Journal of a Voyage in Baffin's Bay in 1850-1851." This accomplished naturalist found the vegetation in both cases to be very similar to the mottled patches of a dark-olive colour, with which rails and wooden structures in this country, exposed to atmospheric changes, are speedily covered, and which form the incipient or the mature stages of the simplest cryptogamic plants. The bleached cells and fibres of the fragment of elm were gorged and interwoven with slender mycelia, while on its different surfaces appeared several dark-coloured specks, referred to the genus Phoma, one of the simplest and minutest fungi. They consisted merely of a grumous nucleus, containing sporidia in a mature state, and included in a naked tubercle,—examples of which may be seen about the end of autumn on withered willow-leaves, decaying stems of dahlias, and very frequently on fallen oak-leaves. As it was exceedingly improbable that these minute plants could have retained, throughout the intense cold of an Arctic winter, their delicate naked spores in the state of perfection in which they were found, it was inferred that they must have been developed during that same summer ; while from four to five years, or even less, in such high latitudes, amid all the severities of stormy ice-covered seas, would suffice to produce the bleached appearance which the wood exhibited. All the circumstances of comparison between similar bleaching processes and similar vegetable growths in this country, are in favour of a recent exposure of the Arctic plank.

As regards the vegetation on the other piece of drift-wood, Mr. Berkeley found on its bleached surfaces a few deeply imbedded minute black spots, very similar to those of the *Lepraria nigra*, which in a confluent state frequently forms wide inky or sooty patches on the squared tops of rails and gate-posts, and especially on the roots of felled oaks smoothed with the axe, in moist situations. On account of this resemblance, this obscure and anomalous production has been called *Sporodermium lepraria*. A closer relation than usual must subsist between it and its matrix, for it is always found to accompany the white spruce, as far as its branches are drifted by the waves. Unlike the Phomas on the Arctic elm, which are very ephemeral, this plant, with its lichen-like habit and appearance, shares the longevity characteristic of that tribe—the same patches lasting for years unchanged on the same piece of wood, and leaving behind traces of their existence for a long time, even when the surrounding tissues are abraded by the elements, and the surfaces worn away. The state in which the specks of it existed on the drifted wood, would seem to indicate that they had not been recently formed, at least during the summer in which they were found, but, on the contrary, that they were the remains of the species which existed on the drift-wood when used for fuel by the crews of the Erebus and Terror. There can be no doubt whatever, considering the circumstances in which they were found, and the peculiar appearances they presented, that both these fragments of wood were connected with the ill-fated ships; and the curious information regarding the course they pursued at a particular time, afforded by such extraordinary and unlikely witnesses as a few tiny, dark specks of cryptogamic vegetation on floating drift-wood, was wonderfully confirmed by the recent discovery of the first authentic account ever obtained of the melancholy history of the lost expedition.

Having thus given a somewhat lengthened and detailed account of the structure, properties, uses, and other peculiarities of this curious and interesting tribe of plants, it may be proper, in conclusion, to glance at the place which they occupy as æsthetic objects in this fair creation. The careful observer will find the universal spirit of beauty sometimes as aptly and richly represented in these productions of corruption and decay, as in the more admired products of the vegetable kingdom. The very commonest fungi, which grow in the darkest and dreariest spots, are invested with a beauty, not absolutely essential to the part which they perform in the operations of nature, or to the efficiency of the organs, whether of absorption or reproduction, with which they are furnished. The fructification of one is a most graceful umbrella, adorned with varied, delicately-shaded hues, and with exquisitely carved veils, fringes, and gills ; that of another presents the most beautifully sculptured ivory pores and sinuosities, or richly-coloured tubes or spikes. One species looks like a ruby cup ; another is embossed with stars ; while the leaves and the grasses of the woods and fields often form niduses for some of the loveliest and strangest forms, which our great Creator has scattered over the earth with lavish hand to delight the intelligent and observant eye. There is not in nature a more picturesque object to the painter, or a more interesting study to the botanist, than the old decaying stump of a tree in some lonely unvisited haunt of a shady ancestral wood, where the soil, enriched by the organic contributions of centuries, is bursting into life through every crevice and in every inch. Such a stump, as Wordsworth beautifully says of the mountain, is "familiar with forgotten years." It is long since the tall massive oak which it supported has been removed by the axe, leaving a gap which the encroaching trees around strive in vain to conceal ; and nature has kindly smoothed away the traces of man's harsh treatment, and brought it back to perish on its own bosom. Every sunbeam and rain-drop that descended upon it, while crumbling it more, increased its picturesqueness, and while depriving it of its own life, helped to develop upon it other forms of life lower in the scale, until now, it not only adds to the air of antique mystery which pervades the scene, but peoples it with all the fantastic tenantry of Shakspere's fairy land. In one corner may be observed a cluster of elegant pearl-like mushrooms, wee elfin-looking things with long, black stalks, and white wheel-like heads; in another, the corky leaves of a Thelephora closely pressed to the wood, with shell-like patterns, and colours as beautifully and dimly shaded on its surface as in a misty rainbow; here the soft, viscid, flesh-like knobs of the *Tremella sarcoides*, resembling tiny teats,—or the wrinkled, quaking, gelatinous mass of the witches' butter, looking more like a frothy exudation from the stump itself than a plant; there a Spathularia protruded from a wide mouth-like gap, like an old woman's tongue, frightening away every young rustic, full of the adventures and transformations of the seven champions of Christendom, from plucking it off, lest the owner, a metamorphosed witch perhaps, should return in proper person to demand her unruly member, and inflict a proportionate punishment; in the middle of the squared top, covered with the minute scurf-like germs of unknown plants, are clustered the beautiful round vermilion balls of the Lycogala, or wolf's milk, which, when bruised, exude a dark, grumous liquor like clotted blood; while springing from the crevices of the bark, near the ground, the *Agaricus necator* overtops the rest, with its zoned and olive-coloured cap and dusky stem, distilling, when broken or injured, a blood-like fluid, as though it were a sensitive creature, thus reminding one of Dante's terrific picture of the living forest in the infernal regions. All these, with a score of other curious microscopic plants, hiding themselves from the superficial observer, but revealing themselves openly to a close and minute scrutiny,—cup-lichens and trailing green mosses, and slimy green dustlike confervæ, surrounded perhaps with a border of dock-leaves, or a fringe of palmy ferns,—invest the aged stump with a nameless charm in the estimation of all true lovers of the picturesque. And returning from the woods and the fields to the retirement of our own homes, we find that there are forms and living things to be seen there as beautiful, interesting, and suggestive of curious thought, as any we have seen in the wider field of nature out of doors. If we examine under the microscope the green or grey covering which spreads over damp walls, or envelopes a stale piece of bread or fruit in a cupboard, or creams over the surface of preserves, what a wonderful scene of beauty suddenly unfolds itself like a miracle to our view! Thousands of plumy trees and feathery fern-like plants rear themselves up in every conceivable attitude, and all so delicate and transparent that the minute seeds are seen lodged in the interior of their stems; luxuriant forests draperied with pendent parasites, and milk-white mosses enveloping the ground, and clothing old, rotten-looking stumps with beauty, all busy in the fulfilment of their offices, lengthening and swelling, and falling, and scattering their minute seeds in little white clouds up and down upon the surrounding air. He who is privileged to feast his eyes on such a beautiful and instructive spectacle as this, must deeply feel with the eloquent Ruskin, that "the Spirit of God works everywhere alike, covering all lonely places with an equal glory, using the same pencil, and outpouring the same splendour in the obscurest nooks, in spots foolishly deemed waste, and amongst the simplest and humblest organisms, as well as in the star-strewn spaces of heaven, and amongst the capable witnesses of His working."

# INDEX OF SCIENTIFIC NAMES.


PAGE

Achlya prolifera, . . . . 234
Æthalium, . . . . . 227
Agaricus campestris, . . . 263
—— deliciosus, . 255, 257
—— eburneus, . . 263
—— esculentus, . . 263
—— Georgii, . . . 263
—— fusipes, . . . 255
—— heterophyllus, . . 255
—— muscarius, . . 250
—— emeticus, . . 246
—— necator, . . . 288
—— olearius, . . . 193
—— oreades, . . . 256
—— procerus, . 212, 263
—— prunulus, . . 263
—— personatus, . . 256
—— ruber, . . . 257
—— rubescens, . . 263
—— virescens, . . 263
Antennaria, . . . . 277
Alectoria jubata, . . . 97
Acetabularia, . . . . 165
Ascomycetes, . . . . 218
Aspergillus glaucus, . . 235

Bartramia fontana, . . . 42
Batrachospermum moniliforme, 162
Bæomyces, . . . . . 66
Boletus edulis, . 255, 258, 263
—— bovinus, . . . 263
—— æneus, . . . 195
Botrytis infestans, . . . 272
—— bassiana, . . . 233
Borrera flavicans, . . . 110
Bovista gigantea, . . . 119
Botrydium granulatum, . . 164
Bryum serpens, . . . 29

Calicium, . . . . . 66
Caulerpa, . . . . . 165
Cetraria Islandica, . . . 96
Chroolepus aureus, . . . 104
—— ebeneus, . . . 141
Cladonia rangiferina, . . 80
Clathrus, . . . . . 206

PAGE

Cladophora mirabilis, . . 165
Chionyphe, . . . . 229
Clavaria coralloides, . . 263
Coleosporium pingue, . . 266
Conferva rivularis, . . 128
—— melagonium, . . 165
Coniomycetes, . . . . 217
Cornicularia aculeata, . . 118
Cyttaria Darwinii, . . . 266

Diatomaceæ, . . . . 174
Dicranum bryoides, . . . 40
Didymium, . . . . . 227

Exidium auricula Judæ, . 210
Enteromorpha intestinalis, . 163
Evernia, . . . . 102, 110

Favularia, . . . . . 60
Fistulina hepatica, . 205, 209
Funaria hygrometrica, . . 44
Fusarium Mori, . . . 278

Gallorrheus, . . . . 216
Gasteromycetes, . . . . 216
Gymnostomum truncatulum, 43
Gyrophora cylindrica, . . 99

Halimeda, . . . . . 165
Helvella crispa, . . . . 260
Hepatica officinarum, . . 53
Hydrodictyon utriculatum, . 132
Hygrocrocis, . . . . 140
Hymenomycetes, . . . 216
Hyphomycetes, . . . . 217
Hydnum, . . . . . 255
Hypochnus rubro-cinctus, . . 91

Ileodictyon, . . . . . 264
Isaria, . . . . . . 230

Jungermannia complanata, . 48

Lecanora esculenta, . . . 102
—— tartarea, . . . 116
—— parella, . . . 118

| | PAGE |
|---|---|
| Lecidea, | 78 |
| Lemania fluviatilis, | 131 |
| Lycopodium clavatum, | 54 |
| —— selago, | 54 |
| —— alpinum, | 54 |
| —— cernum, | 55 |
| —— denticulatum, | 57 |
| —— catharticum, | 58 |
| Lepidodendron, | 59 |
| Lecidea geographica, | 80 |
| Lepraria Jolithus, | 66 |
| —— Kermesina, | 146 |
| —— nigra, | 285 |
| Lanosa nivalis, | 230 |
| Lysurus Mokusin, | 247 |
| Lycogala, | 288 |
| | |
| Marchantia polymorpha, | 51 |
| Merulins lachrymans, | 278 |
| Morchella esculenta, | 259 |
| Mucor Mucedo, | 236 |
| Mycodermata, | 236 |
| Mylitta Australis, | 264 |
| | |
| Neckera crispa, | 44 |
| Nostoc commune, | 159 |
| | |
| Oidium Tuckeri, | 274 |
| —— fructigenum, | 277 |
| Opegrapha scripta, | 67 |
| Oscillatoria nigra, | 135 |
| —— rubescens, | 153 |
| | |
| Parmelia parietina, | 119 |
| Palmella cruenta, | 147 |
| —— prodigiosa, | 151 |
| —— montana, | 161 |
| Peltidea apthosa, | 105 |
| —— canina, | 105 |
| Peziza vesiculosa, | 216 |
| Phoma, | 284 |
| Plica Polonica, | 288 |
| Phallus impudicus, | 199 |
| —— fœtidus, | 206 |
| Polytrichum commune, | 41 |
| Polyporus tuberaster, | 265 |
| —— sanguineus, | 226 |
| —— xanthopus, | 226 |
| —— vesiculosus, | 216 |
| —— squamosus, | 205 |

| | PAGE |
|---|---|
| Polyporus fomentarius, | 247 |
| Protococcus nivalis, | 141 |
| —— viridis, | 146 |
| Phycomyces, | 228 |
| Puccinia graminis, | 269 |
| | |
| Riccia, | 50 |
| Riella, | 51 |
| Racodium cellare, | 228 |
| Rivularia angulosa, | 161 |
| | |
| Sarcina ventriculi, | 167 |
| Selaginella convoluta, | 55 |
| —— mirabilis, | 56 |
| Sigillaria, | 59 |
| Solorina crocea, | 83 |
| Sphagnum, | 42, 46 |
| Sphæria Robertsii, | 231 |
| Sphærobolus stellatus, | 215 |
| Spathularia, | 288 |
| Splachnum, | 42, 46 |
| Sporodesmium lepraria, | 285 |
| Sticta pulmonaria, | 106 |
| Stigmaria, | 59 |
| Spermoedia clavus, | 270 |
| | |
| Tetraspora lubrica, | 164 |
| Tmesipteris, | 55 |
| Torula cervisiæ, | 243 |
| Tremella cerebrina, | 210 |
| —— mesenterica, | 210 |
| —— sarcoides, | 280 |
| Trichostomum lanuginosum, | 48 |
| Trichodesmium Erythræum, | 131 |
| Tuber cibarium, | 267 |
| | |
| Ulodendron, | 60 |
| Ulva crispa, | 163 |
| —— bulbosa, | 163 |
| Uredo rubigo, | 269 |
| —— caries, | 268 |
| —— segetum, | 268 |
| Usnea florida, | 95, 109 |
| —— fasciata, | 77 |
| —— melaxantha, | 78 |
| | |
| Vaucheria dichotoma, | 165 |
| | |
| Zygnema deciminum, | 134 |

# INDEX OF POPULAR NAMES.


| | PAGE |
|---|---|
| Amadou, | 247 |
| Apple Mildew, | 277 |
| Blewitts, | 256 |
| Black Mildew, | 277 |
| Blue Mould, | 235 |
| Boule de Neige, | 256 |
| Bog-moss, | 42-46 |
| Bunt, | 268 |
| Brittleworts, | 170 |
| Caouac, | 176 |
| Cellar-fungus, | 228 |
| Chantarelle, | 255 |
| Champignon, | 256 |
| Club-moss, | 53 |
| Crow-silk, | 166 |
| Cudbear, | 116 |
| Cup-moss, | 67 |
| Dog-lichen, | 105 |
| Dry-rot, | 278 |
| Dust-brand, | 268 |
| Edible-earth, | 176 |
| Electrotype Mould, | 280 |
| Ergot, | 246-269 |
| Fairy-rings, | 256 |
| Fly-Disease, | 281 |
| Flor-de-coco, | 194 |
| Fountain Apple Moss, | 42 |
| Fork-moss, | 45 |
| Fossil-flour, | 176 |
| Fungus-stone, | 265 |
| Geographical Lichen, | 81 |
| Giant Puff-ball, | 199 |
| Gold-fish Disease, | 234 |
| Gory Dew, | 147 |
| Grape Disease, | 274 |
| Green Mould, | 235 |
| Green Snow, | 146 |
| Hair-moss, | 41 |
| Herpette des Tincturiers, | 118 |
| Hop Disease, | 277 |
| Hyssop, | 43 |
| Iceland Moss, | 96 |
| Jew's Ears, | 210 |
| La Charbonniere, | 44 |
| Liverwort, | 106 |
| Liver Fungus, | 209 |
| Lungwort, | 106 |
| Manna, | 102 |
| Marsh Club-moss, | 54 |
| Mentagra, | 238 |
| Meteoric Paper, | 166 |
| Mildew, | 269 |
| Mountain Meal, | 175 |
| Mountain Dulse, | 161 |
| Mountain Cup-moss, | 83 |
| Morell, | 258 |
| Moorball, | 138 |
| Mungo Park Moss, | 43 |
| Mulberry Blight, | 278 |
| Muscardine, | 233 |
| Native Bread, | 264 |
| Nostoc, | 159 |
| Orange Blight, | 276 |
| Orcella, | 255 |
| Orchil, | 112 |
| Perelle-d'Auvergne, | 118 |
| Potato Disease, | 272 |
| Puff-ball, | 248 |
| Red Snow, | 141 |
| Reindeer Moss, | 93 |
| Rock Hair, | 94 |
| Rock Byssus, | 148 |
| Rose-rust, | 266 |
| Rust-corn, | 269 |

| | PAGE |
|---|---|
| Siberian Fungus, | 250 |
| Slaak, | 127 |
| Scotch Bonnets, | 256 |
| Sordes of Teeth, | 238 |
| Snow Mould, | 229 |
| Smut, | 268 |
| Spanish Moss, | 57 |
| Staneraw, | 118 |
| Stinkhorn, | 199 |
| St. John's Bread, | 270 |
| Thrush, | 238 |
| Thyme Moss, | 44 |
| Tinea or Scaldhead, | 238 |
| Tripe de Roche, | 99 |
| Truffle, | 260 |
| Usnech, | 108 |
| Vinegar Plant, | 239 |
| Violet Stones, | 66 |
| Water Flannel, | 132 |
| White Caps, | 256 |
| Witch's Butter, | 288 |
| Woolly Fringe Moss, | 41 |
| Wolf's Milk, | 288 |
| Written Lichen, | 67 |
| Yeast, | 242 |
| Yellow Mould, | 236 |
| Yellow Wall Lichen, | 118 |

---

## *CORRIGENDA.*

Page 7, line 16, *for* is all, *read* are all.

,, 48, title of Illustration, *for* Jungermanniæ *read* Jungermannia.

,, 55, line 19, *delete* a.

,, 129, line 7, *for* less, *read* else.

,, 164, line 13, *for* plane-leaf-like, *read* plain leaf-like.

,, 204, line 1, *for* in its structure, is, *read* as its structure is.

---

EDINBURGH: T. CONSTABLE,
PRINTER TO THE QUEEN, AND TO THE UNIVERSITY.

WORKS PUBLISHED BY

# MESSRS. MACMILLAN AND CO.

---

## The Five Gateways of Knowledge.

A Popular Work on the Five Senses. By GEORGE WILSON, M.D., Regius Professor of Technology in the University of Edinburgh. Eighth Thousand. In fcap. 8vo, cloth, with gilt leaves, 2s. 6d. People's Edition, in ornamental stiff covers, 1s.

"Dr. Wilson unites poetic with scientific faculty, and this union gives a charm to all he writes. In the little volume before us he has described the Five Senses in language so popular that a child may comprehend the meaning, so suggestive that philosophers will read it with pleasure."—*Leader.*

## The Progress of the Telegraph.

By GEORGE WILSON, M.D.

Fcap. 8vo, 1s.

"Most interesting and instructive . . . at once scientific and popular, religious and technical; a worthy companion to the 'Gateways of Knowledge.'"—*Literary Churchman.*

---

*With Portrait, Demy 8vo, cloth, price* 14*s.*

## Memoir of George Wilson, M.D., F.R.S.E.,

Regius Professor of Technology in the University of Edinburgh.

By his Sister, JESSIE AITKEN WILSON.

From *The Athenæum.* Jan. 12, 1861.

"The records of the success of George Wilson, with all its outbreaks of sympathy into other worlds than those of any lecturer—the strong, if silent, power with which he drew to him other men . . . the noble courage with which he fought against a capricious and deluding malady, are all set forth in this book so as to make every one who reads it recollect a true, or entertain a new regard for its object. His memory will nerve the energies of many a student to fight on to the end without any arrogance."

# LIST OF BOOKS

PUBLISHED BY

# MACMILLAN AND CO.

Cambridge,

AND 23, HENRIETTA STREET, COVENT GARDEN, LONDON.

**ABDY.—A Historical Sketch of Civil Procedure among the** Romans. By J. T. ABDY, LL.D. Regius Professor of Civil Law in the University of Cambridge. Crown 8vo. cloth, *4s. 6d.*

**ÆSCHYLI Eumenides.**
The Greek Text with English Notes, and an Introduction, containing an Analysis of Müller's Dissertations. By BERNARD DRAKE, M.A., late Fellow of King's College, Cambridge. 8vo. cloth, *7s. 6d.*

**ADAMS.—The Twelve Foundations and other Poems.**
By H. C. ADAMS, M.A., Author of "Sivan the Sleeper," &c. Royal 16mo. cloth, *5s.*

**AGNES HOPETOUN'S SCHOOLS AND HOLIDAYS.**
The Experiences of a Little Girl. A Story for Girls. By Mrs. OLIPHANT, Author of "Margaret Maitland." Royal 16mo. cloth, gilt leaves, *5s.*

**AIRY.—Mathematical Tracts on the Lunar and Planetary** Theories. The Figure of the Earth, Precession and Nutation, the Calculus of Variations, and the Undulatory Theory of Optics. By G. B. AIRY, M.A., Astronomer Royal. **Fourth Edition,** revised and improved. 8vo. cloth, *15s.*

**AIRY.—Treatise on the Algebraical and Numerical Theory of** Errors of Observations, and the Combination of Observations. By G. B. AIRY, M.A. Crown 8vo. cloth, *6s. 6d.*

**ARISTOTLE on the Vital Principle.**
Translated, with Notes. By CHARLES COLLIER, M.D., F.R.S., Fellow of the Royal College of Physicians. Crown 8vo. cloth, *8s. 6d.*

**ARTIST AND CRAFTSMAN; A Novel.**
Crown 8vo. cloth, *10s. 6d.*

19.6.61.
5,000 cr.

**BAKER.—Military Education in connexion with the Universities.** By JAMES BAKER, Lieutenant-Colonel, Cambridge University Volunteers. 8vo. *6d.*

**BAXTER.—The Volunteer Movement: its Progress and Wants.** With Tables of all the Volunteer Corps in Great Britain, and of their Expenses. By R. DUDLEY BAXTER. 8vo. *1s.*

**BEAMONT.—Catherine, the Egyptian Slave of 1852. A Tale of Eastern Life.** By W. J. BEAMONT, M.A. Fellow of Trinity College, Cambridge, late Principal of the English College, Jerusalem. Fcap. 8vo. cloth, *5s. 6d.*

**BEASLEY.—An Elementary Treatise on Plane Trigonometry:** with a numerous Collection of Examples. By R. D. BEASLEY, M.A., Fellow of St. John's College, Cambridge, Head-Master of Grantham Grammar School. Crown 8vo. cloth, *3s. 6d.*

**BERKELEY.—The Theory of Vision Vindicated and Explained.** By the Right Rev. G. BERKELEY, Lord Bishop of Cloyne. Edited, with Annotations, by H. V. H. COWELL, Associate of King's College, London. Fcap. 8vo. cloth, red leaves, *4s. 6d.*

**BIRKS.—The Difficulties of Belief in connexion with the Creation and the Fall.** By THOMAS RAWSON BIRKS, M.A., Rector of Kelshall, and Author of "The Life of the Rev. E. Bickersteth." Crown 8vo. cloth, *4s. 6d.*

**BLANCHE LISLE, and Other Poems.**
Fcap. 8vo. cloth, *4s. 6d.*

**BOOLE.—The Mathematical Analysis of Logic.**
By GEORGE BOOLE, D.C.L. Professor of Mathematics in the Queen's University, Ireland. 8vo. sewed, *5s.*

**BOOLE.—A Treatise on Differential Equations.**
By GEORGE BOOLE, D.C.L. Crown 8vo. cloth, *14s.*

**BOOLE.—A Treatise on the Calculus of Finite Differences.**
By GEORGE BOOLE, D.C.L. Crown 8vo. cloth, *10s. 6d.*

**BRAVE WORDS for BRAVE SOLDIERS and SAILORS.**
**Tenth Thousand.** 16mo. sewed, *2d.*; or *10s.* per 100.

**BRETT.—Suggestions relative to the Restoration of Suffragan Bishops and Rural Deans.** By THOMAS BRETT (A.D. 1711). Edited by JAMES FENDALL, M.A., Procter in Convocation for the Clergy of Ely. Crown 8vo. cloth, *2s. 6d.*

**BRIMLEY.—Essays, by the late GEORGE BRIMLEY, M.A.** Edited by W. G. CLARK, M.A., Tutor of Trinity College, and Public Orator in the University of Cambridge. With Portrait. **Second Edition.** Fcap. 8vo. cloth, *5s.*

**BROCK.**—Daily Readings on the Passion of Our Lord. By Mrs. H. F. BROCK. Fcap. 8vo. cloth, red leaves, 4*s*.

**BROKEN TROTH, The.**—A Tale of Tuscan Life. From the Italian. By Philip Ireton. 2 vols. Fcap. 8vo. cloth, 12*s*.

**BROOK SMITH.**—Arithmetic in Theory and Practice. For Advanced Pupils. Part First. By J. BROOK SMITH, M.A., of St. John's College, Cambridge. Crown 8vo. cloth, 3*s*. 6*d*.

**BUTLER (Archer).**—Sermons, Doctrinal and Practical. By the Rev. WILLIAM ARCHER BUTLER, M.A. late Professor of Moral Philosophy in the University of Dublin. Edited, with a Memoir of the Author's Life, by the Very Rev. THOMAS WOODWARD, M.A. Dean of Down. With Portrait. **Fifth Edition.** 8vo. cloth, 12*s*.

**BUTLER (Archer).**—A Second Series of Sermons. Edited by J. A. JEREMIE, D.D. Regius Professor of Divinity in the University of Cambridge. **Third Edition.** 8vo. cloth, 10*s*. 6*d*.

**BUTLER (Archer).**—History of Ancient Philosophy. A Series of Lectures. Edited by WILLIAM HEPWORTH THOMPSON, M.A. Regius Professor of Greek in the University of Cambridge. 2 vols. 8vo. cloth, 1*l*. 5*s*.

**BUTLER (Archer).**—Letters on Romanism, in Reply to Mr. NEWMAN'S Essay on Development. Edited by the Very Rev. T. WOODWARD, Dean of Down. **Second Edition,** revised by the Ven. Archdeacon HARDWICK. 8vo. cloth, 10*s*. 6*d*.

**CALDERWOOD.**—Philosophy of the Infinite. A Treatise on Man's Knowledge of the Infinite Being, in answer to Sir W. Hamilton and Dr. Mansel. By the Rev. HENRY CALDERWOOD, M.A. **Second Edition,** 8vo. cloth, 14*s*.

**CAMBRIDGE.** – Cambridge Scrap Book: containing in a Pictorial Form a Report on the Manners, Customs, Humours, and Pastimes of the University of Cambridge. With nearly 300 Illustrations. Second Edition. Crown 4to. half-bound, 7*s*. 6*d*.

**CAMBRIDGE.**—Cambridge Theological Papers. Comprising those given at the Voluntary Theological and Crosse Scholarship Examinations. Edited, with References and Indices, by A. P. MOOR, M.A. of Trinity College, Cambridge, and Sub-warden of St. Augustine's College, Canterbury. 8vo. cloth, 7*s*. 6*d*.

**CAMBRIDGE SENATE-HOUSE PROBLEMS and RIDERS, with SOLUTIONS:—**

| | |
|---|---|
| 1848—1851.—Problems. | By N. M. FERRERS, M.A. and J. S. JACKSON, M.A. of Caius College. 15*s.* 6*d.* |
| 1848—1851.—Riders. | By F. J. JAMESON, M.A. of Caius College. 7*s.* 6*d.* |
| 1854—Problems and Riders. | By W. WALTON, M.A. of Trinity College, and C. F. MACKENZIE, M.A. of Caius College. 10*s.* 6*d.* |
| 1857—Problems and Riders. | By W. M. CAMPION, M.A. of Queen's College, and W. WALTON, M.A. of Trinity College. 8*s.* 6*d.* |
| 1860—Problems and Riders. | By H. W. WATSON, M.A. Trinity College, and E. J. ROUTH, M.A. St. Peter's College. 7*s.* 6*d.* |

**CAMBRIDGE ENGLISH PRIZE POEMS, which have** obtained the Chancellor's Gold Medal from the institution of the Prize to 1858. Crown 8vo. cloth, 7*s.* 6*d.*

**CAMBRIDGE.—Cambridge and Dublin Mathematical Journal.**
*The Complete Work,* in Nine Vols. 8vo. cloth, 7*l.* 4*s.*
ONLY A FEW COPIES OF THE COMPLETE WORK REMAIN ON HAND.

**CAMPBELL.—The Nature of the Atonement and its Rela-** tion to Remission of Sins and Eternal Life. By JOHN M'LEOD CAMPBELL, formerly Minister of Row. 8vo. cloth, 10*s.* 6*d.*

**CHURTON.—The Influence of the Septuagint Version of the** Old Testament upon the Progress of Christianity. By the Rev. WILLIAM R. CHURTON, B.A. Fellow of King's College, Cambridge. Crown 8vo. cloth, 3*s.* 6*d.*

**CICERO.—Old Age and Friendship.**
Translated into English. Two Parts. 12mo. sewed, 2*s.* 6*d.* each.

**CICERO.—THE SECOND PHILIPPIC ORATION.**
With an Introduction and Notes, translated from Karl Halm. Edited with corrections and additions. By JOHN E. B. MAYOR, M.A. Fellow and Classical Lecturer of St. John's College, Cambridge. Fcap. 8vo. cloth, 5*s.*

**CLARK.—Four Sermons Preached in the Chapel of Trinity** College, Cambridge. By W. G. CLARK, M.A. Fellow and Tutor of Trinity College, and Public Orator in the University of Cambridge. Fcap. 8vo. limp cloth, red leaves, 2*s.* 6*d.*

**COLENSO.—The Colony of Natal. A Journal of Ten Weeks'** Tour of Visitation among the Colonists and Zulu Kafirs of Natal. By the Right Rev. JOHN WILLIAM COLENSO, D.D. Lord Bishop of Natal, with a Map and Illustrations. Fcap. 8vo. cloth, 5*s.*

**COLENSO.—Village Sermons.**
**Second Edition.** Fcap. 8vo. cloth, 2*s.* 6*d.*

**COLENSO.—Four Sermons on Ordination, and on Missions.** 18mo. sewed, 1*s*.

**COLENSO.—Companion to the Holy Communion, containing** the Service, and Select Readings from the writings of Mr. MAURICE. Edited by the Lord Bishop of Natal. *Fine Edition*, rubricated and bound in morocco, antique style, 6*s*.; or in cloth, 2*s*. 6*d*. *Common Paper*, limp cloth, 1*s*.

**COOPER.—The Nature of Reprobation, and the Preacher's** Liability to it. A Sermon. By J. E. COOPER, M.A., Rector of Forncet St. Mary, Norfolk, 8vo. 1*s*.

**COTTON.—Sermons and Addresses delivered in Marlborough** College during Six Years by GEORGE EDWARD LYNCH COTTON, D.D., Lord Bishop of Calcutta, and Metropolitan of India. Crown 8vo. cloth, 10*s*. 6*d*.

**COTTON.—Sermons: chiefly connected with Public Events** of 1854. Fcap. 8vo. cloth, 3*s*.

**COTTON.—Charge delivered at his Primary Visitation,** September 1859. 8vo. 2*s*. 6*d*.

**COTTON QUESTION, THE.—Where are the Spoils of the** Slave? Addressed to the Upper and Middle Classes of Great Britain. By λ. 8vo. sewed, 1*s*.

**CRAIK.—My First Journal. A Book for Children.** By GEORGIANA M. CRAIK, Author of "Riverston," &c. Royal 16mo. cloth, gilt leaves, 4*s*. 6*d*.

**CROSSE.—An Analysis of Paley's Evidences.** By C H. CROSSE, M.A. of Caius College, Cambridge. 24mo. boards, 3*s*. 6*d*.

**DAVIES.—St. Paul and Modern Thought:** Remarks on some of the Views advanced in Professor Jowett's Commentary on St. Paul. By Rev. J. LL. DAVIES, M.A.; Rector of Christ Church, Marylebone. 8vo. sewed, 2*s*. 6*d*.

**DAVIES.—The Work of Christ; or the World Reconciled to** God. Sermons Preached in Christ Church, St. Marylebone. With a Preface on the Atonement Controversy. By the Rev. J. LL. DAVIES, M.A. Fcap. 8vo. cloth, 6*s*.

**DAYS OF OLD: Stories from Old English History of the** Druids, the Anglo-Saxons, and the Crusades. By the Author of "Ruth and her Friends." Royal 16mo. cloth, gilt leaves, 5*s*.

**DEMOSTHENES DE CORONA.** The Greek Text with English Notes. By B. DRAKE, M.A. late Fellow of King's College, Cambridge. **Second Edition,** to which is prefixed AESCHINES AGAINST CTESIPHON, with English Notes. Fcap. 8vo. cloth, 5*s*.

**DEMOSTHENES.—Demosthenes on the Crown.** Translated by J. P. NORRIS, M.A. Fellow of Trinity College, Cambridge, and one of Her Majesty's Inspectors of Schools. Crown 8vo. cloth, 3*s*.

**DICEY.—Rome in 1860.**
By EDWARD DICEY. Crown 8vo. cloth, 6*s.* 6*d.*

**DREW.—A Geometrical Treatise on Conic Sections, with** Copious Examples from the Cambridge Senate House Papers. By W. H. DREW, M.A. of St. John's College, Cambridge, Second Master of Blackheath Proprietary School. Crown 8vo. cloth, 4*s.* 6*d.*

**FAWCETT.—Leading Clauses of a new Reform Bill.**
By HENRY FAWCETT, Fellow of Trinity Hall, Cambridge. 8vo. sewed, 1*s.*

**FENDALL.—Exemption from Church Rates on Personal** Grounds, considered in a Letter to J. G. Hubbard, M.P.: together with Suggestions. By JAMES FENDALL, M.A. Proctor for the Diocese of Ely. 8vo. sewed, 6*d.*

**FISHER.—The Goth and the Saracen: a Comparison** between the Historical Effect produced upon the Condition of Mankind by the Mahometan Conquests and those of the Northern Barbarians. By E. H. FISHER, B.A. Scholar of Trinity College, Cambridge. Crown 8vo. 1*s.* 6*d.*

**FORBES.—Life of Edward Forbes, F.R.S.**
Late Regius Professor of Natural History in the University of Edinburgh. By GEORGE WILSON, M.D. F.R.S.E. and ARCHIBALD GEIKIE, F.G.S. of the Geological Survey of Great Britain, 8vo. cloth, with Portrait, 14*s.*

**FROST.—The First Three Sections of Newton's Principia.** With Notes and Problems in illustration of the subject. By PERCIVAL FROST, M.A. late Fellow of St. John's College, Cambridge, and Mathematical Lecturer of Jesus College. Crown 8vo. cloth, 10*s.* 6*d.*

**GILL.—The Anniversaries. Poems in Commemoration of** Great Men and Great Events. By T. H. GILL. Fcap. 8vo. cloth, 5*s.*

**GRANT.—Plane Astronomy.**
Including Explanations of Celestial Phenomena, and Descriptions of Astronomical Instruments. By A. R. GRANT, M.A., one of Her Majesty's Inspectors of Schools, late Fellow of Trinity College, Cambridge. 8vo. boards, 6*s.*

**GROVES.—A Commentary on the Book of Genesis.**
For the Use of Students and Readers of the English Version of the Bible. By the Rev. H. C. GROVES, M.A. Perpetual Curate of Mullavilly, Armagh. Crown 8vo. cloth, 9*s.*

**HAMILTON.—On Truth and Error: Thoughts, in Prose and** Verse, on the Principles of Truth, and the Causes and Effects of Error. By JOHN HAMILTON, Esq. (of St. Ernan's), M.A. St. John's College, Cambridge. Crown 8vo. cloth, 5*s.*

**HARE.—Charges delivered during the Years 1840 to 1854.** With Notes on the Principal Events affecting the Church during that period. By JULIUS CHARLES HARE, M.A. sometime Archdeacon of Lewes, and Chaplain in Ordinary to the Queen. With an Introduction, explanatory of his position in the Church with reference to the parties which divide it. 3 vols. 8vo. cloth, 1*l.* 11*s.* 6*d.*

**HARE.—Miscellaneous Pamphlets on some of the Leading** Questions agitated in the Church during the Years 1845—51. 8vo. cloth, 12*s*.

**HARE.—The Victory of Faith.** **Second Edition.** 8vo. cloth, 5*s*.

**HARE.—The Mission of the Comforter.** **Second Edition.** With Notes. 8vo. cloth, 12*s*.

**HARE.—Vindication of Luther from his English Assailants.** **Second Edition.** 8vo. cloth, 7*s*.

**HARE.—Parish Sermons.** Second Series. 8vo. cloth, 12*s*.

**HARE.—Sermons Preacht on Particular Occasions.** 8vo. cloth, 12*s*.

*** The two following Books are included in the Three Volumes of Charges, and may still be had separately.

**HARE.—The Contest with Rome.** With Notes, especially in answer to Dr. Newman's Lectures on Present Position of Catholics. **Second Edition.** 8vo. cloth, 10*s*. 6*d*.

**HARE.—Charges delivered in the Years 1843, 1845, 1846.** Never before published. With an Introduction, explanatory of his position in the Church with reference to the parties which divide it. 6*s*. 6*d*.

**HARE.—Portions of the Psalms in English Verse.** Selected for Public Worship. 18mo. cloth, 2*s*. 6*d*.

**HARE.—Two Sermons preached in Herstmonceux Church,** on Septuagesima Sunday, 1855, being the Sunday after the Funeral of the Venerable Archdeacon Hare. By the Rev. H. VENN ELLIOTT, Perpetual Curate of St. Mary's, Brighton, late Fellow of Trinity College, Cambridge, and the Rev. J. N. SIMPKINSON, Rector of Brington, Northampton, formerly Curate of Herstmonceux. 8vo. 1*s*. 6*d*.

**HARDWICK.—Christ and other Masters.** A Historical Inquiry into some of the chief Parallelisms and Contrasts between Christianity and the Religious Systems of the Ancient World. With special reference to prevailing Difficulties and Objections. By the Ven. ARCHDEACON HARDWICK. THE RELIGIONS OF CHINA, AMERICA, AND OCEANICA, in one part. RELIGIONS OF EGYPT AND MEDO-PERSIA, in one part 8vo. cloth. 7*s*. 6*d*. each part.

**HARDWICK.—A History of the Christian Church, during the Middle Ages and the Reformation. (A.D. 590-1600.)** By Archdeacon Hardwick. Two vols. crown 8vo. cloth, 21*s*.

Vol. I. History from Gregory the Great to the Excommunication of Luther. With Maps.

Vol. II. History of the Reformation of the Church.

Each volume may be had separately. Price 10*s*. 6*d*.

*** These Volumes form part of the Series of Theological Manuals.

**HARDWICK.—Twenty Sermons for Town Congregations.** Crown 8vo. cloth, 6*s*. 6*d*.

**HAYNES.—Outlines of Equity. By FREEMAN OLIVER** HAYNES, Barrister-at-Law, late Fellow of Caius College, Cambridge. Crown 8vo. cloth, 10*s*.

**HEALY. — God is Light. A Sermon preached at Great** Waldingfield, Suffolk. By J. B. HEALY, B.A. late Curate. Fcp. 8vo. sewed, 6*d*.

**HEDDERWICK.—Lays of Middle Age, and other Poems.** By JAMES HEDDERWICK. Fcp. 8vo. 5*s*.

**HEMMING.—An Elementary Treatise on the Differential** and Integral Calculus. By G. W. HEMMING, M.A. Fellow of St. John's College, Cambridge. **Second Edition.** 8vo. cloth, 9*s*.

**HERVEY.—The Genealogies of our Lord and Saviour Jesus** Christ, as contained in the Gospels of St. Matthew and St. Luke, reconciled with each other and with the Genealogy of the House of David, from Adam to the close of the Canon of the Old Testament, and shown to be in harmony with the true Chronology of the Times. By Lord ARTHUR HERVEY, M.A. Rector of Ickworth. 8vo. cloth, 10*s*. 6*d*.

**HERVEY.—The Inspiration of Holy Scripture.** Five Sermons preached before the University of Cambridge. 8vo. cloth, 3*s*. 6*d*.

**HOLMES.—Elsie Venner; A Tale of Destiny.** By O. W. HOLMES, Author of "The Autocrat of the Breakfast-Table." Fcap. 8vo. cloth, 6*s*.

**HOMER.—The Iliad of Homer Translated into English Verse.** By I. C. WRIGHT, M.A. Translator of "Dante." Vol. I. containing Books I—XII. Crown 8vo. cloth, 10*s*. 6*d*. Books I—VI. in Printed Cover, price 5*s*. also, Books VII—XII, price 5s.

**HOWARD.—The Pentateuch; or, the Five Books of Moses.** Translated into English from the Version of the LXX. With Notes on its Omissions and Insertions, and also on the Passages in which it differs from the Authorised Version. By the Hon. HENRY HOWARD, D.D. Dean of Lichfield. Crown 8vo. cloth. GENESIS, 1 vol. 8*s*. 6*d*.; EXODUS AND LEVITICUS, 1 vol. 10*s*. 6*d*.; NUMBERS AND DEUTERONOMY, 1 vol. 10*s*. 6*d*.

**HUGHES.—Account of the Lock-Out of Engineers, &c.** 1851-2. Preparated for the Social Science Association. By THOMAS HUGHES, Author of "Tom Brown." 8vo. sewed, 1*s*.

**HUMPHRY.—The Human Skeleton (including the Joints).** By GEORGE MURRAY HUMPHRY, M.D. F.R.S., Surgeon to Addenbrooke's Hospital, Lecturer on Surgery and Anatomy in the Cambridge University Medical School. With Two Hundred and Sixty Illustrations drawn from Nature. Medium 8vo. cloth, 1*l*. 8*s*.

**HUMPHRY.—On the Coagulation of the Blood in the Venous** System during Life. 8vo. 3*s*. 6*d*.

**HUMPHRY.—Observations on the Limbs of Vertebrate** Animals, the Plan of their Construction, their Homology, and the Comparison of the Fore and Hind Limbs. 4to. *5s.*

**INGLEBY.—Outlines of Theoretical Logic.** Founded on the New Analytic of SIR WILLIAM HAMILTON. Designed for a Text-book in Schools and Colleges. By C. MANSFIELD INGLEBY, M.A., of Trinity College, Cambridge. In fcap. 8vo. cloth, *3s. 6d.*

**IRETON.—The Broken Troth, a Tale of Tuscan Life, from** the Italian. By PHILIP IRETON. 2 vols. Fcap. 8vo. *12s.*

**JAMESON.—Analogy between the Miracles and Doctrines** of Scripture. By F. J. JAMESON, M.A., Fellow of St. Catharine's College, Cambridge. Fcap. 8vo. cloth, *2s.*

**JAMESON.—Brotherly Counsels to Students. Four Sermons** preached in the Chapel of St. Catharine's College, Cambridge. By F. J. JAMESON, M.A. Fcap. 8vo. limp cloth, red edges, *1s. 6d.*

**JONES.—A Sermon preached at St. Luke's, Berwick Street,** Oxford Street, to the St. Luke's Artisan Rifles (Sixth Company of the Nineteenth Middlesex), on Sunday, October 28, 1860. By the Rev. HARRY JONES, M.A. Incumbent of St. Luke's. 8vo. *1d.*

**JUVENAL.—Juvenal, for Schools.** With English Notes. By J. E. B. MAYOR, M.A. Fellow and Classical Lecturer of St. John's College, Cambridge. Crown 8vo. cloth, *10s. 6d.*

**KINGSLEY.—Two Years Ago.** By CHARLES KINGSLEY, M.A. Rector of Eversley, Chaplain in Ordinary to the Queen, and Professor of Modern History in the University of Cambridge. **Third Edition.** Crown 8vo. cloth, *6s.*

**KINGSLEY.—"Westward Ho!" or, the Voyages and Adventures** of Sir Amyas Leigh, Knight of Burrough, in the County of Devon, in the Reign of Her Most Glorious Majesty Queen Elizabeth. **Fourth Edition.** Crown 8vo. cloth, *6s.*

**KINGSLEY.—Glaucus; or, the Wonders of the Shore.** **New and Illustrated Edition,** corrected and enlarged. Containing beautifully Coloured Illustrations of the Objects mentioned in the Work. Elegantly bound in cloth, with gilt leaves. *7s. 6d.*

**KINGSLEY.—The Limits of Exact Science as Applied to** History. An Inaugural Lecture delivered before the University of Cambridge. By CHARLES KINGSLEY, M.A. Crown 8vo. boards, *2s.*

**KINGSLEY.—The Heroes: or, Greek Fairy Tales for my** Children. With Eight Illustrations, Engraved by WHYMPER. **New Edition,** printed on toned paper, and elegantly bound in cloth, with gilt leaves, Imp. 16mo. *5s.*

**KINGSLEY.—Alexandria and Her Schools: being Four Lectures** delivered at the Philosophical Institution, Edinburgh. With a Preface. Crown 8vo. cloth, *5s.*

**KINGSLEY.—Phaethon; or Loose Thoughts for Loose** Thinkers. **Third Edition.** Crown 8vo. boards, 2*s.*

**KINGSLEY.—The Recollections of Geoffry Hamlyn.** By HENRY KINGSLEY, Esq. **Second Edition,** crown 8vo. cloth, 6*s.*

**LATHAM.—The Construction of Wrought-Iron Bridges,** embracing the Practical Application of the Principles of Mechanics to Wrought-Iron Girder Work. By J. H. LATHAM, Esq. Civil Engineer. 8vo. cloth. With numerous detail Plates. 15*s.*

**LECTURES TO LADIES ON PRACTICAL SUBJECTS.** **Third Edition,** revised. Crown 8vo. cloth, 7*s.* 6*d.* By Reverends F. D. MAURICE, PROFESSOR KINGSLEY, J. LL. DAVIES, ARCHDEACON ALLEN, DEAN TRENCH, PROFESSOR BREWER, DR. GEORGE JOHNSON, DR. SIEVEKING, DR. CHAMBERS, F. J. STEPHEN, Esq., and TOM TAYLOR, Esq.

**LIGHTFOOT.—Christian Progress. A Sermon preached in** the Chapel of Trinity College, Cambridge, at the Commemoration of Benefactors, December 15, 1860. By J. B. LIGHTFOOT, M.A. Fellow and Tutor of Trinity College. 8vo. sewed, 1*s.*

**LITTLE ESTELLA, and other TALES FOR THE** YOUNG. With Frontispiece. Royal 16mo. extra cloth, gilt leaves, 5*s.*

**LONGE.—An Inquiry into the Law of "Strikes."** By F. D. LONGE, Barrister-at-Law. 8vo. sewed, 1*s.*

**LUDLOW.—British India; its Races, and its History,** down to 1857. By JOHN MALCOLM LUDLOW, Barrister-at-Law. 2 vols. fcap. 8vo. cloth, 9*s.*

**LUSHINGTON.—La Nation Boutiquière: and other Poems,** chiefly Political. With a Preface. By the late HENRY LUSHINGTON, Chief Secretary to the Government of Malta. **Points of War.** By FRANKLIN LUSHINGTON. In 1 vol. fcap. 8vo. cloth, 3*s.*

**LUSHINGTON.—The Italian War 1848-9, and the Last** Italian Poet. By the late HENRY LUSHINGTON. With a Biographical Preface by G. S. VENABLES. Crown 8vo. cloth, 6*s.* 6*d.*

**MACKENZIE.—The Christian Clergy of the first Ten Cen-**turies, and their Influence on European Civilization. By HENRY MACKENZIE, B.A. Scholar of Trinity College, Cambridge. Crown 8vo. cloth, 6*s.* 6*d.*

**MACMILLAN'S MAGAZINE. Published Monthly, Price** One Shilling. Volume I to III, are now ready, handsomely bound in cloth, 7*s.* 6*d.* each.

**MANSFIELD.—Paraguay, Brazil, and the Plate.** With a Map, and numerous Woodcuts. By CHARLES MANSFIELD, M.A. of Clare College, Cambridge. With a Sketch of his Life. By the Rev. CHARLES KINGSLEY. Crown 8vo. cloth, 12*s.* 6*d.*

## MACMILLAN'S SERIES OF BOOKS FOR THE YOUNG.

Handsomely bound in cloth. Five Shillings each.

1. **Tom Brown's School days. Seventh Edition.**
2. **Our Year. By the Author of "John Halifax." With** Numerous Illustrations. Gilt leaves.
3. **Professor Kingsley's Heroes; or Greek Fairy Tales.** With Eight Illustrations. Gilt leaves.
4. **Ruth and Her Friends. A Story for Girls. Gilt leaves.**
5. **Days of Old. Stories from Old English History. By the** Author of "Ruth and Her Friends." Gilt leaves.
6. **Agnes Hopetoun's Schools and Holidays. By the Author** of "Margaret Maitland." Gilt leaves.
7. **Little Estella, and other Fairy Tales. Gilt leaves.**
8. **David, King of Israel. A History for the Young. By** J. WRIGHT, M.A. Gilt leaves.

**My First Journal. By G. M. Craik. Gilt leaves, 4s. 6d.**

**M'COY.—Contributions to British Palæontology; or, First Descriptions** of several hundred Fossil Radiata, Articulata, Mollusca, and Pisces, from the Tertiary, Cretaceous, Oolitic, and Palæozoic Strata of Great Britain. With numerous Woodcuts. By FREDERICK McCOY, F.G.S., Professor of Natural History in the University of Melbourne. 8vo. cloth, *9s.*

**MARSTON.—A Lady in Her Own Right.**
By WESTLAND MARSTON. Crown 8vo. cloth, *10s. 6d.*

**MASSON.—Essays, Biographical and Critical; chiefly on the English Poets.** By DAVID MASSON, M.A. Professor of English Literature in University College, London. 8vo. cloth, *12s. 6d.*

**MASSON.—British Novelists and their Styles; being a** Critical Sketch of the History of British Prose Fiction. By DAVID MASSON, M.A. Crown 8vo. cloth, *7s. 6d.*

**MASSON.—Life of John Milton, narrated in Connexion** with the Political, Ecclesiastical, and Literary History of his Time. Vol. I. with Portraits. *18s.*

**MAURICE.—Expository Works on the Holy Scriptures.**
By FREDERICK DENISON MAURICE, M.A. Incumbent of St. Peter's, Vere Street, and late Chaplain of Lincoln's Inn.

I.—**The Patriarchs and Lawgivers of the Old Testament.**
**Second Edition.** Crown 8vo. cloth, *6s.*

This volume contains Discourses on the Pentateuch, Joshua, Judges, and the beginning of the First Book of Samuel.

II.—**The Prophets and Kings of the Old Testament.**
**Second Edition.** Crown 8vo. cloth, *10s. 6d.*

This volume contains Discourses on Samuel I. and II., Kings I. and II., Amos, Joel, Hosea, Isaiah, Micah, Nahum, Habakkuk, Jeremiah, and Ezekiel.

**MAURICE.—Expository Works on the Holy Scriptures.**—*Continued.*

**III.—The Gospel of St. John; a Series of Discourses.** **Second Edition.** Crown 8vo. cloth, 10*s.* 6*d.*

**IV.—The Epistles of St. John; a Series of Lectures on** Christian Ethics. Crown 8vo. cloth, 7*s.* 6*d.*

**MAURICE.—Lectures on the Apocalypse, or, Book of the** Revelation of St. John the Divine. Crown 8vo. cloth, 10*s.* 6*d.*

**MAURICE.—Expository Works on the Prayer-Book.**

**I.—The Ordinary Services.** **Second Edition.** Fcap. 8vo. cloth, 5*s.* 6*d.*

**II.—The Church a Family. Twelve Sermons on the** Occasional Services. Fcap. 8vo. cloth, 4*s.* 6*d.*

**MAURICE.—What is Revelation? A Series of Sermons** on the Epiphany; to which are added Letters to a Theological Student on the Bampton Lectures of Mr. MANSEL. Crown 8vo. cloth, 10*s.* 6*d.*

**MAURICE.—Sequel to the Inquiry, "What is Revelation?"** Letters in Reply to Mr. Mansel's Examination of "Strictures on the Bampton Lectures." Crown 8vo. cloth, 6*s.*

**MAURICE.—Lectures on Ecclesiastical History.** 8vo. cloth, 10*s.* 6*d.*

**MAURICE.—Theological Essays.** **Second Edition,** with a new Preface and other additions. Crown 8vo. cloth, 10*s.* 6*d.*

**MAURICE.—The Doctrine of Sacrifice deduced from the** Scriptures. With a Dedicatory Letter to the Young Men's Christian Association. Crown 8vo. cloth, 7*s.* 6*d.*

**MAURICE.—The Religions of the World, and their Relations** to Christianity. **Third Edition.** Fcap. 8vo. cloth, 5*s.*

**MAURICE.—On the Lord's Prayer.** **Fourth Edition.** Fcap. 8vo. cloth, 2*s.* 6*d.*

**MAURICE.—On the Sabbath Day: the Character of the** Warrior; and on the Interpretation of History. Fcap. 8vo. cloth, 2*s.* 6*d.*

**MAURICE.—Learning and Working.—Six Lectures on the** Foundation of Colleges for Working Men, delivered in Willis's Rooms, London, in June and July, 1854. Crown 8vo. cloth, 5*s.*

**MAURICE.—The Indian Crisis. Five Sermons.** Crown 8vo. cloth, 2*s.* 6*d.*

**MAURICE.—Law's Remarks on the Fable of the Bees.**
Edited, with an Introduction of Eighty Pages, by FREDERICK DENISON MAURICE, M.A. Chaplain of Lincoln's Inn. Fcp. 8vo. cloth, 4*s*. 6*d*.

**MAURICE.—Miscellaneous Pamphlets:—**

**I.—War; How to Prepare Ourselves for It. A Sermon.**
Fcap. 8vo. sewed, 2*d*.

**II.—Death and Life. A Sermon.** *In Memoriam C. B. M.*
8vo. sewed, 1*s*.

**III.—Plan of a Female College for the Help of the Rich** and of the Poor. 8vo. 6*d*.

**IV.—Administrative Reform.**
Crown 8vo. 3*d*.

**V.—Sermon preached to the 19th Middlesex Rifle** Volunteers. Fcap. 8vo. sewed, 2*d*.

**VI.—The Name "Protestant:" and the English Bishopric** at Jerusalem. **Second Edition.** 8vo. 3*s*.

**VII.—Thoughts on the Oxford Election of 1847.**
8vo. 1*s*.

**VIII.—The Case of Queen's College, London.**
8vo. 1*s*. 6*d*.

**IX.—The Worship of the Church a Witness for the** Redemption of the World. 8vo. sewed, 1*s*.

**X.—The Faith of the Liturgy and the Doctrine of the** XXXIX Articles. Two Sermons. Crown 8vo. sewed, 2*s*. 6*d*.

**MAXWELL.—The Stability of the Motion of Saturn's Rings.**
By J. C. MAXWELL, M.A. Professor of Natural Philosophy in the University of Aberdeen. 4to. sewed, 6*s*.

**MAYOR.—Cambridge in the Seventeenth Century.**
2 vols. fcap. 8vo. cloth, 13*s*.
Vol. I. Lives of Nicholas Ferrar.
Vol. II. Autobiography of Matthew Robinson.
By JOHN E. B. MAYOR, M.A. Fellow and Classical Lecturer of St. John's College, Cambridge.

*** The Autobiography of Matthew Robinson may be had separately, price 5*s*. 6*d*.

**MAYOR.—Early Statutes of St. John's College, Cambridge.**
Now first edited with Notes. Royal 8vo. 18*s*.

*** The First Part is now ready for delivery.

**MAYOR.—Juvenal for Schools.**
With English Notes. By JOHN E. B. MAYOR, M.A. Crown 8vo. cloth, 10*s*. 6*d*.

**MAYOR.—Cicero's Second Philippic.**
With English Notes and Introduction translated from Halm, with Corrections and Additions. By JOHN E. B. MAYOR, M.A. Fcap. 8vo. cloth, 5*s*.

**MERIVALE.—Sallust for Schools.**
By C. MERIVALE, B.D. Author of "History of Rome." Second Edition. Fcap. 8vo. cloth, 4*s*. 6*d*.

*** The Jugurtha and the Catilina may be had separately, price 2*s*. 6*d*. each, bound in cloth.

**MOORE.—A New Proof of the Method of Algebra commonly**
called "Greatest Common Measure." By B. T. MOORE, B.A., Fellow of Pembroke College, Cambridge. Crown 8vo. 6*d*.

**MOOR COTTAGE.—A Tale of Home Life.**
By the Author of "Little Estella." Crown 8vo. cloth, 10*s*. 6*d*.

**MOORHOUSE.—Some Modern Difficulties respecting the**
Facts of Nature and Revelation. Considered in Four Sermons preached before the University of Cambridge, in Lent, 1861. By JAMES MOORHOUSE, M.A. of St. John's College, Cambridge, Curate of Hornsey. Fcap. 8vo. cloth, 2*s*. 6*d*.

**MORGAN.—A Collection of Mathematical Problems and**
Examples. Arranged in the Different Subjects progressively, with Answers to all the Questions. By H. A. MORGAN, M.A., Fellow of Jesus College. Crown 8vo. cloth, 6*s*. 6*d*.

**MORSE.—Working for God, and other Practical Sermons.**
By FRANCIS MORSE, M.A. Incumbent of St. John's, Ladywood, Birmingham. **Second Edition.** Fcap. 8vo. cloth, 5*s*.

**NAPIER.—Lord Bacon and Sir Walter Raleigh.**
Critical and Biographical Essays. By MACVEY NAPIER, late Editor of the *Edinburgh Review* and of the *Encyclopædia Britannica*. Post 8vo. cloth, 7*s*. 6*d*.

**NORWAY AND SWEDEN.—A Long Vacation Ramble in**
1856. By X and Y. Crown 8vo. cloth, 6*s*. 6*d*.

**OCCASIONAL PAPERS on UNIVERSITY and SCHOOL**
MATTERS; containing an Account of all recent University Subjects and Changes. Three Parts, price 1*s*. each.

**OLIPHANT.—Agnes Hopetoun's Schools and Holidays.**
The Experiences of a Little Girl. By MRS. OLIPHANT, Author of "Margaret Maitland." Royal 16mo. gilt leaves, 5*s*.

**ORE SEEKER, THE.—A Tale of the Hartz Mountains.**
Handsomely Illustrated, printed on Toned Paper, and bound in super-elegant cloth. Royal 8vo. 15*s*.

**ORWELL.—The Bishop's Walk and the Bishop's Times.** Poems on the Days of Archbishop Leighton and the Scottish Covenant. By ORWELL. Fcap. 8vo. cloth, 5*s.*

**OUR YEAR.—A Child's Book in Prose and Verse.** By the Author of "John Halifax, Gentleman." With Numerous Illustrations by CLARENCE DOBELL. Royal 16mo. cloth, gilt leaves, 5*s.*

**OUT OF THE DEPTHS.—The Story of a Woman's Life.** Crown 8vo. cloth, 10*s.* 6*d.*

**PARKINSON.—A Treatise on Elementary Mechanics.** For the Use of the Junior Classes at the University, and the Higher Classes in Schools. With a Collection of Examples. By S. PARKINSON, B.D. Fellow and Assistant Tutor of St. John's College, Cambridge. Crown 8vo. cloth, 9*s.* 6*d.*

**PARKINSON.—A Treatise on Optics.** Crown 8vo. cloth, 10*s.* 6*d.*

**PARMINTER.—Materials for a Grammar of the Modern** English Language. Designed as a Text-book of Classical Grammar for the use of Training Colleges, and the Higher Classes of English Schools. By GEORGE HENRY PARMINTER, of Trinity College, Cambridge; Rector of the United Parishes of SS. John and George, Exeter. Fcap. 8vo. cloth, 3*s.* 6*d.*

**PEROWNE.—The Christian's Daily Life a Life of Faith. A** Sermon preached in the Chapel of Corpus Christi College, Cambridge, on Sunday Morning, October 21, 1860. By the Rev. EDWARD HENRY PEROWNE, B.D. Fellow and Tutor. 8vo. sewed, 1*s.*

**PEROWNE.—"Al-Adjrumiieh."** An Elementary Arabic Grammar. By J. J. S. PEROWNE, B.D. Lecturer in Divinity in King's College, London, and Examining Chaplain to the Lord Bishop of Norwich. 8vo. cloth, 5*s.*

**PERRY.—Five Sermons preached before the University of** Cambridge, in November, 1855. By CHARLES PERRY, D.D. Bishop of Melbourne. Crown 8vo. cloth, 3*s.*

**PHEAR.—Elementary Hydrostatics.** By J. B. Phear, M.A. Fellow of Clare College, Cambridge. **Second Edition.** Accompanied by numerous Examples, with the Solutions. Crown 8vo. cloth, 5*s.* 6*d.*

**PHILLIPS.—Life on the Earth: Its Origin and Succession.** By JOHN PHILLIPS, M.A. LL.D. F.R.S. Professor of Geology in the University of Oxford. With Illustrations. Crown 8vo. cloth, 6*s.* 6*d.*

**PHILOLOGY.—The Journal of Sacred and Classical Philology.** Four Vols. 8vo. cloth, 12*s.* 6*d.* each.

**PLAIN RULES ON REGISTRATION OF BIRTHS AND** DEATHS. Crown 8vo. sewed, 1*d.*; 9*d.* per dozen; 5*s.* per 100.

**PLATO.—The Republic of Plato.**
Translated into English, with Notes. By Two Fellows of Trinity College, Cambridge (J. Ll. Davies M.A. and D. J. Vaughan, M.A.). **Second Edition.** 8vo. cloth, 10*s*. 6*d*.

**PLATONIC DIALOGUES, THE.—For English Readers.**
By W. WHEWELL, D.D. F.R.S. Master of Trinity College, Cambridge. Vol. I. **Second Edition,** containing **The Socratic Dialogues.** Fcap. 8vo. cloth, 7*s*. 6*d*. Vol. II. containing **The Anti-Sophist Dialogues,** 6*s*. 6*d*. Vol. III. containing **The Republic.** Fcap. 8vo. cloth, 7*s*. 6*d*.

**PRATT.—Treatise on Attractions, La Place's Functions,** and the Figure of the Earth. By J. H. PRATT, M.A. Archdeacon of Calcutta, and Fellow of Gonville and Caius College, Cambridge. **Second Edition.** Crown 8vo. cloth, 6*s*. 6*d*.

**PRAYERS FOR WORKING MEN OF ALL RANKS;**
Earnestly designed for Family Devotion and Private Meditation and Prayer. Fcap. 8vo. cloth, red leaves, 2*s*. 6*d*. Common Edition, 1*s*. 9*d*.

**PRINCIPLES of ETHICS according to the NEW TESTAMENT.** Crown 8vo. sewed, 2*s*.

**PROCTER.—A History of the Book of Common Prayer: with** a Rationale of its Offices. By FRANCIS PROCTER, M.A., Vicar of Witton, Norfolk, and late Fellow of St. Catherine's College. **Fourth Edition,** revised and enlarged. Crown 8vo. cloth, 10*s*. 6*d*.
*** This forms part of the Series of Theological Manuals.

**PUCKLE.—An Elementary Treatise on Conic Sections and** Algebraic Geometry. With a numerous collection of Easy Examples progressively arranged, especially designed for the use of Schools and Beginners. By G. HALE PUCKLE, M.A., Principal of Windermere College. **Second Edition,** enlarged and improved. Crown 8vo. cloth, 7*s*. 6*d*.

**RAMSAY.—The Catechiser's Manual; or, the Church Cate-**chism illustrated and explained, for the use of Clergymen, Schoolmasters, and Teachers. By ARTHUR RAMSAY, M.A. of Trinity College, Cambridge. 18mo. cloth, 3*s*. 6*d*.

**RAWLINSON.—Elementary Statics.**
By G. RAWLINSON, M.A. late Professor of the Applied Sciences in Elphinstone College, Bombay. Edited by EDWARD STURGES, M.A. Rector of Kencott, Oxon. Crown 8vo. cloth, 4*s*. 6*d*.

**RAYS OF SUNLIGHT FOR DARK DAYS. A Book of** Selections for the Suffering. With a Preface by C. J. VAUGHAN, D.D. Vicar of Doncaster and Chaplain in Ordinary to the Queen. Royal 16mo. elegantly printed with red lines, and bound in cloth with red leaves, 4*s*. 6*d*. or in morocco antique, 10*s*. 6*d*.

**REICHEL.—The Lord's Prayer and other Sermons.**
By C. P. REICHEL, B.D., Professor of Latin in the Queen's University; Chaplain to his Excellency the Lord-Lieutenant of Ireland; and late Donnellan Lecturer in the University of Dublin. Crown 8vo. cloth, 7*s*. 6*d*.

**ROBINSON.—Missions urged upon the State, on Grounds** both of Duty and Policy. By C. K. ROBINSON, M.A. Fellow and Assistant Tutor of St. Catherine's College. Fcap. 8vo. cloth, 3*s*.

**ROUTH.—Treatise on Dynamics of Rigid Bodies.** With Numerous Examples. By E. J. ROUTH, M.A. Fellow and Assistant Tutor of St. Peter's College, Cambridge. Crown 8vo. cloth, 10*s*. 6*d*.

**ROWSELL.—THE ENGLISH UNIVERSITIES AND THE** ENGLISH POOR. Sermons Preached before the University of Cambridge. By T. J. ROWSELL, M.A. Rector of St. Margaret's, Lothbury, late Incumbent of St. Peter's, Stepney. Fcap. 8vo. cloth limp, red leaves, 2*s*.

**ROWSELL.—Man's Labour and God's Harvest.** Sermons preached before the University of Cambridge in Lent, 1861. Fcap. 8vo. limp cloth, red leaves, 3*s*.

**RUTH AND HER FRIENDS. A Story for Girls.** With a Frontispiece. **Third Edition.** Royal 16mo. extra cloth, giltleaves, 5*s*.

**SALLUST.—Sallust for Schools.** With English Notes. **Second Edition.** By CHARLES MERIVALE, B.D.; late Fellow and Tutor of St. John's College, Cambridge, &c., Author of the "History of Rome," &c. Fcap. 8vo. cloth, 4*s*. 6*d*.

"THE JUGURTHA" AND "THE CATILINA" MAY BE HAD SEPARATELY, price 2*s*. 6*d*. EACH IN CLOTH.

**SALMON.—Sermons preached in the Chapel of Trinity** College, Dublin. By GEORGE SALMON, D.D. Fellow and Tutor. Crown 8vo. cloth, 6*s*.

**SANDARS.—BY THE SEA, AND OTHER POEMS.** By EDMUND SANDARS, of Trinity Hall, Cambridge. Fcap. 8vo. cloth, 4*s*. 6*d*.

**SCOURING OF THE WHITE HORSE; or, The Long** Vacation Ramble of a London Clerk. By the Author of "Tom Brown's School Days." Illustrated by DOYLE. **Eighth Thousand.** Imp. 16mo. cloth, elegant, 8*s*. 6*d*.

**SELWYN.—The Work of Christ in the World.** Sermons preached before the University of Cambridge. By the Right Rev. GEORGE AUGUSTUS SELWYN, D.D. Bishop of New Zealand, formerly Fellow of St. John's College. **Third Edition.** Crown 8vo. 2*s*.

**SELWYN.—A Verbal Analysis of the Holy Bible.** Intended to facilitate the translation of the Holy Scriptures into Foreign Languages. Compiled for the use of the Melanesian Mission. Small folio, cloth, 14*s*.

**SIMEON.—Stray Notes on Fishing and on Natural History.** By CORNWALL SIMEON. Crown 8vo. cloth, 7*s*. 6*d*.

**SLOMAN.—Claims of Leibnitz to the Invention of the** Differential Calculus. By DR. H. SLOMAN. Royal 8vo. cloth, 8*s*. 6*d*.

**SIMPSON.—An Epitome of the History of the Christian** Church during the first Three Centuries and during the Reformation. With Examination Papers. By WILLIAM SIMPSON, M.A. **Third Edition.** Fcp. 8vo. cloth, *5s.*

**SMITH.—A Life Drama, and other Poems.** By ALEXANDER SMITH. Fcap. 8vo. cloth, *2s. 6d.*

**SMITH.—City Poems.** By ALEXANDER SMITH, Author of "A Life Drama," and other Poems. Fcap. 8vo. cloth. *5s.*

**SMITH.—Arithmetic and Algebra, in their Principles and** Application: with numerous systematically arranged Examples, taken from the Cambridge Examination Papers. By BARNARD SMITH, M.A., Fellow of St. Peter's College, Cambridge. **Eighth Edition.** Crown 8vo. cloth, *10s. 6d.*

**SMITH.—Arithmetic for the use of Schools.** **New Edition.** Crown 8vo. cloth, *4s. 6d.*

**SMITH.—A Key to the Arithmetic for Schools.** **Second Edition.** Crown 8vo. cloth, *8s. 6d.*

**SMITH.—Exercises in Arithmetic.** By BARNARD SMITH. With Answers. Crown 8vo. limp cloth, *2s. 6d.* Or sold separately, as follows:—Part I. *1s.* Part II. *1s.* Answers, *6d.*

**SMITH.—Pilate's Wife's Dream, and other Poems.** By HORACE SMITH. Fcap. 8vo. cloth, *2s. 6d.*

**SMITH.—An Outline of the Theory of Conditional Sentences** in Greek and Latin. For the use of Students. By R. HORTON SMITH, M.A. Fellow of St. John's College, Cambridge. 8vo. *2s. 6d.*

**SMITH.—The Koran in India. A Comparison of the Religious** Policies of Akbar and Aurengzebe. By LUMLEY SMITH, B.A. Fellow of Trinity Hall. 8vo. sewed, *2s.*

**SNOWBALL.—The Elements of Plane and Spherical** Trigonometry. By J. C. SNOWBALL, M.A. Fellow of St. John's College, Cambridge. **Ninth Edition.** Crown 8vo. cloth, *7s. 6d.*

**SNOWBALL.—Introduction to the Elements of Plane Trigo-**nometry for the use of Schools. **Second Edition.** 8vo. sewed, *5s.*

**SNOWBALL.—The Cambridge Course of Elementary** Mechanics and Hydrostatics. Adapted for the use of Colleges and Schools. With numerous Examples and Problems. **Fourth Edition.** Crown 8vo. cloth, *5s.*

**SPRAY.** Crown 8vo. boards, *3s.*

**SWAINSON.—A Handbook to Butler's Analogy.** By C. A. SWAINSON, M.A. Principal of the Theological College, and Prebendary of Chichester. Crown 8vo. sewed, *1s. 6d.*

**SWAINSON.—The Creeds of the Church in their Relations** to Holy Scripture and the Conscience of the Christian. 8vo. cloth, 9*s*.

**SWAINSON.—THE AUTHORITY OF THE NEW TESTAMENT;** The Conviction of Righteousness, and other Lectures, delivered before the University of Cambridge. 8vo. cloth, 12*s*.

**TAIT and STEELE.—A Treatise on Dynamics, with numerous Examples.** By P. G. TAIT, Fellow of St. Peter's College, Cambridge, and Professor of Mathematics in Queen's College, Belfast, and W. J. STEELE, late Fellow of St. Peter's College. Crown 8vo. cloth, 10*s*. 6*d*.

**TEMPLE. — Sermons preached in the Chapel of Rugby** School. In 1858, 1859, and 1860. By F. TEMPLE, D.D. Chaplain in Ordinary to her Majesty, Head Master of Rugby School, Chaplain to Earl Denbigh. 8vo. cloth, 10*s*. 6*d*.

**THEOLOGICAL Manuals.**

**I.—History of the Church during the Middle Ages.** By ARCHDEACON HARDWICK. With Four Maps. Crown 8vo. cloth, 10*s*. 6*d*.

**II.—History of the Church during the Reformation.** By ARCHDEACON HARDWICK. Crown 8vo. cloth, 10*s*. 6*d*.

**III.—The Book of Common Prayer: Its History and** Rationale. By FRANCIS PROCTER, M.A. Fourth Edition. Crown 8vo. cloth, 10*s*. 6*d*.

**IV.—History of the Canon of the New Testament.** By B. F. WESTCOTT, M.A. Crown 8vo. cloth, 12*s*.

**V.—Introduction to the Study of the Gospels.** By B. F. WESTCOTT, M.A. Crown 8vo. cloth, 10*s*. 6*d*.

*** Others are in progress, and will be announced in due time.

**THRING.—A Construing Book.** Compiled by the Rev. EDWARD THRING, M.A. Head Master of Uppingham Grammar School, late Fellow of King's College, Cambridge. Fcap. 8vo. cloth, 2*s*. 6*d*.

**THRING.—The Elements of Grammar taught in English.** **Third Edition.** 18mo. bound in cloth, 2*s*.

**THRING.—The Child's Grammar.** Being the substance of the above, with Examples for Practice. Adapted for Junior Classes. **A New Edition.** 18mo. limp cloth, 1*s*.

**THRING.—Sermons delivered at Uppingham School.** By EDWARD THRING, M.A. Head Master. Crown 8vo. cloth, 5*s*.

**THRING.—School Songs.** A Collection of Songs for Schools. With the Music arranged for four Voices. Edited by EDWARD THRING, M.A., Head Master of Uppingham School and H. RICCIUS. Small folio, 7*s*. 6*d*.

**THRUPP.—Antient Jerusalem: a New Investigation into the** History, Topography, and Plan of the City, Environs, and Temple. Designed principally to illustrate the records and prophecies of Scripture. With Map and Plans. By JOSEPH FRANCIS THRUPP, M.A. Vicar of Barrington, Cambridge, late Fellow of Trinity College. 8vo. cloth, 15*s.*

**THRUPP.—Introduction to the Study and Use of the** Psalms. By the REV. J. F. THRUPP, M.A. 2 vols. 8vo. 21*s.*

**THRUPP.—The Christian Inference from Leviticus xviii.** 16, sufficient ground for holding that Marriage with a Deceased Wife's Sister is unlawful. By J. F. THRUPP, M.A. 8vo. sewed, 1*s.*

**THRUPP.—Psalms and Hymns for Public Worship.** Selected and Edited by the REV. J. F. THRUPP, M.A. 18mo. cloth, 2*s.* limp cloth, 1*s.* 4*d.*

**THUCYDIDES, BOOK VI. With English Notes, and a Map.** By PERCIVAL FROST, Jun. M.A. late Fellow of St. John's College, Cambridge. 8vo. 7*s.* 6*d.*

**TODHUNTER.—A Treatise on the Differential Calculus.** With numerous Examples. By I. TODHUNTER, M.A., Fellow and Assistant Tutor of St. John's College, Cambridge. **Third Edition.** Crown 8vo. cloth, 10*s.* 6*d.*

**TODHUNTER.—A Treatise on the Integral Calculus.** With numerous Examples. Crown 8vo. cloth, 10*s.* 6*d.*

**TODHUNTER.—A Treatise on Analytical Statics, with** numerous Examples. **Second Edition.** Crown 8vo. cloth, 10*s.* 6*d.*

**TODHUNTER.—A Treatise on Conic Sections, with** numerous Examples. **Second Edition.** Crown 8vo. cloth, 10*s.* 6*d.*

**TODHUNTER.—Algebra for the use of Colleges and Schools.** **Second Edition.** Crown 8vo. cloth, 7*s.* 6*d.*

**TODHUNTER.—Plane Trigonometry for Colleges and** Schools. **Second Edition.** Crown 8vo. cloth, 5*s.*

**TODHUNTER.—A Treatise on Spherical Trigonometry for** the Use of Colleges and Schools. Crown 8vo. cloth, 4*s.* 6*d.*

**TODHUNTER.—Critical History of the Progress of the** Calculus of Variations during the Nineteenth Century. By I. TODHUNTER, M.A. 8vo. cloth, 12*s.*

**TODHUNTER.—Examples of Analytical Geometry of Three** Dimensions. Crown 8vo. cloth, 4*s.*

**TOM BROWN'S SCHOOL DAYS.**
By AN OLD BOY. **Seventh Edition.** Fcap. 8vo. cloth, 5*s.*
COPIES OF THE LARGE PAPER EDITION MAY BE HAD, PRICE 10*s.* 6*d.*

## TRACTS FOR PRIESTS AND PEOPLE.

By VARIOUS WRITERS.

**No. I.—Religio Laici.**
By THOMAS HUGHES, Author of "Tom Brown's School Days." Price One Shilling.

**No. II.—The Mote and the Beam: a Clergyman's** Lessons from the Present Panic. By the REV. F. D. MAURICE, Incumbent of St. Peter's, St. Marylebone. Price One Shilling.

**No. III.—The Atonement as a Fact and as a Theory.**
By the REV. FRANCIS GARDEN, Sub-Dean of Her Majesty's Chapels Royal. Price One Shilling.

**No. IV.—The Signs of the Kingdom of Heaven: An** Appeal to Scripture on the Question of Miracles. By the Rev. J. Ll. DAVIES, Rector of Christ Church, St. Marylebone. Price One Shilling.

*** Others are in Preparation.

**TRENCH.—Synonyms of the New Testament.**
By The Very Rev. RICHARD CHENEVIX TRENCH, D.D. Dean of Westminster. **Fourth Edition.** Fcap. 8vo. cloth, *5s.*

**TRENCH.—Hulsean Lectures for 1845—46.**
Contents. 1.—The Fitness of Holy Scripture for unfolding the Spiritual Life of Man. 2.—Christ the Desire of all Nations; or the Unconscious Prophecies of Heathendom. **Fourth Edition.** Foolscap 8vo. cloth, *5s.*

**TRENCH.—Sermons Preached before the University of Cambridge.** Fcap. 8vo. cloth, *2s. 6d.*

**TUDOR.—The Decalogue viewed as the Christian's Law,** with Special Reference to the Questions and Wants of the Times. By the REV. RICHARD TUDOR, B.A. Curate of Helston. Crown 8vo. cloth, *10s. 6d.*

**UNDERWOOD.—Short Manual of Arithmetic.**
By the REV. C. W. UNDERWOOD, M A. Vice-Principal of the Liverpool Collegiate Institution. Fcap. 8vo. limp cloth, *2s. 6d.*

**VACATION TOURISTS IN 1860.**
Edited by F. GALTON, F.R.S. Crown 8vo. cloth, with Map and Illustrations, *14s.* **CONTENTS**:—NAPLES. By W. G. Clark, M.A. CROATIA. By G. A. Spottiswoode. SCLAVONIC RACES. By R. D. SUTHERLAND. By G. H. K. PERU. By C. C. Bowen. GRAIAN ALPS. By J. J. Cowell, F.R.G.S. ALLELEIN-HORN. By L. Stephen, M.A. MONT-CERVIN. By F. V. Hawkins, M.A. LAUTERBRUNNEN TO ÆGGISHORN. By J. Tyndall, F.R.S. ICELAND. By J. W. Clark, M.A. NORWAY. By H. F. Tozer, M.A. SPAIN. By the Editor. SYRIA. By Hon. R. Noel.

**VAUGHAN.—Notes for Lectures on Confirmation. With** suitable Prayers. By C. J. VAUGHAN, D.D. Chaplain in Ordinary to the Queen, Vicar of Doncaster, and late Head Master of Harrow School. **Third Edition.** Limp cloth, red edges, *1s. 6d.*

**VAUGHAN.—St. Paul's Epistle to the Romans.** The Greek Text with English Notes. By C. J. VAUGHAN, D.D. Second Edition. Crown 8vo. cloth, red leaves, 5*s.*

**VAUGHAN.—MEMORIALS OF HARROW SUNDAYS.** A Selection of Sermons preached in Harrow School Chapel. By C. J. VAUGHAN, D.D. With a View of the Interior of the Chapel. **Third Edition.** Crown 8vo. cloth, red leaves, 10*s.* 6*d.*

**VAUGHAN.—Epiphany, Lent, and Easter. A Selection of** Expository Sermons. By C. J. VAUGHAN, D.D. **Second Edition.** Crown 8vo. cloth, red leaves, 10*s.* 6*d.*

**VAUGHAN.—Revision of the Liturgy. Four Discourses.** With an Introduction. I. ABSOLUTION. II. REGENERATION. III. ATHANASIAN CREED. IV. BURIAL SERVICE. V. HOLY ORDERS. By C. J. VAUGHAN, D.D. **Second Edition.** Crown 8vo. cloth, red leaves, 4*s.* 6*d.*

**VAUGHAN.—Four Sermons preached before the University** of Cambridge, May, 1861.

**No. I.—The Two Departures of Christ, and the Three** Returns.

**No. II.—Suspense.**

**No. III.—The Seven Spirits of God.**

**No. IV.—Choice of Professions.**

By CHARLES JOHN VAUGHAN, D.D. Crown 8vo. sewed, 1*s.* 6*d.*

**VAUGHAN.—The Joy of Success corrected by the Joy of** Safety. An Ordination Sermon preached in York Cathedral. By C. J. VAUGHAN, D.D. Chancellor of the Cathedral. Fcap. 8vo. sewed, 2*d.*

**VAUGHAN.—Sermons preached in St. John's Church,** Leicester, during the years 1855 and 1856. By DAVID J. VAUGHAN, M.A. Fellow of Trinity College, Cambridge, and Vicar of St. Martin's, Leicester. Crown 8vo. cloth, 5*s.* 6*d.*

**VAUGHAN.—Sermons on the Resurrection. With a Preface.** By D. J. VAUGHAN, M.A. Fcap. 8vo. cloth, 3*s.*

**VAUGHAN.—Three Sermons on The Atonement. With a** Preface. By D. J. Vaughan, M.A. Limp cloth, red edges, 1*s.* 6*d.*

**VAUGHAN.—Sermons on Sacrifice and Propitiation, preached** in St. Martin's Church, Leicester, during Lent and Easter, 1861. By D. J. VAUGHAN, M.A. Fcap. 8vo. cloth limp, red edges, 2*s.* 6*d.*

**VOLUNTEER'S SCRAP BOOK.** By the Author of "The Cambridge Scrap Book." Crown 4to. half-bound, 7*s.* 6*d.*

**WAGNER.—Memoir of the Rev. George Wagner, late of St.** Stephen's, Brighton. By J. N. SIMPKINSON, M.A. Rector of Brington, Northampton. **Second Edition.** Crown 8vo. cloth, 9*s.*

**WATSON AND ROUTH.—CAMBRIDGE SENATE HOUSE** PROBLEMS AND RIDERS. For the Year 1860. With Solutions by H. W. WATSON, M.A. and E. J. ROUTH, M.A. Crown 8vo. cloth, 7*s.* 6*d.*

**WESTCOTT.—History of the Canon of the New Testament** during the First Four Centuries. By BROOKE FOSS WESTCOTT, M.A., Assistant Master of Harrow School; late Fellow of Trinity College, Cambridge. Crown 8vo. cloth, 12*s.* 6*d.*

*** This forms part of the Series of Theological Manuals.

**WESTCOTT. — Characteristics of the Gospel Miracles.** Sermons preached before the University of Cambridge. **With Notes.** By B. F. WESTCOTT, M.A., Author of "History of the New Testament Canon." Crown 8vo. cloth, 4*s.* 6*d.*

**WESTCOTT.—Introduction to the Study of the Four Gospels.** By B. F. WESTCOTT, M.A. Crown 8vo. cloth, 10*s.* 6*d.*

*** This forms part of the series of Theological Manuals.

**WHEWELL.—THE PLATONIC DIALOGUES FOR** ENGLISH READERS. By W. WHEWELL, D.D. Vol. I. **Second Edition,** containing "The Socratic Dialogues," fcap. 8vo. cloth, 7*s.* 6*d.* Vol. II. containing "The Anti-Sophist Dialogues," 6*s.* 6*d.* Vol III. containing the Republic, 7*s.* 6*d.*

**WHITMORE.—Gilbert Marlowe and Other Poems.** With a Preface by the Author of "Tom Brown's Schooldays." Fcap. 8vo. cloth, 3*s.* 6*d.*

**WILSON.—Memoir of George Wilson, M.D. F.R.S.E.** Regius Professor of Technology in the University of Edinburgh. By his Sister. 8vo. cloth, with Portrait, 14*s.*

**WILSON.—The Five Gateways of Knowledge.** By GEORGE WILSON, M.D., F.R.S.E., Regius Professor of Technology in the University of Edinburgh. **Second Edition.** Fcap. 8vo. cloth, 2*s.* 6*d.* or in Paper Covers, 1*s.*

**WILSON.—The Progress of the Telegraph.** Fcap. 8vo. 1*s.*

**WILSON.—A Treatise on Dynamics.** By W. P. WILSON, M.A., Fellow of St. John's, Cambridge, and Professor of Mathematics in the University of Melbourne. 8vo. bds. 9*s.* 6*d.*

**WOLFE.—ONE HUNDRED AND FIFTY ORIGINAL** PSALM AND HYMN TUNES. For Four Voices. By ARTHUR WOLFE, M.A., Fellow and Tutor of Clare College, Cambridge. Oblong royal 8vo. extra cloth, gilt leaves, 10*s.* 6*d.*

**WOLFE.—Hymns For Public Worship.** Selected and Arranged by ARTHUR WOLFE, M.A. 18mo. cloth, red leaves, 2*s.* Common Paper Edition, limp cloth, 1*s.* or twenty-five for 1*l.*

**WOLFE.—Hymns For Private Use.** Selected and Arranged by ARTHUR WOLFE, M.A. 18mo. cloth, red leaves, 2*s.*

**WORKING MEN'S COLLEGE MAGAZINE.** Monthly, 2*d.* Vol. I. (1859) and Vol. II. (1860) handsomely bound in cloth, 2*s.* 6*d.* each.

## WORSHIP OF GOD AND FELLOWSHIP AMONG MEN.

A Series of Sermons on Public Worship. Fcap. 8vo. cloth, 3*s*. 6*d*.

By F. D. MAURICE, M.A. T. J. ROWSELL, M.A. J. LL. DAVIES, M.A. and D. J. VAUGHAN, M.A.

## WRATISLAW.—Middle-Class and Non-Gremial Examinations.

Cui Bono? By A. H. WRATISLAW, M.A. Head-Master of the Grammar School, Bury St. Edmunds, and formerly Fellow and Tutor of Christ's College, Cambridge. 8vo. sewed, 6*d*.

## WRIGHT.—The Iliad of Homer.

Translated into English Verse by J. C. WRIGHT, M.A. Translator of Dante. Crown 8vo. Vol. I. containing Books I.—XII., 10*s*. 6*d*. Books I.—VI., 5*s*. Books VII.—XII., 5*s*.

## WRIGHT.—Hellenica; or, a History of Greece in Greek,

as related by Diodorus and Thucydides, being a First Greek Reading Book, with Explanatory Notes, Critical and Historical. By J. WRIGHT, M.A., of Trinity College, Cambridge, and Head-Master of Sutton Coldfield Grammar School. **Second Edition,** WITH A VOCABULARY. 12mo. cloth, 3*s*. 6*d*.

## WRIGHT.—David, King of Israel.

Readings for the Young. With Six Illustrations after SCHNORR. Royal 16mo. extra cloth, gilt leaves, 5*s*.

## WRIGHT.—A Help to Latin Grammar;

or, the Form and Use of Words in Latin. With Progressive Exercises. Crown 8vo. cloth, 4*s*. 6*d*.

## WRIGHT.—The Seven Kings of Rome:

An easy Narrative, abridged from the First Book of Livy by the omission of difficult passages, being a First Latin Reading Book, with Grammatical Notes. Fcap. 8vo. cloth, 3*s*.

## WRIGHT.—A Vocabulary and Exercises on the "Seven

Kings of Rome." Fcap. 8vo. cloth, 2*s*. 6*d*.

*** The Vocabulary and Exercises may also be had bound up with "The Seven Kings of Rome." Price 5*s*. cloth.

## Yes and No; or Glimpses of The Great Conflict.

3 vols. crown 8vo. cloth, 1*l*. 11*s*. 6*d*.

---

*ONE SHILLING, MONTHLY.*

## MACMILLAN'S MAGAZINE.

EDITED BY DAVID MASSON.

Volumes I., II., and III., are now ready, handsomely bound in cloth, price 7*s*. 6*d*. each.

---

R. CLAY, SON, AND TAYLOR, PRINTERS, BREAD STREET HILL.

CPSIA information can be obtained
at www.ICGtesting.com
Printed in the USA
BVHW070140120819
555624BV00025B/4369/P